AIDS: a guide to the law

The views and legal opinions of this book are those of the authors and do not necessarily represent the policies of The Terrence Higgins Trust. Neither can the trust accept liability for any omissions or incorrect statements made in the book which is a guide to the law.

AIDS: a guide to the law

Edited by
Dai Harris and Richard Haigh
for
The Terrence Higgins Trust

Routledge
London and New York

To
People with AIDS
and
In Memory of
Colin d'Eça

First published 1990
by Routledge
11 New Fetter Lane, London EC4P 4EE

Simultaneously published in the USA and Canada
by Routledge
a division of Routledge, Chapman and Hall, Inc.
29 West 35th Street, New York, NY 10001

© 1990 The Terrence Higgins Trust

Photoset by Mayhew Typesetting, Bristol, England
Printed and bound in Great Britain by
Biddles Ltd, Guildford and King's Lynn

British Library Cataloguing in Publication Data

Aids : a guide to the law.
  1. Great Britain. Man. Aids. Legal aspects
  I. Harris, Dai II. Haigh, Richard
  344.104'439792

  ISBN 0-415-04667-X
  ISBN 0-415-04668-8 (pbk)

Library of Congress Cataloging in Publication Data also available

Contents

Contents

Preface

This book was written for advisers, and not legal specialists. It is intended to give an overview of the law, to guide and to help the professional adviser, be they insurance brokers or welfare-benefits advisers, Health and Safety Officers or social workers; professionals who are increasingly called upon to advise their clients about the legal issues of AIDS. Hence, we have written this book for them, with as little legalese as the law and English language allows.

The view of the law for advice purposes is a description of what the law is, and not how we would like it to be. Advisers should try to provide the best advice and arguments on the present laws, although this is difficult as our laws offer little protection to people affected by AIDS. Presently, many people who have AIDS have lost over £50 per week in benefit through changes in the law. The future is bleak as many young people with HIV cannot afford the food or accommodation necessary to maintain their health and well-being. It is nothing short of a social-welfare disaster. People are now campaigning for the laws to be changed, for a welfare benefit which can meet the needs of people with AIDS, and laws to outlaw discrimination in insurance, immigration, and employment practice.

The law and practice described in each chapter may not necessarily apply to Northern Ireland or Scotland: Appendix 1 provides a list of agencies which may be able to provide referral advice.

There are a number of people we would like to thank individually for their help and support in the making of this book: Kuki Hahndel, Tim Proctor, Martin Eede, Robin Dormer, Nuala Mole, Peter Chadwick, Talia Rodgers, David Campbell, Robin Gorna, Dr Virginia Bieluch, Terry Munyard, David Taylor, and Russell Campbell. We are also very grateful to our colleagues at Threshold Housing Advice, the Terrence Higgins Trust, and Hillingdon Legal Resource Centre. We wish to thank the Board of Directors at the Terrence Higgins Trust, who gave us the support to publish this book, and to acknowledge the help and advice of the World Health Organization, the Institute of Advanced Legal Studies, Professor Rideout at University College London, and the Department of Business Studies at Aston University.

Finally, but not least, we would like to thank our authors who wrote this book, our publishers who printed it, and Apricot Computers in Birmingham for their generosity.

We have attempted to state the law as of March 1989.

Dai Harris
Richard Haigh

April 1989

Editors and contributors

Dai Harris, LL.B(Hons), is a barrister who has worked as an employment adviser at Brixton Community Law Centre and as an AIDS researcher for Paddington Law Centre. In 1985, he set up a volunteer legal advice service at the Trust to help people affected by AIDS. Two years later, he was appointed as the first Legal Adviser on AIDS in the UK. In the supervening years, at the Trust, he has undertaken anti-discrimination casework in the employment, medico-legal, immigration, and insurance areas. He presently co-ordinates the Trust's welfare-rights, housing, and legal-advice services.

Richard Haigh has been a volunteer to the Terrence Higgins Trust since 1983. He co-ordinated the Buddy Group and was Chair of the Trust's Steering Committee before becoming a Director in 1987.

Medico-legal aspects of AIDS

Colin A.M.E. d'Eca, MD MSc BSc DipLL Barrister, initially studied Genetics and Microbiology before undergoing medical training in Canada. He did research in medical immunogenetics and practised for a brief period as a paediatrician. He then switched to law and was called to the Bar in 1981. His first legal practice was at a Legal Advice Centre (3 years) where he specialized in welfare law. In 1984 he joined the DHSS and worked in the branch dealing with the means-tested benefits and was heavily involved in drafting the Income Support and Housing Benefit legislation. He was a legal adviser in the Department of Health Medicines Division. He was a founder member of the Legal Services Group of the Terrence Higgins Trust and specialized in medico-legal matters and welfare law. He was Director of the Board of the Trust and a member of its Personnel Committee.

Colin d'Eca died in June 1989.

Social-welfare law

Derick Bird has extensive knowledge of AIDS and is a skilled advocate of

Social-welfare Law, having worked in the field for many years. He was a member of the Legal Services Group of the Terrence Higgins Trust. Derick is dedicated to the welfare of people with AIDS and is a tireless campaigner for their rights. He is currently co-ordinator of 'Hartley Munro Advocacy Service' based in Birmingham, which is an organization seeking Law Centre Federation status offering legal and social-welfare representation for people with AIDS or HIV infection.

Housing law and people with HIV infection

Ginny O'Brien, **Jane Carrier**, and **David Ward** have between them over 20 years of housing-service experience in agencies as diverse as Law Centres, Citizen Advice Bureaux, and Local Authority Housing Aid Centres. Working at Threshold Advice Centres in the west and south-west of London, on housing advice and development for people without dependent children, they have a wide experience of helping people with HIV infection. Ginny O'Brien and Jane Carrier have also developed training courses for housing-advice workers and the staff of housing projects, which seek to assist these organizations in providing services to people with AIDS.

AIDS and immigration

Michael Shrimpton, LL.B (Hons), of Gray's Inn is a barrister and part-time Lecturer in Law at Ealing College of Higher Education. He is a member of the Immigration Law Practitioners Association, the Administrative Law Bar Association, and the Joint Council for the Welfare of Immigrants. He has had a number of legal articles published and is Rapporteur of the Justice Committee on Immigration. Apart from law, his interests extend to politics, which led him to contest Horsham in the 1987 General Election and West Sussex in the 1989 Elections for the European Parliament.

Powers of attorney, wills, and probate

Nigel A. Clarke qualified as a Solicitor in 1975, and since then has been a partner in a provincial firm of family solicitors. He deals with the day-to-day problems of those no longer able, physically or mentally, to deal with their own affairs and with preparation of wills and the administration of estates. In 1986 he became a member of the Legal Services Group of the Terrence Higgins Trust.

AIDS and insurance

Wesley Gryk is an American lawyer who has lived in England for 10 years. A graduate of Harvard College and Harvard Law School, he is a member of the Bar of New York and worked in New York and Hong Kong as a companies' and banking lawyer. For much of his time in England he has specialized in international human rights law, working for the United Nations and Amnesty International. He is currently working at the London solicitors' firm of B.M. Birnberg & Co.

Legal structures of voluntary organizations

Timothy Costello is a solicitor. He has been advising people with AIDS and others affected by HIV for the past 3 years as a volunteer with the Terrence Higgins Trust and honorary legal adviser to the Hartley Munro Advocacy Service. He is a partner in the firm Boodle Hatfield.

Abbreviations

AIDS	Acquired Immune Deficiency Syndrome
AO	Adjudication Officer
AR	Additional Requirement
ARC	AIDS-related Complex
CBI	Confederation of British Industry
CCG	Community-Care Grant
DHSS	Department of Health and Social Security
DSS	Department of Social Security
EEC/EC	European Economic Community/European Community
EHD	Environmental Health Department
EHO	Environmental Health Officer
EOC	Equal Opportunities Commission
FC	Family Credit
GP	General Practitioner
HB	Housing Benefit
HIV	Human Immunodeficiency Virus
ICA	Invalid-Care Allowance
IS	Income Support
LA	Life Assurance
NCIP	Non-contributory Invalidity Pension
NHS	National Health Service
PCP	Pneumocystis Carinii Pneumonia
PGL	Persistent Generalized Lymphadenopathy
PHI	Permanent Health Insurance
SB	Supplementary Benefit
SDA	Severe-Disablement Allowance
SF	Social Fund
SFO	Social Fund Officer
SSP	Statutory Sick Pay
STD	Sexually transmitted diseases
TUC	Trades Union Congress
WHO	World Health Organization

Chapter one

AIDS, people with AIDS, and legal advice
Dai Harris

AIDS and HIV transmission

AIDS is an abbreviation for Acquired Immune Deficiency Syndrome. It means the body's immune system is no longer able to protect itself against certain infections and cancers. Although some of the infections of AIDS can be treated, the syndrome itself is incurable. AIDS was first noticed as a new disease in 1981 in the USA. Between June and November of that year 159 people were found to have AIDS. Most of the cases came from the major cities of the USA and 92 per cent were gay men. In 1983, people from Africa treated in Europe were found to have AIDS, and subsequent investigation revealed a large number of people with AIDS in central Africa.

The immune deficiency in AIDS is caused by a virus called Human Immunodeficiency Virus (HIV). This virus was discovered in 1983 and it attacks the helper cells which are the fighting cells of the blood. It is a retrovirus, which means that it is slow-acting and not highly infectious. Occasionally, infection with HIV causes short-lived immediate 'flu-like symptoms. Nearly all people with HIV remain well for several years after infection; there is a very very small chance of people developing AIDS in the first 3 years (less than 1 per cent per year). By the seventh year of infection there is thought to be a 33 per cent chance of developing AIDS. However, in general it remains uncertain whether everyone with HIV infection will develop AIDS or even become ill.

HIV causes a range of illnesses of which AIDS is one. The other diseases include a relatively non-serious inflammation of the glands called Persistent Generalized Lymphadenopathy (PGL), and AIDS-related Complex (ARC) which causes some debilitating conditions like fevers, oral thrush, night sweats, and loss of weight. HIV may also cause dementia, which can be significant in people with AIDS/ARC but is otherwise rare in people with unsymptomatic HIV infection.

HIV infection is more common than AIDS. It was estimated at the beginning of 1989, that between 60,000 and 100,000 people were infected with HIV in the UK, compared with less than 2,000 diagnosed with AIDS.

1

Worldwide it is estimated that up to 5 million could be infected with HIV, and by 1991 the figure may be nearer 10 million. The WHO has received reports of 132,976 individual cases of AIDS in the world (January 1989).

HIV affects the world's population unevenly. Central Africa continues to have a most serious problem of infection, with some of its urban populations reported to be 20 per cent infected (Panos Institute, March 1987). In the USA, 30 per cent of those with AIDS are now heterosexual and the remainder gay or bisexual men. In the UK, about 70 per cent of people with AIDS live in London and most are gay, but outside London a high level of infection with HIV exists in Edinburgh amongst its drug-injecting population.

HIV transmission

HIV is not easily passed from one person to another: it is a blood-borne virus, and is spread in fluids like semen, vaginal fluids, and blood. HIV can be spread through unsafe sexual contact, the sharing of needles, and from an infected mother to her baby. A very small number of people has become infected in the UK through unscreened and infected blood or blood products. In the past, the risk of HIV infection in the UK occurred almost exclusively amongst homosexual men having anal sex, drug-users sharing needles, and haemophiliacs who received factor VIII and cryoprecipitate blood-clotting products. Today, the risk of infection extends to anyone, anywhere, who has vaginal or anal sex without using a condom, which acts as a barrier to HIV. There is no risk of infection from daily contact with someone who has HIV as the virus is not spread by sharing cups, cutlery, toilet seats, or from kissing or touching.

Preventing infection – a private and public issue

Both community-based and nationwide public-health campaigns have succeeded in preventing people from becoming infected with HIV in Europe, Africa, the USA, and Australia. Health-education initiatives in the UK have altered behaviour which previously put people at risk. Gay and bisexual males in the UK, for example, have less anal sex: we know this from the decrease in reports of rectal venereal disease.

Despite the success of information campaigns in preventing infection, there have been suggestions that control measures should be introduced against those people who have HIV or AIDS. The measures include compulsory screening and the isolation of people with HIV or AIDS. These arguments are based on the false premiss that those with HIV are solely responsible for putting others at risk. Everyone who has consensual sex with new partners is 'a risk' and 'at risk'. It is impossible to deter people from having sex, and most people become infected, as much as they infect others, through consensual sex. So far, reason has won the day and people realize that the law cannot prevent infection: only people can do that. People who have listened to and acted on the health-education message of safer sex have not become infected.

Preventing discrimination – a private and public issue

A negative test-result is now becoming a common precondition for work or residence in other countries, for employment in some UK companies, for life-insurance and endowment mortgages. People who are antibody-positive are being refused insurance and employment, as well as being denied the right to visit or remain in many countries. These discriminatory policies have serious social implications in the UK. People who have HIV and many more suspected to be at risk, are finding it impossible to obtain an endowment mortgage to buy a house. There have also been cases, albeit decreasing in number, of doctors and dentists refusing to treat people with AIDS or HIV.

In Chapter 8 AIDS and insurance, Wesley Gryk examines in detail the policy of UK insurance companies requiring applicants to take an HIV-antibody test. Elsewhere a few employers have said that the test is necessary because of the loss of expectation of life of employees with HIV, but it is rarely a financial liability for them. In most cases the discrimination is based on an unnecessary fear of infection. Many countries, including the USA, have laws barring people with AIDS or HIV from visiting or remaining, yet these countries have some of the highest rates of HIV infection.

At a policy level, organizations including the WHO, the Department of Health, and the Terrence Higgins Trust are seeking to persuade employers, insurance companies, and the Immigration Service not to discriminate against those perceived to be at risk from HIV, or with HIV infection. At an individual level, as the chapters of this book will reveal, there are few laws which prohibit discrimination. Nevertheless, discriminatory conduct can in many cases be challenged with letters, telephone calls, or meetings. To threaten immediate legal action will accomplish little save to antagonize the discriminator still further. When it comes to AIDS, defeating prejudice and creating understanding through persuasion and education is the objective.

People with AIDS

People with AIDS are typically diagnosed at a young age as having an incurable disease, and must endure uncomfortable symptoms of sweats, diarrhoea, bad vision, and nausea, sometimes accompanied by disfiguring cancers or sores. The drugs taken to prolong life also increase physical suffering and impede a person's ability to accomplish everyday tasks. A diagnosis itself is shocking and may lead to mental depression; people who are young and active are ill-prepared for AIDS both emotionally and financially. Many people with AIDS have to face a world which views AIDS as little more than a death sentence. For the person with AIDS a diagnosis brings into focus the past, present, and future. It is the job of the adviser to help a person with AIDS to live the present and future as comfortably as possible.

At the Terrence Higgins Trust we try to treat people with AIDS as normal people who have some superhuman problems. Our aim is to give sensitive as well as professional advice. Sometimes, people's legal problems will be a direct consequence of their condition. Being told that you have AIDS may lead to an attitude of helplessness. A person may lose or resign his or her job and will need to adjust to a low standard of living. When a person with AIDS contacts an adviser, the immediate legal or financial problems will be one of many. In Chapter 3 on Social-welfare law, Derick Bird notes that people with AIDS, like anybody else, are not likely to reveal these problems unless they have confidence in their advisers, and the advisers are sensitive to them.

Legal problems for people with AIDS arise when they wish to adjust or prepare for a change in their lives. They may wish to buy a house, go on holiday, make a will, resign or change jobs – in fact, make changes in their lives which are part of any 'normal' life. They may also have more critical problems, such as living in bad housing which is detrimental to health, or being homeless, or being without enough money to keep warm, or to eat properly, or to visit friends or to go to hospital.

An important principle of advice work is to listen, and discover the real issue for the person with AIDS; and as Ginny O'Brien, Jane Carrier, and David Ward state in Chapter 4 on housing and AIDS, the person with AIDS also needs to be kept fully informed about his or her case and the courses of legal and practical action available. People with AIDS should be given plenty of time to consider the implications of any option or advice. The whole purpose of professional intervention is to empower people with AIDS to regain control of their lives.

The adviser

Providing advice to a group of people who suffer discrimination, to people who are young and who have AIDS, or to people who may dement before death, is undeniably stressful. Many of the legal problems seen by an adviser are caused by AIDS, yet the adviser is not always qualified to address the underlying emotional issues, and nor is it really appropriate. It is important for advisers to realize that it is proper for the psychological issues to be left to other people to be 'solved'. Indeed, it is the experienced adviser who will know when and how to make a referral to the social worker when someone needs help, to the doctor when someone is ill, to a counsellor when a person wishes to talk, and to a carer when a person needs care.

Despite the existence of a multidisciplinary force in the AIDS field, the adviser will still suffer much strain and stress. He or she may have personal concerns about AIDS or infection with HIV: advisers often become attached to the people they are helping and advising, and almost without exception they are well motivated and conscientious. Yet these emotions and efforts can remain unacknowledged in the structures and activities of the voluntary organization and workers become exhausted and frustrated as a result. Support, emotional and managerial, is essential in the AIDS field to sustain and nurture the helpers and advisers.

Legal advice at the Terrence Higgins Trust

For 4 years, the Terrence Higgins Trust has pioneered work in the legal-advice field. Back in 1985, six advisers and lawyers banded together to offer legal advice to people affected by AIDS. New legal problems emerged as a result of AIDS. People were losing their jobs and accommodation and were refused medical care because they were thought to be infectious. People with AIDS needed advice on benefits and financial matters. There were public-policy issues around the law. In March 1985, the government passed laws providing for the detention and removal of people with AIDS to hospitals.

The demand for legal help was small then – only forty-eight requests in 1985; but by the end of 1987 over 600 legal-advice calls had been answered. The Trust responded to the increase in work by appointing a qualified lawyer as full-time adviser. The group of volunteer lawyers expanded its number to forty and was designated as a Legal Advice Centre by the Bar Council. In the following year, the Centre completed an advice campaign on the social-security changes, and then insurance, and opened the Legal Line, which offered advice in the evening.

The following chapters express the experience and knowledge of advisers at the Terrence Higgins Trust Legal Centre and Threshold Housing Advice. We feel that our understanding of how the law can, and cannot, meet the needs of people directly affected by AIDS should be shared with everyone dealing with the public issues of AIDS. We hope it will advance the cause of assistance and education against one of suffering or discrimination.

Dai Harris
April 1989

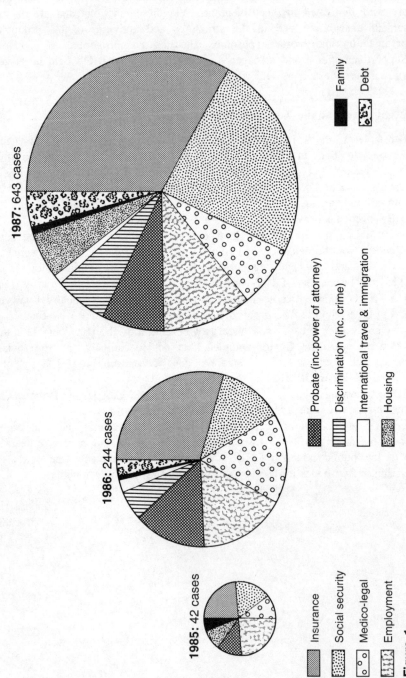

1987: 643 cases

1986: 244 cases

1985: 42 cases

Family

Debt

Probate (inc.power of attorney)

Discrimination (inc. crime)

International travel & immigration

Housing

Insurance

Social security

Medico-legal

Employment

Figure 1

Chapter two

Medico-legal aspects of AIDS
Colin A.M.E. d'Eca

Introduction

Apart from the law of negligence in relation to death and personal injury, the law relating to medical issues is poorly developed in England and Wales. The lack of case-law concerning specific issues, which have become highlighted because of the AIDS epidemic, has made it difficult to be specific about what the law actually is. Experience of other common-law jurisdictions such as the United States of America, Canada, Australia, and New Zealand is not particularly helpful in this area. The few decisions made often rely upon specific state legislation outlawing discrimination in the provision of services or other human-rights legislation. In so far as decisions are based solely on common law, it has to be recognized that they are reached in the historical and social context of that jurisdiction. Whether an English court would take the same approach must be a matter for speculation.

Aspects of treatment and consent

The courts have recognized the fundamental right of all adults of sound mind to have control over their bodily integrity and protect that right through the civil wrong of trespass to the person, that is to say assault and battery, and by the criminal law relating to offences against the person.

The threat of unlawful physical force against the person (assault) or the application of that force (battery) can give rise to a legal action in the courts for damages unless the touching is negligible, no more than can be expected in the normal course of life, or there is consent or there is statutory sanction for the touching. All medical treatment, including examination and diagnostic procedures, is thus potentially an act of battery in the absence of consent or statutory sanction.

Of particular interest in the context of this volume is the issue of HIV antibody or antigen testing, both of which rely on the touching of the subject to remove a sample of blood. It is the act of taking the blood, not the actual blood testing, which can give rise to the action for battery. This is an important distinction as will be seen below.

In English law, consent may be either express or implied. The courts have circumscribed the circumstances in which consent will be implied and are reluctant to extend the concept, where a defence of implied consent is raised. However, the limits are not closed. The most obvious circumstance covered by implied consent is 'necessity', where the patient is unconscious or otherwise unable to indicate consent and the treatment is essential to save life or preserve the health of the person. The word 'essential' within the concept of necessity is important: it is not sufficient if the action is simply desirable or expedient. Implied consent may arise from the nature of the conduct of the parties: where a patient requests treatment from a doctor and does not query the doctor's actions, it will be implied that the patient has consented to all the subsequent procedures even if unaware of the extent or nature of those procedures. As a result, attending for a check-up at an STD clinic and consenting to the drawing of blood, either expressly or by acquiescence, is sufficient consent to an HIV test. However, it would probably not constitute consent to such a test if the person came to the doctor for another condition to which HIV status was irrelevant for proper treatment and management.

There is much discussion amongst the medical profession and the general public to the effect that informed consent is the only valid consent. English law rejects the concept of informed consent, although it is accepted in some US jurisdictions and in Canada. The doctrine requires that the patient shall have been informed of all material factors which might influence the patient's decision to consent to the treatment. It is subject to a therapeutic defence – namely, the exercise of clinical judgement that revelation of certain facts might be prejudicial to the patient. The House of Lords, in the Sidaway case, has decisively rejected the concept and approved Lord Donaldson's words in his judgment in the Court of Appeal:

> I am wholly satisfied that as a matter of English law a consent is not vitiated by a failure on the part of the doctor to give his patient sufficient information before consent is given. It is only if the consent is obtained by fraud or misrepresentation of the nature of what is to be done that it can be said that an apparent consent is not a true consent.

In so affirming the Master of the Rolls was merely following precedent established as early as 1878. The principle also applies where the doctor is in breach of his or her common-law duty of care to the patient to inform him or her of substantial factors which may influence the giving of consent (of which more below).

Accordingly, where a person agrees to have blood taken for tests without enquiring as to the nature of the tests or procedures being taken in relation to the sample, no action lies in battery if an HIV antibody or antigen test is subsequently performed, even though consent would have been refused had the patient known that such a test were to be performed. This probably applies to HIV tests carried out on surplus blood samples taken for other purposes, at least where such testing is truly anonymized, because there is no proprietary interest in the blood once taken.

Apart from instances of fraud or misrepresentation as to HIV testing, a person's remedy in law for any testing, where the person actually or impliedly consented to the taking of the blood, lies in an action for negligence and not trespass to the person. This is an important distinction. In an action for trespass to the person, once the unlawful touching is proved, damages flow without establishing anything else. However, in an action for negligence, there must be a breach of a duty of care owed to the person making the claim and damages will only be awarded if the loss concerned was foreseeable and not too remote.

How can an action in negligence lie against a doctor for testing without consent? Part of a doctor's duty of care to the patient is to inform the patient of the nature and purpose of any proposed treatment and of the risks and implications of the treatment. The extent to which information should be given to any individual patient depends upon the circumstances and is essentially a matter of clinical judgement. A doctor is not obliged to explain the proposed treatment in detail, for example every test which might be performed on a blood sample, nor to advise upon every risk involved in a particular treatment. If a patient asks specific questions, they must be answered fully and truthfully by the doctor; otherwise, the extent of the explanation given is a matter of clinical judgement. The yardstick used is based upon what a responsible body of medical opinion practising in the area concerned believes should have been done in the same circumstances (the Bolam test). There need not be universal acceptance of the procedure, even amongst practitioners of the same speciality.

In the case of HIV testing, whether and to what extent there is a duty to give full information when obtaining consent is still an open question. In general it appears that the profession has accepted that express consent must be obtained and further that there should be adequate pre-test counselling. The General Medical Council gave guidance that doctors are expected to obtain patients' consent to investigative procedures or invasive techniques. This general principle is especially important in the case of testing for HIV infection. Only in the most exceptional circumstances, when a test is imperative to secure the safety of persons other than the patient, can testing without explicit consent be justified. It also dealt with the testing of children, which raises additional ethical and legal issues. Because one of the parents may have been the source of infection, if the child is not old enough to give consent and it is in the best interests of the child, it is considered proper to test without parental consent.

At its 1988 conference, the British Medical Association, the professional body of a large number of doctors, adopted the following resolution:

HIV testing should be performed only on clinical grounds and with the specific consent of the patient. There may be individual circumstances where a doctor believes that in the best interests of a particular patient it is necessary to depart from this general rule, but if the doctor does so he or she must be prepared to justify this action before the courts and the General Medical Council.

However, the craft union representing consultant surgeons and anaesthetists at its conference adopted a similar resolution, but one which emphasized the qualification and also included in the qualification reference to the health interests of the medical-care team. Thus, a surgeon or anaesthetist, who considered that the health of any member of the medical-care team would be at risk unless the HIV status of the patient were known and could justify that position, might successfully defend an action for negligence. However, it is hard to envisage any circumstances in which express consent could not be obtained. Where consent is refused, the health-care team is entitled to proceed as if the patient were HIV-antibody-positive, an assumption which could be adopted also where it was not possible to obtain express consent. Further, apart from suggesting the taking of additional precautions, such as double gloving and the surgeon's picking up all sharps rather than them being passed by a theatre nurse, knowledge of the patient's antibody status should have no practical effect. The guidance of the General Medical Council makes it clear that it is a doctor's duty to extend to patients with AIDS or HIV infection the same standard of care and support that they would offer to any other patient.

Although it is proper for a doctor who has a conscientious objection to undertaking a particular course of treatment to refer a patient to a professional colleague, it is otherwise unethical to refuse treatment or investigation on the grounds that the patient has a condition which might expose the doctor to personal risk or to withhold treatment on the basis of a moral judgement about the patient's life-style. Any such refusal would constitute grounds for a charge of serious professional misconduct.

Finally, the official view of the government as expressed by the then DHSS is that:

> As a positive HIV test has serious implications, counselling of patients prior to carrying out the test is essential, and further counselling must be offered if the test proves positive. . . . Routine screening of all patients for HIV infection is not desirable.

That view is incompatible with testing without consent. In view of the general opinion of the health authorities and medical profession, testing without express consent will, except in the most rare circumstances, be a breach of a duty of care and actionable in negligence. The difficulty in such an action will be proving damage and quantifying any loss.

Confidentiality of medical records

There is no law of privacy in the United Kingdom. Protection of a person's 'right' not to have information disclosed or published lies in the law of libel and slander or, in certain circumstances, in the law of confidence. In some circumstances information is protected by statutory provision.

In the main, medical information about a person is protected by the codes of professional conduct under which most of the health-care team, to whom confidential information is given, operate. The General Medical Council rules provide:

It is a doctor's duty, except in the exceptional circumstances mentioned below, strictly to observe the rule of professional secrecy by refraining from disclosing voluntarily to any third party any information he has learnt directly or indirectly in his professional capacity as a registered medical practitioner. The death of the patient does not absolve him from this obligation.

The exceptions concern disclosure with the consent, or in the best interests, of the patient, in compliance with a court order or other legally enforceable duty and, in very limited circumstances, where the public interest so requires. Circumstances in which the public interest overrides the duty of confidentiality are in the investigation and prosecution of serious crime or where there is a current or future (but not a past and non-current) health risk to others.

The General Medical Council in its guidance on HIV infection and AIDS stated:

When diagnosis has been made by a specialist and the patient, after appropriate counselling, still refuses permission for the General Practitioner to be informed of the result, that request for privacy should be respected. The only exception would be when failure to disclose would put the health of the health-care team at serious risk. All people receiving such information must consider themselves to be under the same obligations of confidentiality as the doctor principally responsible for the patient's care. Occasionally the doctor may wish to disclose a diagnosis to a third party other than a health-care professional. The Council think that the only grounds for this are when there is a serious and identifiable risk to a specific person, who, if not so informed would be exposed to infection. . . . A doctor may consider it a duty to ensure that any sexual partner is informed regardless of the patient's own wishes.

The provisions governing nurses, midwives, and health visitors are in similar terms.

These ethical codes do not have statutory force and can be changed at any time. Breach of the codes is not something which, of itself, entitles the patient to recover damages from the doctor in court, although it would probably form the basis for proceedings for serious professional misconduct before the General Medical Council. In serious cases this could result in the doctor's losing the right to practise medicine. However, the codes are also of relevance in determining whether the common-law duty of confidentiality has been breached.

The common-law duty of confidence

The duty of confidence arises whenever information is imparted by one person to another, either expressly in confidence or in circumstances where such confidentiality is implicit. In the case where the information passes from a patient to a health-care professional, in part because of the professional rules referred to above, there will be found an implied understanding that the information will be kept in confidence. Although the duty of confidence between a health-care worker and a patient arises out of the special nature of that relationship, there does not have to be a special relationship between the parties: communications between friends can be covered by the law, if circumstances so warrant.

The duty of confidentiality is however not absolute. The courts recognize a number of exceptions – namely, where the law requires disclosure; to assist in the investigation or prosecution of a serious crime; to prevent a continuing and serious threat to health of either specific identifiable persons or the public at large; where disclosure is necessary in the performance of a public or statutory duty, and where it is necessary in the public interest.

The public-interest or health-risk argument may be raised as a defence by a doctor for disclosure to third parties of a patient's HIV-antibody status. This is particularly likely to succeed where the sexual partner of the patient is also a patient of the doctor and the patient is unwilling to inform the partner of a positive test-result or allow the doctor to do so. If the doctor did not ensure that the sexual partner was informed, the sexual partner might have a cause of action against the doctor, especially if the sexual partner were also the doctor's patient. The General Medical Council considers that breach of confidentiality in these circumstances could be justified.

Where breach of confidentiality is anticipated, the subject can restrain any breach by injunction. Where, as will be the case in the vast majority of cases, the first thing the subject knows about the breach of confidence is that the disclosure has been made, the only remedy is damages. The courts have recently shown themselves very willing to preserve the confidentiality of medical records and, in particular, information relating to AIDS. In the recent case of *X vs. Y [1988] 2 AER 479*, a health authority sought to restrain a national newspaper from publishing information relating to the fact that two doctors employed by the health authority were still practising although they had both been diagnosed with AIDS. The information had been obtained as a consequence of the breach of confidentiality by an employee of the health authority. The Judge said:

> In the long run, preservation of confidentiality is the only way of securing public health; otherwise doctors will be discredited as a source of education, for future patients will not come forward if doctors are going to squeal on them. Consequently, confidentiality is vital to secure public as well as private health, for unless those infected come forward they cannot be counselled and self-treatment does not provide the best care; opportunistic infections such as shortness of breath and signs of disease in the nervous system . . . are better detected and responded to by observation, investigation, and management in hospital.

> I keep in the forefront of my mind the very important public interest in the freedom of the Press. And I accept that there is some public interest in knowing what the defendants seek to publish. . . . But in my judgment those public interests are substantially outweighed when measured against the public interest in relation to loyalty and confidentiality both generally and in relation to AIDS patients' hospital records. The records of hospital patients, particularly those suffering from this appalling condition should in my judgment be as confidential as the courts can properly keep them, in order that the plaintiffs may be free from suspicion that they are harbouring disloyal employees.

The National Health Service (Venereal Diseases) Regulations 1974 (as amended)

In the HIV field there is also some statutory protection of confidential information through the operation of the National Health Service (Venereal Diseases) Regulations 1974 (as amended). These Regulations only apply to regional and area health authorities, not to general practitioners or private hospitals or clinics. Health authorities are required to take all necessary steps to secure that any information capable of identifying an individual obtained by officers of the authority with respect to persons examined or treated for any sexually transmitted disease shall not be disclosed except:

- for the purpose of communicating the information to a medical practitioner, or to a person employed under the direction of a medical practitioner in connection with the treatment of persons suffering from such disease or the prevention thereof; and
- for the purpose of such treatment or prevention.

Those provisions would cover disclosure to the health authority's contact tracers or a general practitioner's practice nurse. The Regulations apply not only to Venereal Diseases, a limited list of prescribed diseases, but also to all sexually transmitted diseases: although HIV infection is not transmitted exclusively through sexual relations, the general view is that the Regulations apply to all cases of HIV infection. The Regulations do not prevent disclosure with the consent of the patient or where the law requires disclosure.

Specific AIDS legislation

There is little legislation in force specifically concerning AIDS and HIV infection in the United Kingdom. This in part reflects the fact that AIDS has only recently been recognized as a specific disease syndrome. Other factors include the view that the law is inappropriate to many of the issues raised. The government seems to believe that the current law is adequate and gives a low political priority to the subject.

The first legislation specifically relating to AIDS was the Public Health (Infectious Diseases) Regulations 1985. These were produced in an atmosphere of near hysteria induced by ill-informed press comment at a time when medical knowledge of the causes and infectious nature of AIDS and HIV infection was less advanced than it is now. It was a minimal response using what powers were available to the Secretary of State without new primary legislation, so as to stave off the calls for more draconian measures.

The Regulations were made under the Public Health (Control of Diseases) Act 1984. They do not make AIDS a notifiable disease but they apply Sections 35 (medical examination), 37 (removal to hospital), 38 (detention in hospital), 43 (death in hospital), and 44 (isolation of the body) of the Act to AIDS.

Sections 35, 37, and 38 have common requirements for their application. In order to obtain an order applying the section concerned, the appropriate officer must make an application, which may be made without informing the person against whom the order is sought, to a magistrate, who must determine whether or not to make the order.

Section 35, Medical examination

The application for an order for medical examination must be made by a medical practitioner nominated by the local authority for the district and be supported by a written certificate signed by the medical practitioner to the effect that the requirements of Section 35 are satisfied.

This section is applied by Regulation 2 of the 1985 Regulations not only to those with AIDS but to those who are HIV-antibody-positive or suspected of being so but only if it can be shown that:

- it is expedient to examine the person medically in the person's own interest or that of his or her family or the public generally; and
- either that the person is not under the care of a doctor or, if so, that the doctor consents

The crucial issue is thus the question of 'interest'. Because there is at present

no means either of preventing (other than by avoiding infection) or curing HIV
infection and there is no treatment available for HIV infection, it is difficult
to argue that examination is in the interest of the person concerned or the
public. The family interest is more problematical. A person having a sexual
relationship with the person concerned may wish to avoid infection.
Moreover, the fact of transmission of infection from mother to child before
or during birth is well known as is the increased risk of a pregnant woman
who is HIV-antibody-positive developing AIDS: in the case of couples where
one is, or may become, pregnant, she may well have an even greater interest
in knowing the HIV-antibody status of her male partner. However, even
though it may be argued that a sexual partner has an interest, there is nothing
in the legislation which permits the disclosure of the result of an examination
without the consent of the person examined, so it is not an interest which can
be satisfied.

Section 35 orders can be supplemented by an order under Section 61 of the
Act. This provides that a magistrate may issue a warrant to support the entry,
if necessary by force, of an authorized officer into any premises in order to
discharge the officer's duties under the Act. Wilful obstruction of an officer
in the discharge of his duty under the Act or of a warrant is a criminal offence
punishable by a fine. Section 15 of the Act also makes wilful neglect or refusal
to obey or obstruction of the execution of the Regulations an offence
punishable by a fine, and in the case of a continuing offence by a further fine
of up to £50 per day.

Although there are penalties for failure to comply with an order for medical
examination, there is no provision in the legislation for the dispensation of
consent to treatment. Thus, a medical practitioner carrying out such an
examination in the face of express refusal of consent is at risk of being sued
for assault. It is doubtful whether any doctor would proceed in such
circumstances.

Section 37, removal to hospital

This section is applied by the Regulations only to those who have been
diagnosed as having AIDS (being HIV-antibody-positive or having ARC is
insufficient). The magistrate, before making an order on application by the
local authority, must be satisfied that:
- the person is suffering from AIDS;
- the person's circumstances are such that proper precautions to prevent
  the spread of infection cannot or are not being taken;
- as a result there is a serious risk of infection to other people;
- that there is National Health Service hospital accommodation available;
  and
- the area or district health authority responsible for the proposed hospital
  of admission consents to that person's admission.

The conditions are cumulative. The implication of the section is that hospitalization will reduce or eliminate the risk of infection. Because of the limited ways in which HIV is transmitted (see Chapter 1), infection can only be avoided by avoiding risk activities. It is therefore likely that, except perhaps in the case of haemorrhage or where other large volumes of body fluids are being produced, the section will never apply.

Section 38, Detention in hospital

This section has been specifically modified by Regulation 3 of the 1985 Regulations to apply in AIDS cases only where specific circumstances justify detention in hospital. The local authority must show that:

- the person is suffering from AIDS;
- the person is an in-patient in hospital;
- on leaving hospital:
  - the person would not be provided with suitable lodging or accommodation to allow proper precautions to be taken to prevent the spread of infection; or
  - proper precautions will not be taken in other places to which the person might be expected to go to prevent the spread of AIDS.

This additional criterion is widely drawn and would apply to any place to which a person might go – for example, a cinema, public swimming pool, pub, club, or shop; but whether the section applies is likely to be qualified by the possible activities of the person and the risk which he or she poses to others. Those who habitually abuse drugs administered by injection may well be caught by this provision.

It should be noted that the section refers to spreading the disease, in this case AIDS and not the wider term 'infection' which is used in Section 37. It could be argued that because HIV infection does not necessarily *per se* result in AIDS, the section does not apply. However, the courts may not accept such a technical argument where public health is concerned.

This section has been applied once in relation to AIDS, in Manchester. The case went to appeal in the Crown Court with a High Court Judge presiding. However, because the case was dealt with by consent, no case-law was created. The remarks of the Judge that the Magistrate was correct in issuing the order can only be said not to be binding authority. There are grave doubts whether the person who was the subject of the order (and who was said to be explosively haemorrhaging) fell within the ambit of the section: in particular there was no evidence that he actually had AIDS, as opposed to being HIV-antibody-positive.

An order is made for a specific period but there can be applications to extend the period of the original order and any subsequent order. Leaving the hospital in breach of an order is punishable by a fine. In addition the court can order forcible removal back to hospital.

Appeals

Appeals can be made against any order issued under Sections 35, 37, and 38 initially to the Crown Court. Judicial review would also be available to challenge procedural errors or matters of jurisdiction but not on matters of fact or applicability.

Section 43, Removal of body of person who has died of AIDS

Where a person dies of AIDS in hospital, a proper officer of the local authority or a doctor can certify that, in his or her opinion, it is desirable, in order to prevent the spread of infection, that the body should not be removed from the hospital except for the purpose of being taken directly to a mortuary or to be cremated or buried. Where there is such a certificate, it is a criminal offence, punishable by a fine, to remove the body except for the purpose of immediate disposal.

Section 44, Isolation of the body of a person who has died of AIDS

The section imposes a duty upon the person in charge or in control of the premises (for example, the hospital manager, mortician, or undertaker) in which the person who has died as a result of a condition associated with AIDS to take such steps as are reasonably practical to prevent persons unnecessarily coming into contact with the body. Failure to take such steps is a criminal offence punishable by a fine.

These two sections together can prohibit the body of a person who has died from AIDS remaining in the home, or being viewed in an open coffin.

The AIDS Control Act 1987

This Act, introduced into Parliament as a private-member's bill, came into force on 15 May 1987. It has been amended by regulations made under Section 1(5) with effect from 28 February 1988. Essentially it provides for the collection and reporting of statistics relating to the number of people diagnosed as having AIDS, of those dying as a consequence of AIDS, of those known to be HIV-antibody-positive, the facilities and staff available for testing for HIV infection, offering counselling, treatment, and other measures, in particular health education, designed to prevent the spread of HIV infection. The reports are to be drawn up by each district health authority in England and Wales and each health board in Scotland. The reports are to be produced in accordance with the requirements of the Secretary of State at least once a year. The reports are to be published.

The Health and Medicines Act 1988

Section 23 of this Act prevents the sale, supply, or administration of any equipment or reagents whose purpose is to detect antibodies to any Human Immunodeficiency Virus except by, or under the direction of, a doctor. This provision is intended to prohibit the sale of do-it-yourself HIV-antibody-test kits and to curtail the establishment of 'cowboy' testing centres, where there is no medical supervision and so no guarantee of adequate pre- and post-test counselling.

The National Health Service (Charge to Overseas Visitors) (No.2) Regulations

These Regulations as amended impose a duty upon a health authority or board to make and recover prescribed charges for health services provided to overseas visitors. For the purpose of the Regulations, a person is an overseas visitor if not ordinarily resident in the United Kingdom. Case-law in the immigration field may be relied upon where there is doubt as to residence. Clearly such residence must be lawful residence. A person is exempt from the overseas visitors provisions if he or she:

- has been lawfully resident in the United Kingdom for the 12 months preceding the date treatment is given; or
- is a refugee or, having applied for that status, has not had the result of the application determined by the authorities; or
- is a member of HM forces, a Crown servant, or a British Council employee; or
- has been working overseas but has not done so for more than 5 years or, where the person has worked overseas for more than 5 years, employment is under a contract which provides for home leave at least once every 2 years and that the person has lived in the United Kingdom for a period of at least 10 years; or
- is working in a Member State of the European Community and is paying national-insurance contributions; or
- is an EEC national or the member of the family of an EEC national to whom regulations EEC 1408/71 or 1396/81 apply; or
- is a prisoner or detained under immigration legislation; or
- is a national of a state with reciprocal health arrangements with the United Kingdom and whose need for treatment arose after arrival in the United Kingdom; or
- is an EEC national whose need for treatment arose after arrival in the United Kingdom.

Certain services are exempt from charges including amongst other things emergency treatment on an out-patient basis at a hospital, treatment of any notifiable disease under the Public Health (Control of Disease) Act 1984, certain specified infections not being notifiable diseases, food poisoning and food-borne infections, sexually transmitted diseases, other than AIDS or HIV, and treatment given under the provisions of the Mental Health Act 1983.

Charges are imposed for accommodation, diagnostic procedures, medical and surgical treatment of various kinds, and the supply of drugs or medicines which are designed to eliminate, prevent the replication of, or in any way inhibit the mode of action of any human immunodeficiency virus. The amount of the charge is specified in the regulations. The liability to meet them rests on the patient receiving the treatment except in the case of an employee of a vessel or aircraft, in which case the liability is that of the employer.

Medical complaints

The forum for bringing complaints relating to medical treatment varies according to the nature of the complaint, the status of the person against whom the complaint is made, and the type of service involved. The complaint may relate to a claim for personal injury or death, professional conduct, clinical judgement, or administrative matters: it may be against an independent practitioner, such as a general practitioner, dentist, optician, or pharmacist and it may relate to medical, dental, optical, or pharmaceutical services. Different complaints procedures have developed, each with their own and often critical time limits. It is essential to identify the correct forum and ensure that action is taken within the prescribed time limits and in the required manner.

Personal injury

Where damages are sought for physical injuries or death arising out of medical treatment, the claim is based on negligence and action must be brought in the courts, either the county court or, more likely, the High Court, depending on the amount of damages sought. Negligence actions and the procedure for prosecuting them lie outside the scope of this chapter.

Failure of independent practitioners to provide service adequately or at all

General practitioners, dentists, opticians, and retail pharmacists are all independent contractors who provide services to the National Health Service in accordance with the statutory terms and conditions for service prescribed by the relevant set of regulations.

The duties owed by a doctor are generally owed to those persons who have been accepted or agreed to be accepted to his or her list drawn up by the Family Practitioner Committee contracting the doctor's services, persons assigned to the doctor by the Family Practitioner Committee, temporary residents, those given immediate treatment because of accident or other emergency, and patients of another doctor for whom the doctor is acting as deputy. A doctor can terminate his or her responsibilities to a particular individual by having the person removed from his or her list in accordance with the prescribed procedure. It is not possible to terminate responsibility earlier than the date of assignment of the patient to another doctor or the eighth day after the treatment of the patient ceases, which ever is the earlier date.

The primary duty imposed is for the doctor to render to patients all necessary and appropriate personal medical services of the type usually provided by general medical practitioners. Such services are to be provided at the doctor's practice premises or, if the condition of the patient otherwise requires, elsewhere within the doctor's practice area. A doctor is under no contractual duty to provide such services outside that area. Except where prevented by an emergency, a doctor must attend and treat a patient at the places and during the hours approved by the Family Practitioner Committee, unless an appointments system is in operation and the patient attends without an appointment: in this case, if the patient's health will not be jeopardized, treatment can be refused and the patient given an appointment to attend within a reasonable time. When a doctor is going to be absent or unable to provide medical services, he or she must ensure that his or her patients have access to such services, either by the employment of an assistant or deputy or by making suitable arrangements with another doctor. The doctor is also required to provide proper and sufficient accommodation at the practice premises. A doctor must keep adequate records of the illnesses and treatment of patients, forward those records on request to the Family Practitioner Committee (to whom they belong), and forward them to the Family Practitioner Committee within 14 days of notification of the death of a patient on the doctor's list. The doctor is required to issue certain certificates to patients free of charge and may not demand or accept fees or remuneration for any treatment provided to patients except where authorized by the Regulations.

Dentists are required by their terms of service to employ a proper degree of skill and attention, except where providing occasional treatment, to provide treatment necessary to ensure dental fitness and satisfactorily complete that treatment and in general to give the treatment personally. The dentist is under an obligation when administering a general anaesthetic in connection with any operation to provide the services of a doctor or another dentist and is also under a duty to make home visits to patients within a 5-mile radius of the surgery when the patient's condition so requires. When the services required cannot be provided by a dentist who knows that the services can be provided by another dentist or by a hospital, the dentist must inform the patient. If the patient wishes, the dentist must take all necessary steps to arrange for those services to provided. A dentist has to keep records in respect of each patient.

Fees and remuneration must not be demanded or accepted from a patient by a dentist except as provided by the Regulations. Approved treatment is to be provided within 6 months from approval (12 months where there are extractions and the consequent provision of dentures), provided that no delay is caused by the patient. A dentist is required to provide a proper, sufficient, and suitably equipped surgery, and waiting-room accommodation for patients. Dentists, where unable to provide services personally, may do so by a partner or the employment of assistants or deputies.

The complaints procedure for independent contractors

Complaints involving breach of the terms and conditions for the supply of services, such as failure to attend a patient, must be made to the Family Practitioner Committee contracting for the professional's services.

The Family Practitioner Committees are established under the National Health Service Act and Article 2 of the Family Practitioner Committee (Establishment) Order 1985. There are now some 180 Family Practitioner Committees with members appointed by the Secretary of State for Health. Each committee consists of professional and lay members: the former are drawn from the local district health authority and the latter from local authorities lying within the locality of the committee.

Each Family Practitioner Committee must establish for its area one or more medical, pharmaceutical, dental and, joint-service committees. These service committees, other than the joint service committee, consist of a chair and six members; the joint committee has a chair and ten members. The six members consist of three lay members appointed by and from the lay members of the Family Practitioner Committee and three professional members appointed as is relevant by the local medical, dental, and pharmaceutical committees. The chair is appointed by the service committee from amongst its lay members or, if the committee cannot agree, by the Family Practitioner Committee. If the service committee does not agree with the Family Practitioner Committee's appointment, the Secretary of State determines the matter after consultation.

The ophthalmic service committee consists of a chair and ten members, four lay members appointed by and from the lay members of the Family Practitioner Committee, two ophthalmic medical practitioners appointed by the local medical committee, two ophthalmic opticians, and two dispensing opticians appointed by the local optical committee. The joint-services committee consists of a lay chair, two lay members, two doctors, two dentists, two pharmacists, and two ophthalmic medical practitioners or opticians. Any of the members of the service committee can be represented by deputies. The chair serves for one year but can be reappointed.

Time limit for complaints

Complaints must be made in writing to the Family Practitioner Committee and, except where the late claim provisions apply, within 8 weeks from the event giving rise to the complaint. For dentists the complaint must be made within 6 months of completion of the treatment or within 8 weeks after the event giving rise to the complaint, whichever is the earlier date. The Family Practitioner Committee has a discretion to accept late complaints if satisfied that illness or other reasonable cause contributed to the delay and either the person complained against or the Secretary of State consents to the admission of a late claim. Where the Family Practitioner Committee seeks the Secretary of State's consent, the person complained against will be supplied with a copy of the complainant's notice, statement, and reasons for making the late application, and has 14 days to forward a statement to the Secretary of State stating why the investigation should not take place. Where the Secretary of State's consent is not sought, the Family Practitioner Committee must give reasons for its decision, notify the complainant of the decision, the reasons for it, and the complainant's right to appeal to the Secretary of State.

Where the Family Practitioner Committee decides not to investigate the complaint, the complainant may within 14 days make an appeal in writing setting out the grounds of appeal. Once the appeal is received by the Secretary of State, the person complained against will be notified and will have 14 days in which to make written representations. The decision of the Secretary of State is given with reasons and, subject to judicial review, is final.

Procedure where the complaint is initially accepted by the Family Practitioner Committee

If the complaint is accepted by the Family Practitioner Committee, the Secretary will forward the complaint to the chair of the relevant service committee. If the complaint relates to more than one service committee's jurisdiction, it will be referred to the joint-service committee.

If the chair considers that no complaint is made out he or she will inform the secretary of the Family Practitioner Committee, who will then write to the complainant inviting a further statement amplifying the complaint to be submitted within 14 days. If no response is received from the complainant within the 14 day period or if the chair is still not satisfied that there is a complaint within the service committee's jurisdiction, the matter will be referred to the committee for determination without a hearing. Where the original or subsequent complaint does disclose an issue for determination, the secretary of the Family Practitioner Committee will send a copy of the complaint to the person complained against, inviting comments in writing within 4 weeks or such longer period as the committee may allow. A copy of any response made is sent to the complainant who has 14 days in which to respond in writing.

The chair, having read the papers, will then decide whether there should be a hearing or the matter ought to be determined by the committee on the papers. A hearing will be held if no comments are received in response to the papers or comments are received and the chair considers that a hearing is necessary or there is a dispute as to the facts.

Where the complaint concerns the acts or omissions of a deputy or assistant, that person will become a party to the proceedings, upon application to be so treated within 14 days of being notified of the complaint. However, the service committee can take no formal action against such a person who has no right of appeal against the service committee's decision. Where the principal is not personally in breach, the service committee can dispense with a hearing in relation to the principal but continue the investigation of the deputy.

Where it is decided to hold a hearing, the secretary of the Family Practitioner Committee must give all interested parties at least 21 days' written notice of the date, time, and place of the hearing. The chair can postpone the date fixed (whether or not either party applies for a postponement) if satisfied that the attendance of either party or of any witnesses or the date fixed is not practicable, or for any other reason.

If either party fails to attend the hearing on the date fixed and the service committee is satisfied that such absence is due to illness or some other reasonable cause, the service committee may adjourn the hearing after inviting the observations of the party who did attend.

The hearings are always held in private and only the parties may be present. Witnesses may only be present while giving their evidence. The complainant can be represented by any person other than a barrister or solicitor, whether acting in that capacity or not.

Before the hearing commences, the chair will ask members of the service committee whether any of them has a direct or indirect interest in the case: if so, they will be required to withdraw from the committee and a deputy substituted.

If, during the course of the proceedings, the complainant introduces any issue which the chair considers was not sufficiently disclosed in the written statement(s) sent to the person complained against, the chair has a discretion to admit or exclude the issue. If he or she decides to admit the issue, he or she must give the person complained against or the representative of that person or the representative of any of the local committees an opportunity to seek an adjournment to consider the new matters. Where a hearing is adjourned for any reason, no member of the service committee may be present who was not present at the earlier hearing.

The quorum for the service committee is the chair, one lay member, and one professional member.

After having heard the parties and any witnesses and after considering any documents submitted, the service committee draws up a report setting out the relevant facts as found, the inference drawn from those facts, and states whether in the committee's opinion there has been a breach of the terms and conditions for service, and must make such recommendations as to the actions (if any) which the Family Practitioner Committee ought to take. The service committee is also entitled to bring to the attention of the Family Practitioner Committee past breaches of service by the person against whom the complaint is made.

The Family Practitioner Committee must accept as conclusive any findings of fact made by the service committee and must consider the report. The Family Practitioner Committee may decide to take any of the following actions:

- limit a doctor's list to a particular number;
- recommend to the Secretary of State recovery from the doctor, optician, or pharmacist, by deduction from any remuneration, of an amount to meet any expenses, except those incurred in connection with the investigation by the Family Practitioner Committee, which have been reasonably and necessarily incurred by any person by reason of the practitioner's failure to comply with the terms of service, such monies to be paid to that person;
- in the case of a dentist, may recommend to the Secretary of State deduction from remuneration or otherwise any expenses reasonably and necessarily incurred because of the dentist's default. This is subject to a maximum which can be recovered in respect of obtaining further dental treatment;
- recommend to the Secretary of State the withholding of any amount of remuneration;
- may make representations to the National Health Service Tribunal established under Section 42 of the National Health Service Act as amended that the practitioner's name should be removed from the list;
- in the case of dentists, that, apart from emergency treatment or examination, the dentist for a specified period seek prior approval from the Dental Estimates Board for all specified forms of treatment; and
- recommend to the Secretary of State that the practitioner be warned to comply with the terms and conditions for service more closely in future.

Where the Family Practitioner Committee does not adopt the service committee's recommendations or decides to take action not recommended, it must give reasons for that decision. The parties involved as well as the Secretary of State are given copies of the report and notice of the Family Practitioner Committee's decision, together with notice of either party's right to appeal to the Secretary of State and of his or her powers to make one party pay the expenses of the other. The practitioner has a right, instead of exercising appeal rights, to make representations to the Secretary of State against any recommendations to withhold an amount from the practitioner's remuneration or, in the case of a dentist, the requirement for prior approval of the Dental Estimates Board before commencing any specified treatment.

Appeal to the Secretary of State

The Secretary of State will examine the notice of appeal and any further particulars furnished by the appellant. If it is considered that they do not disclose any reasonable grounds for appeal or that the appeal is frivolous and vexatious, the appeal may be dismissed forthwith. Any such decision is final. If the appeal is to be considered, the Secretary of State decides whether to hold an oral hearing or not. An oral hearing must be held where any of the recommendations are to limit the practitioner's list, deduct expenses from remuneration, withhold remuneration, or limit the scope of dental treatment without prior approval from the Dental Estimates Board.

Where there is an oral hearing, the Family Practitioner Committee or any person who has received notice of appeal (the parties to the original hearing) can appear and take part in the proceedings. Any party may be represented by any person, including a barrister or solicitor.

The hearing is conducted by officers of the Department of Health appointed by the Secretary of State. The inquiry is conducted by a panel of three officers, a legal chair, and two professionals, one of whom must be from the same branch of service as the professional appearing before the inquiry.

It is not possible to rely on any facts or matters not raised before the service committee except with the consent of the Secretary of State, unless 7 days' written notice has been given to all interested parties.

The inquiry is held in private. The inquiry panel can compel the testimony of witnesses and the production of documents, and failure to appear can be punished either by a fine or committal to prison for contempt.

The members of the inquiry will draw up a report and present it to the Secretary of State for his or her consideration. The ultimate decision is that of the Secretary of State and will be notified in writing with reasons to the parties concerned. His or her decision is final and conclusive.

Complaints about National Health Service hospital treatment

There are no fixed legal procedures for making complaints about hospital treatment. The Secretary of State has issued directions to health authorities pursuant to the Hospital Complaints Procedure Act 1985. These directions are however more like guidelines and urge each authority to establish and publish the procedures to be operative in their area. Thus, all that can be said here is the general nature of the complaints procedure: each hospital will have its own procedure which must be adhered to.

The procedures differ as to whether the complaint relates to minor matters,

matters not concerning clinical judgement, and those matters which do concern clinical judgement.

Many minor complaints can be resolved informally by discussing the matter with the personnel involved. Where matters cannot be dealt with in this way, the ward sister should be involved if it concerns nursing or non-medical staff. If the complaint relates to the medical staff, the consultant in charge must be informed.

Where a patient wants to make a complaint to the health authority, this must be done in writing and the complaint should be addressed to the area or district administrator of the relevant authority. Information about making complaints should generally be available to all patients in the 'hospital booklet', which ought to be provided on admission, and in any event at out-patient departments.

Formal complaints should usually be made within a year of the event giving rise to the complaint.

All complaints are to be investigated thoroughly, fairly, and as promptly as circumstances allow. The investigating members of staff should keep the complainant and all those concerned with the complaint informed as to the reasons for unavoidable delay in resolving the complaint. Any member of staff involved in the complaint should be informed of the allegations made at the outset, given the opportunity to reply, and advised of the right to seek the advice and assistance of the staff member's professional association or union.

Where there is a possibility of litigation, the advice of the legal adviser of the authority should be obtained so as to avoid or minimize the risk of prejudicing civil proceedings by the manner or conduct of the investigation. The likelihood of litigation should not prevent investigation of the complaint.

Where the complaint is made orally to the consultant, the consultant will attempt to resolve it initially and will make a record of the complaint and the resolution in the patient's notes. If the matter cannot be resolved, the consultant will advise that a formal written complaint be made to the area or district administrator. Where the complainant is unable or unwilling to make a complaint in writing, the consultant should arrange for a written report to be made which the complainant should sign. A copy will be given to the complainant. Any written complaint should be notified to the chair of the authority by the district administrator or secretary of the board of governors where local arrangements have been made for administrative staff to deal with complaints. Any reply to the complainant following investigation must be referred to the district management team, who will either agree or reply on behalf of the authority. In cases of serious concern the chair of the authority may reply personally. The reply will explain the action taken or why no action was taken, as appropriate. All members of staff involved in the complaint will be informed of the outcome. A complainant who is still dissatisfied should be informed of the right to seek the assistance of the National Health Service Commissioner (NHS Ombudsman).

Complaints concerning the clinical judgement of staff

Where a complaint concerns the clinical judgement of a member of staff, the consultant must deal with the issue. The member of medical staff involved should be consulted from the outset and throughout the complaint procedure. In some cases the patient's general practitioner may be involved. If the consultant feels that litigation is likely, the consultant must also involve the district administrator who must in turn seek the advice of the authority's legal adviser. Any non-clinical aspects of the complaint should be referred to the district administrator to be resolved as explained above.

The district administrator, on behalf of the authority, will send the terms of any reply to the complainant, having agreed the text concerning any clinical matter with the consultant in charge.

A complainant who is still dissatisfied with the reply may renew the complaint either to the authority or one of its administrators or the consultant. If the complaint has not yet been reduced to writing, this will be requested. The Regional Medical Officer will now be informed by the consultant. The Regional Medical Officer, consultant, and other professional colleagues brought in by the consultant will then discuss whether stage III of the procedure should be activated.

Only complaints of a substantial nature which are not likely to be the subject of formal action by the authority or the courts get to stage III.

The Regional Medical Officer will arrange for two independent consultants in active practice in the appropriate speciality or specialities to consider all aspects of the case. These two consultants will be nominated by the Joint Consultants Committee. One of them should be a doctor working in a comparable hospital in another region.

These consultants will have access to all the clinical records. They will discuss the complaint with the consultant in charge, the other medical staff involved, and the complainant. The discussion with the complainant is in the nature of a complete medical examination and will be carried out in the absence of the consultant in charge and any other medical staff involved. The complainant may be accompanied by anyone of his or her choosing, including his or her own general practitioner. The two consultants will then report in confidence to the Regional Medical Officer.

On completion of the review by the independent consultants, the district administrator, on behalf of the authority, will write formally to the complainant with copies to the consultant and medical staff involved. The district administrator will explain what (if any) formal action is to be taken. The reply is treated as confidential unless the complainant seeks to make it public or prior or subsequent publicity necessitates the authority's commenting publicly.

Chapter three

Social-welfare law
Derick Bird

Preamble

AIDS is a wretched, unpredictable disease confounded by any number of secondary complications. There is no time-scale from diagnosis to death: it just depends upon the type of opportunistic infection contracted. Whether they have just discovered they have the virus, or have the full-blown symptoms, people with AIDS have immediate needs. They may appear perfectly healthy one day, but be close to death the next. The advice worker will experience many painful personal challenges. To achieve effective results he or she will not only have to advocate, litigate, and negotiate but may also have to counsel.

It is the recognition of the immediate needs of a person with AIDS which will generate within the advice worker much frustration. At a time when they should avoid stress at all costs, people with AIDS are faced with numerous problems covering all aspects of living – employment, accommodation, finance, and all too often relationships.

Many people believe AIDS is only attacking 'high-risk' groups such as homosexuals and intravenous drug-users. This is not so. Many women, whether single, married, or a lone parent, are infected. Paediatric cases have already been reported involving young children living at home or in care. There are incidences of pensioners who either have the virus or have developed full-blown symptoms. The presence of HIV and AIDs is reported in most ethnic communities. Certainly the majority of those infected are relatively young. Many have had good jobs but have not had the opportunity to create the resources adequate to sustain themselves when they become ill. Others have always been socially disadvantaged, particularly young 'rootless' people who may resort to prostitution for survival.

Introduction

A great deal has already been expressed about the changes of the 1986 Social Security Act introduced on 11 April 1987. It would be beneficial to enter the arena of dialogue by explaining exactly what has happened to a person with AIDS since that date.

Income Support (IS), together with its incumbent premiums, replaced Supplementary Benefit (SB). As with Income Support, Supplementary Benefit provided a basic scale rate known as 'Normal Requirements' and related

to all items of normal expenditure on day-to-day living including in particular food, household fuel, the purchase, cleaning, repair and replacement of clothing and footwear, normal travel costs, weekly laundry costs, miscellaneous household expenses such as toilet articles, cleaning materials, window cleaning and the replacement of small household goods (for example crockery, cutlery, cooking utensils, light bulbs) and leisure and amenity items such as television licence and rental, newspapers, confectionary and tobacco.

The 1980 Social Security Act recognized that the basic weekly allowance could only cover normal expenses. Some claimants would have special expenses which simply could not be met out of the basic weekly entitlement. Additional Requirements (ARs) met these special expenses on a weekly basis. Additional Requirements had the following features:

– they were paid on top of basic weekly Supplementary Benefit;
– they were assessed at the same time the DHSS assessed normal requirements;
– they could not be claimed separately from Supplementary Benefit;
– there were fourteen different additional requirements – ten covered extra expenses related to disability and therefore applied to people with AIDS;
– some Additional Requirement rates were static and accordingly it was only necessary to show the qualifying condition was met;
– other additional requirements were calculated on an individual basis. The amount depended on circumstances and the ability to calculate accurately (and prove) the actual expenses involved. This could be actual cost but also a general principle. R(SB) 1/84 at para. 5 provides an indication of the meaning of this.

It was therefore possible under Supplementary-benefit regulations to maximize the following on behalf of a person with AIDS:

(1) An AR for more than one bath per week owing to constant and chronic diarrhoea, profuse sweating by both day and night, and skin complaints requiring bathing in a solution.
(2) Where laundry could not be done at home because the adult members of the household were too ill, disabled, or infirm, or because there were no suitable washing facilities, or the quantity was substantially greater than would normally be generated (for example, incontinence), the amount by which the average weekly cost exceeded £0.55p was payable. A claim for the cost of washing powder could also be lodged.

(3) A claim was naturally lodged for the higher heating addition of £5.55 per week for a person deemed to be chronically sick and virtually housebound.

(4) It was recognized and accepted by the DHSS-designated Medical Officer that it was imperative for a person with AIDS to follow a diet to counter rapid weight loss, dehydration resulting from fluid loss by diarrhoea, together with the need to prevent the person with AIDS becoming malnourished. The actual cost varied but on average a claim for £32.75 per week was lodged with actual cost substantiated by the hospital Senior Dietitian and supported by the medical practitioner.

(5) It was possible to claim for an additional requirement of £5.80 per week for wear and tear on clothing.

It was also possible to claim for 'Domestic Assistance', where expenses were incurred for ordinary domestic tasks (for example, cleaning, cooking) and such assistance was essential because all adult members of the 'assessment unit' were incapable of performing these tasks.

It has been argued that Income Support makes the same provision as Supplementary Benefit. However, additional requirements as from 11 April 1987 have been predetermined by the rather arbitrary and ominous weekly premiums. The rates apply to everyone irrespective of individual needs. But even the basic scale rate of Income Support is dependent on age. This would suggest that a 16-year-old person with AIDS has less needs than a person with AIDS who is 30 years old!

Certainly, the legislators of Income Support recognized that chronically sick and disabled people would incur additional weekly expenses to meet their needs as a result of either their illness and/or disability with the introduction of a 'Disability Premium' and a 'Severe Disability Premium'. There is however a qualification period of some 28 weeks to be satisfied before the premiums become payable either via receipt of Invalidity Benefit or Attendance Allowance. Consequently, it can prove difficult to lift a person with AIDS on to the relevant premium because of not satisfying the conditions for receipt of Attendance Allowance or not having satisfied the 28-week waiting period.

Quite often, during this waiting period, a person with AIDS will die and therefore will not experience any degree of financial security. Death is compounded by financial insecurity, inability to maintain a proper diet, and inability to afford the necessary comfort of adequate warmth. In consequence people with AIDS are dying in the most tragic circumstances.

Further, actual disposable income has been eroded under Income Support since 20 per cent rates plus water rates is now payable by every householder. Consequently, Income Support has had further devastating effects on the person with AIDS. Previous to April 1987 it was possible to maximize weekly entitlement to approximately £115 per week, irrespective of age. Under Income Support however, a newly diagnosed 18 year old will only receive the basic 'applicable amount' for the age-group and their circumstances could be similar or even worse than someone over 25 who would be in receipt of over £15 more per week.

As with any other debilitating disease, the course and progress of AIDS differs from person to person. There is however a common denominator of physical symptoms of debilitating fatigue. AIDS also produces predictable cognitive effects including higher levels of distractability, memory impairment, poor concentration, impaired orientation, and general confusion.

The usual response, following diagnosis and not being in a position to follow gainful employ, will be negative. Various indebtedness will usually accumulate. The life-style will radically alter and it is not unknown for the person with AIDS to encounter phenomenal debts.

The question of confusion and disorientation is an important indicator when making representation. This feature of the disease can be used in favour of a backdated claim because the original claim did not declare the true circumstances. This will obviously become 'good cause for late claim', which can usually be substantiated with a backdated medical certificate (MED 3). It may be possible to lodge a claim as if it were under the regulations for Supplementary Benefit to include all additional requirements. Periods of sickness from employment can be 'linked' and combined to extend the date of the original claim.

It may be found that people with AIDS have simply stopped work because they could not cope with the physical effects of the virus in the work situation. They may have had a 'benefit stop' for 6 weeks. They may be 'signing-on' as unemployed and therefore will never satisfy the conditions for obtaining a disability premium. In these circumstances it would be better to advise people to declare themselves sick and backdate the claim to when they actually ceased working. The argument against signing-on is whether they would be capable of sustaining employment given the symptomatology of AIDS. Should it be possible to backdate the claim beyond 6 months, the person with AIDS will immediately qualify for Invalidity Benefit and any other incumbent benefit including housing costs and so on.

Recent successful claims with high awards have been attained on behalf of people with AIDS where it has been possible to backdate the claim prior to 11 April 1988. The 52-week rule should be ignored in this respect provided there is sufficient evidence to substantiate the claim. A further method, where a backdated claim has been accepted and the 6-month qualification period satisfied prior to 11 April 1988, is to claim for single payments under the old Single-Payment Regulations. Use can be made of the existing Single-Payment Regulations or Regulation 30, or, if the Single-Payment general conditions are not satisfied, consideration and determination could be made under the old Urgent Cases Regulations. It is important to construct the argument and detail the reasons why the claim is being made. This will give the Adjudication Officer an idea of the substance of the appeal, should the claim be refused. Always appeal and gather as much documentary evidence as possible with witnesses if necessary, including people with AIDS, who have already received the items requested.

It will be recalled that single payments were lump-sum payments or single grants paid to people in receipt of, or entitled to but not claiming, Supplementary Benefit or Housing Benefit Supplement (HBS). In some circumstances, help could be obtained under the Urgent-case Regulations. It is always expedient to become acquainted with the old system and regulations.

Debts, and interest on them, can be written off or repayments rescheduled if lenders are contacted early and the financial circumstances of the person with AIDS explained. Some creditors will take a realistic view of the circumstances of a person with AIDS. Bearing in mind that the life expectancy of a person with AIDS is short, the creditors will not want to appear unreasonable, uncompassionate, or unrealistic in negotiating a settlement of a debt. Another remedy to explore where property is owned by the person with AIDS is to raise a bank loan with charge against the property but request suspension of interest and capital repayments to be paid on death. Where life insurance is secured against mortgage and if the property has considerably appreciated in value, and there are no dependants to necessitate continual protection of the mortgage, the life policy could be surrendered to realize disposable capital to discharge any indebtedness.

Income support

It is assumed the advice worker reading this chapter is already conversant with the basic rudiments of both Income Support (IS) and the Social Fund (SF). It is not therefore the intention to duplicate the context and commentary concerning IS and the SF as many excellent publications are already available on the subject. It is intended to provide indicators with specific reference to people with AIDS or HIV infection.

General conditions of entitlement to income support

1. The claimant must be living in Great Britain, but
   (a) IS can still be paid to a claimant who is temporarily absent from home;
   (b) Claimants who are incapable of work through illness or disability will continue to receive IS while abroad only if the claimant goes for the 'sole purpose' of receiving treatment from an 'appropriate qualified person'. This ruling could present a problem when

advising a person with AIDS who may wish to explore 'alternative medicine' offered abroad which will not necessarily be recognized by the DHSS as being treatment from an 'appropriate qualified person'.

2. The claimant must be aged 18 or over but a young person of 16 or 17 may have an entitlement.

3. The claimant must not be engaged in remunerative work or full time (non-advanced) education.

4. Certain groups are *not* treated as in remunerative work and therefore escape this exclusion and are:
   (a) disabled people whose earning capacity is reduced by 25 per cent or more;
   (b) volunteers or charity/voluntary-organization workers receiving expenses only;
   (c) carers looking after a person receiving Attendance Allowance or someone who has claimed Attendance Allowance in the last 6 months.

5. The general rule for claiming IS is that the unemployed person must be available for employment for 24 hours or more per week. Certain groups are excluded from the need to be available for employment:
   (a) a person looking after a member of the family who is temporarily ill;
   (b) a person who is regularly and substantially engaged in caring for another person if:
       (i) the person doing the caring is in receipt of an Invalid Care Allowance;
       (ii) the person being cared for is in receipt of Attendance Allowance;
       (iii) the person being cared for has claimed Attendance Allowance but only for the period to determination of claim or for a period of 26 weeks from the date of claim, whichever date is earlier;
   (c) a person who, by reason of some disease or bodily or mental disablement, is incapable of work, which includes any period during which they are appealing against a decision that they are so incapable;
   (d) a person who is mentally or physically disabled and whose earning capacity is, by reason of that disability, reduced to 75 per cent or less of what, but for that disability, he or she could reasonably be expected to earn;
   (e) a person who is a student and who, by reason of any mental or physical disability would, in comparison with other students, be unlikely to obtain employment within a reasonable period of time.

The family unit for Income Support purposes

1. A person can claim IS for his or her family if it consists of:
   (a) any partner, married or unmarried, with whom they share a common household.
   (b) an unmarried couple is treated as a family unit where the two are living together as man and wife; or
   (c) a child or young person who is a member of the same household for whom the claimant and/or their partner is responsible.

The income and capital of the family are subject to exceptions and are therefore treated as belonging to the claimant. Further, entitlement by one family member to IS, Family Credit, or Housing Benefit generally excludes entitlement to that benefit to any other member of the family for the same period.

Children

2. A claimant or partner is treated as responsible for a child if he or she has 'primary responsibility'. If it is unclear who has primary responsibility for a child this will be decided by reference to who is receiving child benefit.

   A child can continue to count as part of the household (thus enabling the claimant to receive IS) while temporarily absent, the main exception being when the child is in care or custody, although IS will be paid for the period when the child returns home.

Equal treatment

3. A couple can choose which partner makes the claim for both of them. 'In default of agreement', the Secretary of State can decide which one is to be the claimant. There are still circumstances in which the choice of claimant can be important – for example, entitlement to a disability premium on the basis of incapacity for work.

Calculation of Income Support

1. The amount of IS a person receives is the difference between income and the 'applicable amount'. There is a capital cut-off point.

Applicable amounts

2. A person's applicable amount consists of three elements:
   (a) personal amount;
   (b) premiums; and
   (c) eligible housing costs.

Premiums

The system of premiums in effect replaced the long-term SB scale rate and Additional Requirements. Premiums were introduced to resolve conflict between means testing combined with recognition of wide divergences of need according to individual circumstances. It is debatable whether premiums compensate for loss of the long-term scale rate and Additional Requirements which were more flexible by making allowance for a broader range of health and disability problems. The current system relies heavily on either the claimant or disabled member of the family unit satisfying conditions for other social-security benefits for chronically sick or disabled people. Premiums are awarded essentially on the basis of structure of the family unit, lone parents, old age (two rates of ordinary and higher), disability, severe disability, and disabled children.

Disability premium

3. A person (but not a partner) will qualify for this premium if under 60 and is:
   (a) registered as a blind person;
   (b) in receipt of Attendance Allowance, Constant Attendance Allowance, Mobility Allowance, Invalidity Pension, or Severe Disablement Allowance;
   (c) in receipt of grant from the invalid vehicle or war pensioners' vehicle scheme, or purchasing or leasing a car under 'Motability'; or
   (d) has been treated as incapable of work for a continuous period of 28 weeks.

   Once the premium applies, any gap of up to 8 weeks is ignored.

Severe disability premium

4. It should be noted that this premium can be *added* to a disability or higher pensioner premium. It is paid at the same rate as Invalid Care Allowance (ICA) and is in essence a substitute for ICA. A single claimant or lone parent must satisfy three conditions:
   (a) the person must be receiving Attendance Allowance;
   (b) there must be no non-dependants aged 18 or over living in the same household; but the following are excluded from this rule:
      (i) a joint occupier, a subtenant, or boarder;
      (ii) any other person receiving Attendance Allowance; or
      (iii) a person employed by a charitable or voluntary body to care for the claimant or partner and for whom the claimant or partner pay a charge;
   (c) there must be no person receiving ICA for looking after the claimant. In the case of a couple, either no ICA must be in payment or only one partner can have someone receiving ICA to take care of them.

Eligible housing costs

1. Eligible housing costs are:
   (a) mortgage-interest payments;
   (b) interest on loans for home repairs and improvements;
   (c) rent or ground rent in the case of a long lease;
   (d) payments under a co-ownership scheme;
   (e) payments of Crown tenants;
   (f) service charges;
   (g) tent and site charges where the tent is a home; and
   (h) analogous payments.
2. Two basic conditions must be satisfied for housing costs to be added to the applicable amount. The initial condition is that the claimant must be responsible for housing costs. The second condition is that the person responsible for housing costs must occupy the house as his or her home. The circumstances in which a person is treated as responsible for costs are when:
   (a) liability is to someone outside the household;
   (b) there is a necessity to meet the costs because the person liable is not able to meet his or her commitment by way of (perhaps) mental incapacity and it is necessary to retain the home. This is particularly important where a homosexual couple reside together and the mortgagor is a person with AIDS in the advanced stages of the disease and the partner, whether joint mortgagor or a person merely living in the same household, does not have enduring power of attorney but housing costs are still liable;
   (c) the person in practice shares the costs with other household members who are not close relatives or a partner and it is reasonable to treat the person as responsible.

Mortgage interest

3. Interest will be payable on a loan taken out to acquire an interest in the home or to carry out repairs or improvements to the home. An equivalent amount will be met on a re-mortgage of such loans:
   (a) the 50 per cent rule applies to the first 16 weeks of a claim of interest on a loan for the purpose of 'acquiring an interest in the dwelling occupied as a home'. The 50 per cent rule excludes anyone over 60;
   (b) following the 16-week period the claimant is entitled to interest on the arrears accumulated during the period;
   (c) the application of the 50 per cent rule will lead to loss of entitlement to Income Support where the applicable amount has been reduced to a level below relevant income. Regulations provide, where the 50 per cent rule was sole reason for refusal of

a claim, that the claimant is entitled to make a second claim 16 weeks after the first claim but no later than 20 weeks following the first claim. Assessable housing costs will include full interest together with 50 per cent interest on arrears of interest;

(d) the interest payable on loans for repairs and improvements can be included in assessable housing costs. 'Repairs and improvements' are defined as 'major repairs necessary to maintain the fabric of the dwelling' but also include damp-proofing, installation of a bath or shower or sink or lavatory which has been executed to improve fitness for occupation. This is an important provision for a person with AIDS who may require adaptation to his or her home to accommodate the effects of the disease.

Restrictions and deductions

4. Assessable housing costs cannot include anything in respect of Housing Benefit expenditure.

5. For a claimant in receipt of Income Support, who has security of tenure and purchases his or her home from a private landlord or, as a tenant of the public sector exercising the 'right to buy' option, assessable housing costs will be the interest on the loan and will be limited to the 'eligible rent' used to calculate Housing Benefit.

6. An Adjudication Officer (AO) may disallow 'excessive' housing costs where:

(a) the dwelling is 'larger than required . . . having regard in particular to suitable alternative accommodation occupied by a household of the same size'. It is difficult to predict, at the time of writing, whether in practice this rule will be vigorously applied. Many single people acquire and live in a larger than average family house. There may be an instance when it will be necessary for the advice worker to argue against the application of this rule where AIDS has been diagnosed. It would be unreasonable to expect someone, given the symptoms of AIDS, to move into accommodation acceptable to the DSS. From 10 April 1989 the wording in the amendment relating to this restriction of high rents has been changed from 'may' to 'will'.

(b) There are 'relevant factors' which would make it unreasonable for the claimant to seek alternative accommodation. The AO is required to have regard to the 'availability of suitable accommodation and the level of housing costs in the area' and 'the circumstances of the family including in particular the age and state of health of its members, the employment prospects of the claimant', and 'effect on any child or young person'.

Non-dependant deductions

7. This refers to someone who 'normally resides' with the claimant and
reduces assessable housing costs where part of the latter are met, or
deemed to be met, by other persons.
   (a) A person shall be treated as residing with the claimant if he or
   she shares any accommodation excepting a bathroom, lavatory, or
   common access area, but will exclude:
       (i)   a child or young person living with the claimant;
       (ii) a joint occupier (shared responsibility);
       (iii) a tenant (rent payable treated as income);
       (iv) a person engaged by a charity or voluntary body to care for
       the claimant or partner and who is paid by the claimant or
       partner.

Assessment of income

Notional income

1. To deal with problems of abuse or collusive behaviour, account is
taken of notional income in addition to or instead of actual income.
   (a) Claimants will be treated as possessing income which they have
   deprived themselves of, for the purpose of securing entitlement to
   IS or increasing the amount of that benefit. Other notional income
   includes;
   (b) income available to the claimant upon application. The claimant is
   treated as being in possession of this from the date when it would
   have been paid;
   (c) 'earnings' where the claimant performs an unpaid service for
   another or is paid less remuneration than is typically earned in the
   locality: claimant is treated as receiving earnings reasonable for
   that employment;
   (d) payments to a third party for the claimant's family which is used
   for food, fuel, clothing, shoes, rent, and rates or housing costs
   met by IS;

there is provision for Income Support to be paid at a reduced 'urgent
cases' rate where a person is treated as possessing income which is due
but has not yet been paid and the income is not readily available. These
payments are however only available if hardship would otherwise result.

Maintenance payments

2. A periodic payment (including arrears) from a liable relative (usually
parent or former spouse), whether by court order or agreement, is almost
always counted in full as income. The definition of a liable

relative includes a sponsor who, pursuant to immigration rules, has agreed on or after 23 May 1980 to be responsible for a person from abroad. The definition of a payment made by a liable relative has been broadened to include 'any payment which would be so made . . . upon application being made by the claimant which has not been acquired by him'. In theory it would appear possible for an AO to reduce a woman's benefit to take account of notional maintenance.

Other benefits

Most benefits are counted in full but not Mobility Allowance, Attendance Allowance, Housing Benefit, Social Fund payments, and Christmas Bonus.

Payments from work other than earnings

Statutory Sick Pay, Statutory Maternity Pay, and other sick/maternity payments are counted in full. Expenses paid to a volunteer or a charity/voluntary organization worker are ignored if they are the only payment received.

Charitable/voluntary payments

If made irregularly, the first £250 paid in a year is treated as capital, and any other extra is counted in full as income spread over a fixed 52-week period. If payments are made (or due to be made) regularly, £5 per week is ignored.

Income of a child or young person

Usually the income of a child is aggregated with that of the claimant, except:

(i)   the earnings of a child still at school (newspaper round, Saturday job) are totally ignored:
(ii) where earnings and/or income exceed the personal allowance applied to the applicable amount, the excess is ignored.

Board-and-lodging regulations

There are special rules for calculating the needs of boarders and since April 1985 there has been a number of controversial changes in response to the escalating costs of meeting boarding charges. Fraud teams were deployed to deal with the so-called abuse by boarders and lodgers and there have been constant amendments following political pressure resulting from successful appeals to tribunals and the courts.

Further changes in the Board and Lodging amending Regulations took effect on 10 April 1989. Charges for board and lodging was transferred to the Housing Benefit scheme and Income Support merely meets the 'applicable amount' for boarders. This resulted in a more complex claiming process as two different agencies are involved (the DSS and HB). It is necessary for Housing Benefit administrators to deal with a more difficult and sensitive assessment.

The 1989 Housing Act now applies pressure on Housing Benefit administrators to 'restrict' rent, and Housing Benefit Officers will need to refer rent details on new claims to a Rent Officer. It is the Rent Officer who determines a 'subsidizable rent'.

Housing Benefit

1. Entitlement to Housing Benefit (HB) depends upon whether there is liability to make payments in respect of a dwelling in Great Britain which is defined as 'any residential accommodation, whether or not consisting of the whole or part of a building and whether or not comprising separate or self contained premises';
   (a) a person can be treated as occupying a dwelling as a home while being temporarily absent for a maximum period of 52 weeks, but only if;
      (i)   there is intention to return to occupy the dwelling as home;
      (ii) it has not been let or sublet;
      (iii) the period of absence is unlikely to exceed 52 weeks or in exceptional circumstances is unlikely substantially to exceed 52 weeks. This is an extremely important clause for a person with AIDS as it allows hospitalization without loss to HB entitlement.
2. Liability to make payment in respect of a dwelling is variable:
   (a) it can be the partner of the person who is liable;
   (b) it can be someone else who has to pay rent or rates because:
      the person normally liable is not making payment and the someone else is either:
      – an ex-partner of the person liable; or
      – a person who it is reasonable to treat as liable.
3. HB will not be paid where capital exceeds a specified HB limit, including capital of the partner.
4. In calculating HB the assessment is dependent on income against the appropriate IS level.
   (a) Calculations for HB are based on net earnings and will include Statutory Sick Pay and Statutory Maternity Pay but excludes Mobility Allowance and Attendance Allowance.

The advice worker should pay particular note to Regulation 69(8) in relation to a person with AIDS where 'the appropriate authority may, if the claimant's circumstances are exceptional, increase the weekly amount of any Housing Benefit to be paid'. This paragraph enables the authority to exercise power to treat the claimant as entitled to more HB than is due if the circumstances are 'exceptional'. Consideration may only be given on an individual basis and is therefore not on a predefined basis. Circumstances considered to be exceptional are given as high outgoings or high rent and/or rate arrears.

Another regulation of particular importance to a person with AIDS is Regulation 18 concerning patients who have a period of hospitalization of more than 6 weeks. The applicable amount is radically reduced after the 6-week period.

There may be an instance of a person with AIDS who is a full-time student an element of whose grant provides for rent. For the purpose of calculating eligible rent, liability is reduced by a weekly amount which, according to whether or not the claimant is attending a course in the City of London and/or Metropolitan Police area, has two rent-deduction figures. This regulation is naturally applicable to all students, but where a chronically sick student has higher outgoings, and his or her circumstances are 'exceptional', it may be an argument for using Regulation 69(8).

Given the established fact that people with AIDS can be confused, and suffer clinical dementia, a late claim for HB may be made. There may also be a possibility, where payment of HB has been made, that the person with AIDS may not have declared his or her true and full circumstances. Regulation 75(15) makes provision for backdating a claim and it is important that the advice worker is familiar with the procedure.

The procedure for making a backdated claim is exactly the same as for any other Social Security benefit (Regulation 14 of the Social Security [Claims and Payments] Regulations 1979); that there must be 'continuous good cause'. A good excuse is not good cause. There is a 52-week provision and it must be shown that the claimant with 'continuous good cause' was entitled to HB for the whole of that period.

There is for HB an appeals procedure where a review of a determination by the appropriate authority may be requested under Regulation 79(2) by written representation within 6 weeks of notification of determination. A further review under Regulation 81 may be requested in writing 4 weeks following the decision given under Regulation 79. This review will be conducted by a 'Review Board' which is appointed by the authority, so it is not necessarily an independent decision-making body. The minimum quorum of the Review Board is three and the hearing should be oral within 6 weeks of the request (or 'as soon as reasonably practicable'). The person requesting the hearing may make further written representation and take part in the oral hearing. The 'Review Board' can confirm or revise a determination, and where there is error in law either by procedure, misdirection, or failure, judicial review becomes an option as the final appeal process.

An overpayment is an amount which has been paid by way of HB to which there was no entitlement. This is a common occurrence and recovery tends to be handled very badly by the local authority, even where the overpayment has been caused by 'official error'. This is because if the Secretary of State considers that the local authority has unreasonably refused to recover an overpayment, it may affect its subsidy.

Official error refers to an overpayment caused by 'a mistake made or something done or omitted to be done by the appropriate authority'. The criteria for recovery of an overpayment depends on whether a person could 'reasonably be expected to realize' that he or she was being overpaid. This assumes knowledge of the complexity of the housing benefit system; as this chapter is devoted to the person with AIDS one should conclude that they could not be reasonably 'expected to realize' they were being overpaid.

The regulation distinguishes between overpayments which are 'recoverable' and those which are 'to be recovered' by the local authority. The discretion to recover must be exercised judicially, based on the merits of each individual case. There cannot be a blanket recovery policy and where recovery of an overpayment is exercised, the advice worker should use the review procedure until exhausted.

Board-and-lodging regulations

As previously mentioned, that part of The Housing Act 1989 which will affect boarders was implemented on 10 April. Boarders not only have to make application for IS but also for HB thus effectively receiving money from two sources. The 'moving-on' provisions concerning young people's maximum period of entitlement have now quietly been dropped. Time limits and charge limits will therefore no longer apply. However, new housing regulations are just as horrendous and will result in many people being evicted because of administrative difficulties in applying the new HB scheme.

1. The situation for boarders on IS is as follows:
   (a) boarders will have their benefit assessed from IS as other IS claimants;
   (b) boarders on IS will need to claim to the local authority for HB in the same way as non-income support boarders;
   (c) new HB rules have been introduced on the weekly deduction for meals and fuel. The new rules will apply to existing and new claimants.
2. The envisaged problems that a person with AIDS will experience with this new ruling may be:
   (a) greater poverty, financial hardship/stress, frustration, anger;
   (b) confusion as to how and where to claim benefit and entitlement;
   (c) two claims are now necessary instead of one, with more form-filling and an increase in bureaucracy;
   (d) a lack of security of tenure leading to an increase of homelessness;

(e) where there is an inability to pay for ineligible housing costs, arrears will occur leading to eviction, and further homelessness;
(f) benefit entitlement linked to age with radical differences of pay even where circumstances are similar;
(g) inadequacy and confusion over Transitional Protection;
(h) inconsistency between HB and IS as one benefit is paid in advance and the other in arrears;
(i) where a person with AIDS is a boarder, he or she will become highly susceptible to opportunistic infection due to insecurity, financial stress, and exceptional hardship.

Social-security benefits

Statutory Sick Pay (SSP)

1. It is employers who are responsible for paying SSP to their employees for the first 28 weeks of sickness. The general conditions of entitlement are therefore discussed in Chapter 5 on AIDS and employment.

Sickness Benefit

1. Sickness Benefit is not automatically payable to everyone as it is a 'contributory' benefit.
2. Entitlement depends on having sufficient class 1 and/or class 2 national-insurance contributions during any one tax year.
3. Payment for incapacity is based on a working day forming part of a period of interruption of employment.
4. Four or more consecutive days of incapacity are necessary to constitute a period of interruption of employment.
5. Periods of incapacity may be linked provided separation is not more than 8 weeks.
6. There can be disqualification for failure to attend for medical examination by the DSS Regional Medical Officer.
7. The Medical Officer can rule the claimant to be 'fit for light work'.
8. Otherwise the same rules apply as for SSP.

Invalidity Benefit

1. Invalidity Benefit is a contributory benefit payable to people who have been incapable of work for at least 28 weeks.
2. There are three component parts to the overall name of Invalidity Benefit:

(a) *Invalidity Pension* is the basic benefit replacing SSP or Sickness Benefit following 28 weeks of incapacity;

(b) *Invalidity Allowance* is payable in addition to Invalidity Pension, with the rate being dependent on age and only payable where the claimant is incapacitated for more than 5 years before pension age;

(c) *Additional Earnings-related Pension* is payable to former employees who have become entitled to Invalidity Benefit on or after 6 April 1979.

Severe-Disablement Allowance (SDA)

1. SDA replaced Non-contributory Invalidity Pension for men (NCIP) and women in November 1984.
2. SDA is a weekly cash benefit for people who have been incapable of work for a period of 196 consecutive days and who do not qualify for Invalidity Benefit.
3. There are four routes to qualify for SDA: the claimant
   (a) must be incapable of work; or
   (b) must have been so incapable when young; or
   (c) must be severely disabled, meaning:
   'if he suffers from loss of physical or mental faculty such that the assessed extent of the resulting disablement is not less than 80 per cent'.
   Normally a medical examination will be necessary but there is exemption if:
   (i) disablement has already been assessed at 80 per cent or more under the industrial injury or war-pension scheme;
   (ii) the claimant is in receipt of Attendance Allowance or Mobility Allowance;
   (iii) the claimant has been provided with a DHSS invalid tricycle or car or private car allowance;
   (iv) the claimant is registered as blind or partially sighted;
   (v) the claimant receives payment under the Vaccine Damage Payments Act 1979; or
   (d) the claimant has previously been entitled to NCIP.
4. SDA is not payable to those under 16 years or who are in full-time education (which includes those who are aged 16–19 and attending an educational course of more than 21 hours per week).

Invalid-Care Allowance (ICA)

1. ICA is a benefit for people of working age who are unable to work because they are caring for a severely disabled person.

2. It is not necessary to be related to the person or to live at the same address.
3. ICA can only be awarded if the person is spending at least 35 hours each week caring for the disabled person.
4. No person can receive ICA if they are working or in full-time education, but 'limited' part-time earnings will not affect benefit.
5. Married women can receive ICA.
6. ICA cannot be paid twice to different people looking after the same disabled person.
7. In order to qualify for ICA:
   (a) the disabled person must be in receipt of Attendance Allowance (at either rate) or Constant Attendance Allowance;
   (b) the applicant must be aged between 16 and 60 for women, and 65 for men.

Attendance Allowance

This benefit is a tax-free allowance which is totally ignored as income for IS purposes. There is a lower and higher rate and to qualify the claimant should be so severely disabled, physically or mentally, that he or she requires from another person:

- for the lower rate, at least one of the following from either (a) or (b);
- for the higher rate, at least one of the following from both (a) and (b).

DURING THE DAY
(i) frequent attention throughout the day in connection with bodily functions; or
(ii) continual supervision throughout the day in order to avoid substantial danger to self or to others.

DURING THE NIGHT
(i) prolonged or repeated attention during the night in connection with bodily function; or
(ii) 'another person to be awake for a prolonged period or at frequent intervals for the purpose of watching over the claimant'.

1. The operative word to watch out for in the legislation is 'requires', and it should be noted that the statutory conditions are 'required' rather than 'provided'. The test therefore is based on the objective existence of the need rather than actual provision of a service. Further, the need should be 'reasonably required', which is not necessarily based on medical reasons. Physical comfort of the claimant should be sufficient.

2. Attention in connection with bodily functions must be 'frequent', which, interpreted, means 'several times' and not once or twice. Further, for night, attention must be prolonged, which means lasting 'for some little time', or 'repeated'. It should therefore be concluded, as quoted from R vs. National Insurance Comr, ex-parte Secretary of State for Social Services (the Packer case), that attention means 'something more than personal service, something involving care, consideration and vigilance for the person being attended . . . a service of a close and intimate nature'.

   Perhaps more helpful are the words of Lord Denning, MR, in the same case when he spoke of bodily functions as:

   > include breathing, hearing, seeing, eating, drinking, walking, sleeping, getting in and out of bed, dressing, undressing, eliminating waste products, and the like, all of which an ordinary person, who is not suffering from any disability, does for himself. But they do not include cooking, shopping or any of the other things which a wife or daughter does as part of her domestic duties, or generally which one of the household normally does for the rest of the family.

3. Attention must be *in connection with* these bodily functions. An indication of the meaning of 'in connection with' is again contained in the Packer case:

   > duties that are out of the ordinary, doing for the disabled person what a normal person would do for themselves, such as cutting up food, lifting the cup to the mouth, helping to dress or undress or at the toilet.

4. Continual supervision to avoid substantial danger is one of the requirements of day-time attention, a condition which, according to a Tribunal of Commissioners, must contain four elements:
   (a) 'the claimant's medical condition must be such it gives rise to a substantial danger either to himself or to someone else';
   (b) 'the substantial danger must not be a too remote possibility';
   (c) supervision by another must be necessary to avoid the danger;
   (d) 'the supervision must be continual'.

5. These are phrases which do not have a specific or precise meaning. Therefore 'by day . . . throughout the day . . . at night . . . during the night' is not substantiated by any given number of days or nights during the week. The test, to qualify for Attendance Allowance, for someone with renal failure, is a need to have three sessions per week of dialysis.

Mobility Allowance

This benefit is non means-tested, and is not treated as income for IS purposes. The criteria to be satisfied to qualify for Mobility Allowance are as follows:

A person shall only be treated . . . as suffering from physical disablement such that he is either unable to walk or virtually unable to do so, if his physical condition as a whole is such that, without having regard to circumstances peculiar to that person as to place of residence or as to place of, or nature of, employment –

(i)   he is unable to walk; or

(ii) his ability to walk out of doors is so limited, as regards the distance over which, or the speed at which, or the length of time for which, or the manner in which he can make progress on foot without severe discomfort, that he is virtually unable to walk; or

(iii) the exertion required to walk would constitute a danger to his life or would be likely to lead to a serious deterioration in his health.

1. Note that Mobility Allowance is restricted to physical disablement and therefore must exclude conditions such as agoraphobia where the inability to walk would be regarded as mental disablement.

2. Personal circumstances do not include where the claimant lives or the nature of his or her employment.

3. Not everyone who is severely disabled will be awarded Mobility Allowance. This is because the Mobility Regulations stipulate 'such as permits him from time to time to benefit from enhanced locomotion'. Consequently the wording will exclude that category of disabled people who are totally bedridden. A person with AIDS who is so advanced with the disease may not qualify or even, on review for Mobility Allowance, have entitlement withdrawn.

4. The exact meaning of 'total inability to walk' is 'inability to move by means of a person's legs and feet or a combination of them'.

5. Virtual inability to walk is based on the ability to walk outdoors without severe discomfort. However, the designated medical practitioner must take into regard the distance, speed, length, and time it takes the claimant to walk, and disregard any outdoor walking which the claimant could only accomplish with severe discomfort.

6. Therefore, in essence, Mobility Allowance is awarded to a person with AIDS on the criterion of their virtual inability to walk. AIDS, it should be remembered, is an unpredictable disease and affects all parts of the bodily system and secondary complications associated with the disease are many and varied. Many drugs are prescribed which have many side-effects. 'Zidovudine' (AZT) is a very widely used drug which, although shown to prolong life, also causes confusion. Balance problems and dizziness caused by drugs should not be forgotten, together with debilitating fatigue common to people with AIDS.

7. On the basis of the arguments in paragraph 6, it is often argued that *exertion* on walking constitutes a risk to life and health for a person with AIDS, and this entitles them to Mobility Allowance.

The Independent-Living Fund

On 9 February 1988, Nicholas Scott, Minister of State for Social Services, announced in Parliament the setting up of 'a special fund in co-operation with the Disablement Income Group . . . to make payments to those *very* severely disabled people who need extensive help to live in the community'. This is *not* a social-security benefit and is *not* part of IS. It is not given as of right and it is rigidly means-tested solely for a specific purpose or a specific need.

There is only one specific target group, and to qualify for financial assistance from the Fund:

1. the applicant is so severely disabled, whether physically, mentally, or in a sensory way, to the extent that he or she needs help with domestic tasks and/or personal care to enable the applicant to live independently in his or her own home;
2. the applicant should be living alone; or
   (a) living with a partner, parent or parents, or any other person or persons who are unable because of old age, ill-health, disability, other responsibilities, or the extent of the care needed, to provide the total amount of personal care and domestic assistance required;
3. the applicant:
   (a) must be in receipt of Attendance Allowance or Constant Attendance Allowance;
   (b) must have claimed and been found to satisfy the Attendance Allowance eligibility criteria even though the 6-month qualification period has not been satisfied.
4. the applicant is severely restricted in the ability to perform normal personal care and/or domestic tasks because of disablement without extensive help;
5. the applicant or partner (or parent in the case of a dependent child) is:
   (a) in receipt of IS; or
   (b) not in receipt of IS but has net income which even though in excess of IS level is less than the amount needed to pay for essential personal care or domestic assistance and has capital of less than a specified limit;
6. that part of personal care and domestic assistance provided by a close relative who incurs only minimal expenses, or provided by a local authority, is not normally eligible;
7. personal care and domestic assistance must be paid for;
8. the above criteria having been satisfied, the trustees may give such assistance with the cost of provision of personal care and domestic assistance having regard to receipt of Attendance Allowance, Invalid Care Allowance, Income Support Severe Disablement Premium, excess income, net housing costs, to other care needs and to other such factors as the trustees think fit;

9. Not withstanding that the above criteria may not all be met, the trustees may exceptionally make payments as they think fit if such payments would prevent a severely disabled person's admission to institutional care.

Conclusion

One or more of the above social-security benefits may be payable to a person with AIDS. It is for advice workers to guide the person with AIDS through the complexity of the system to achieve the highest income levels for their clients. There is no hard and fast rule as circumstances will differ considerably.

It is important that the advice worker does not dismiss an enquiry without initially looking at the available options and alternatives. Imagine a student in full-time education diagnosed with AIDS, who is diabetic, but without the necessary resources to afford a special diet. He or she could become malnourished and highly susceptible to opportunistic infection. The student is therefore worthy of in-depth casework to establish whether he or she could qualify for any one of a number of social-security benefits.

The Social Fund

Introduction

No one could have been aware of the hostile criticism generated by the introduction of the Social Fund (SF). Its hallmarks are discretionary powers and uncertainty of what exactly is available to the claimant and the evidence of need. The SF is 'cash limited' and already there is presenting evidence of diversity of administration by local Department of Social Security offices.

It is therefore fair comment that the administration of the SF is an inequitable system which has caused those who are in greatest need further financial hardship. The concept of budget loans strikes at the very heart of social welfare, where repayments must be made from the IS 'applicable amount'. This can only serve to exacerbate exceptional hardship. It is now questionable whether there are welfare rights available to the poor, given that 'relief' is no longer afforded under the current social-security system. The Social Security Act 1986 has re-introduced the provision of 'less eligibility', as was contained in the Poor Law Amendment Act 1834.

Legislation for the SF is contained in The Social Security Act 1986 and Section 2 of the Act made provision for the establishment of a fund to be known as the 'Social Fund' (SF) to meet:

1. 'in prescribed circumstances, maternity expenses and funeral needs'; and

2. 'other needs in accordance with direction given or guidance issued by the Secretary of State'.
3. Financial arrangements of the SF provide for:
   (a) maternity and funeral payments;
   (b) loans known as Budgeting Loans and Crisis Loans;
   (c) grants known as Community Care Grants;
   (d) payments for maternity and funeral expenses are 'demand led';
   (e) any expenditure over the annual amount allocated in the national SF budget is met from a standing balance;
   (f) other payments are subject to budget constraints;
   (g) a DSS office receives an annual budget allocation which is divided between loans and grants which are separate and distinct and it is not possible to move funds between them; and thus
       (i) the SFO (Social Fund Officer) must have regard to the relevant budget allocation when determining whether to make an award and the amount or value of the payment. Therefore, bearing in mind the state of the budget, the SFO is expected to assess the relative priority of every application and to meet those needs which have the highest priority;
       (ii) expenditure is spread throughout the year by dividing the budget into monthly spending limits;
       (iii) the suggested level of expenditure for any month is not to be used as a limit, but managers are advised to adjust plans, if actual expenditure is above or below that expected, by spreading any deficit or excess over the remaining months of the year;
   (h) waiting-lists are forbidden but SFOs are advised that they may hold back borderline applications to allow other applications to come forward, or to judge better whether the budget can afford a payment, given other demands.
       Direction 7 of the Secretary of State states:
       'A social fund officer shall not make an award in respect of a repeat application within 26 weeks of a previous application for a loan or a grant for the same item of service for which a payment has already been awarded or refused unless there has been a change in the applicant's circumstances'.
4. Adjudication
   (a) Determination by AOs on maternity and funeral payments are subject to the normal rules:
       (i) determination should be within 14 days of submission, or 'so far as is practicable';
       (ii) notification of determination should be in writing together with reasons;
       (iii) there is right of appeal to a Social Security Appeal Tribunal to

be lodged within 3 months of notification of decision.

(b) In the case of budget loans and community-care grants, SFOs are advised to make determination within 28 days of receipt of an application 'whenever practicable' and decisions on crisis loans should be taken 'without delay', with investigations being carried out on the date of request or the next day.

(c) The guidance states that claimants (referred to as applicants) should be given a 'micro-produced notification' of a determination. This is a reference to the microcomputer in each office which records payments made and offered and hence the state of the SF budget.

(d) There is no indication in the SF manual that an applicant will automatically be sent reasons for a determination. SFOs are merely advised to explain the reasons for a decision if it is queried by the applicant.

(e) An applicant has 28 days from the date of determination by an SFO to request a review. The request must be in writing and must contain 'the particulars of the specific grounds' for a review. It must be signed by the applicant. The time limit can be extended for special reasons. The SFO is required to review a decision in examining the facts as they existed at the time of the original decision. If the decision cannot be changed wholly in the applicant's favour, the SFO is advised to invite the applicant to an interview at which they may be accompanied by a friend or representative.

(f) At the review interview the SFO must give the applicant an explanation of the reasons for the decision and the opportunity for the applicant to make representation. The SFO is also directed to make a written record of the representations and to agree the record with the applicant. The SFO will pass the papers to a higher executive officer for a final decision unless the matter has been decided wholly in favour of the applicant.

(g) An applicant who is dissatisfied with the SFO's determination on review can request a further review within 28 days of the determination (or longer if there are special reasons). The request must be in writing, contain the grounds for the request, and be signed by the applicant. This further review is carried out by an SF inspector who is likely to be based at the DSS regional office.

Demand-led payments of funeral expenses:

1. Eligibility

The claimant or partner must be in receipt of IS, Family Credit (FC), or HB at the date of the claim. A payment will be made where the claimant or one of the family is taking responsibility for the cost of a funeral taking place in the UK.

2. Claims

A claim for funeral payment must be made within 3 months of the funeral.

3. Amount

(a) Payment will only cover the basic expenses of a funeral to include:

   (i) the cost of necessary documentation;

   (ii) the cost of an ordinary coffin;

   (iii) the cost of transport for the coffin and bearers and one additional car;

   (iv) the reasonable cost of flowers provided by the claimant;

   (v) undertaker's fees and gratuities, chaplain's, organist's, and cemetery or crematorium fees;

   (vi) additional expenses (a set limit) arising from the religious faith of the deceased;

   (vii) (if the death occurred away from the deceased's home) the cost of transporting the body within the UK;

   (viii) reasonable travelling costs for one return journey incurred by the claimant in connection with arrangement of, or attendance at, the funeral.

(b) Deductions will be made if the claimant has capital over a set limit and also in respect of the following:

   (i) the value of any assets of the deceased which are available to the claimant without probate or letters of administration;

   (ii) lump sums due to the claimant which become payable on death from an insurance policy, occupational pension scheme, burial club, or similar;

   (iii) any surplus sum which is left over from a payment by a charity, after meeting expenses other than those for which a funeral payment is made;

   (iv) a funeral grant from public funds for a war-disabled pensioner.

4. Capital

Capital over a set limit will reduce the amount of the funeral payment pound for pound. Capital is calculated in the same way as IS except:

   (i) any capital acquired by the claimant (including a loan) for the express purpose of paying for the funeral is ignored;

   (ii) a widow's lump payment is ignored if the claim for funeral expenses is made within 12 months of the husband's death; and,

   (iii) other capital already spent on the funeral expenses is still counted as capital.

5. Recovery of payments

The Secretary of State has power to recover funeral payments from the estate of the deceased. Recovery of funeral expenses will take priority over any other liability but personal possessions left to relatives together with the value of a home occupied by a surviving partner (gay lover) are disregarded.

Cold-weather payments

Although not yet in force, there is a proposed amendment to SSA 1986 s32 to allow payments for heating expenses incurred or likely to be incurred in cold weather. Such payments will be governed by regulations with a right of appeal against determination to a Social Security Appeal Tribunal.

Other payments

There are certain general considerations to which, by law, an SFO must have regard when determining whether to make a loan or grant and how much to award:

1. the nature, the extent, and the urgency of the need;
2. the existence of resources from which the need may be met;
3. the possibility that some other person or body may meet the need, whether wholly or in part;
4. where the payment is recoverable, the likelihood of repayment, and the time within which this is likely;
5. the budget allocation.

Community-Care Grants

A Community-Care Grant (CCG) is designed to 'promote community care' by:

1. assisting an eligible person with expenses . . . where such assistance will:
   (a) help that person, or a member of his or her family, to re-establish him- or herself in the community following a stay in residential or institutional care; or
   (b) help that person, or a member of his or her family, to remain in the community rather than enter institutional or residential care;
   (c) ease exceptional pressure on that person and family; or
   (d) by assisting an eligible person, or a member of his or her family, with expenses of travel within the United Kingdom in order to . . . visit someone who is ill . . . attend a relative's funeral . . . ease a domestic crisis . . . visit a child who is with the other

parent pending a custody decision . . . or . . . move to suitable accommodation.

2. Eligible person:
   (a) the applicant must be in receipt of IS at date of application. An applicant, however, is considered eligible if he or she is to be discharged from a relevant institution within 6 weeks and in the opinion of the SFO, is likely to receive IS on such discharge.
   (b) A person involved in a trade dispute can apply for CCG only in limited circumstances for certain travel expenses.

3. Capital:
   The same rules for capital which govern the award for a budget loan, apply to a CCG.

4. Exclusion:
   Exclusions specific to CCGs are:
   (a) installation, rental, and call charges for a telephone;
   (b) expenses which the local authority has a statutory duty to meet;
   (c) costs of fuel consumption and associated standing charges; and
   (d) housing costs, including deposits to secure accommodation, boarding charges, rates, water rates, and service charges.

5. Minimum amount:
   Direction 28` stipulates a minimum payment, except for travel expenses.

6. Deciding priorities:
   The SF Manual catalogues certain vulnerable groups which it is suggested should in general be given priority. These are:
   (a) elderly people, especially ones with restricted mobility or who have difficulties doing personal tasks;
   (b) mentally handicapped people;
   (c) mentally ill people;
   (d) physically disabled people;
   (e) chronically sick people, especially the terminally ill;
   (f) people who have misused drugs or alcohol;
   (g) ex-offenders requiring resettlement;
   (h) people without a settled way of life undergoing resettlement;
   (i) families under stress; and
   (j) young people leaving local authority care.

The SF Manual lists priority situations. For each situation, priority people and priority items are identified. The priorities are in the form of guidance, not directions. SFOs are told, 'The guidance cannot be expected to cover every contingency that will arise and the absence of guidance on a particular situation does not mean that help must be refused.' Therefore an advocate could seek to persuade an SFO that the client's situation, although not specifically mentioned, still comes within the criteria for a grant, for example where a family under stress or the need of a 'whole-cost diet' for a person with AIDS. The argument could be based on the assumption that without a high protein/high calorie diet, the person with AIDS will become malnourished, dehydrated, and as a consequence highly susceptible to opportunistic infection which will necessitate hospitalization.

The provision of Budget Loans and Crisis Loans is inequitable and resort to claims should be avoided as the repayment schedule will cause a person with AIDS exceptional financial hardship resulting in considerable stress. It is for the advice worker to develop and apply his or her skills in making an application for a CCG on behalf of a person with AIDS or HIV infection. It is possible to substantiate an argument with an independent social worker's report, a medical report, and other reports from, for instance, a senior hospital dietitian.

The government claimed that single payments presented several problems of, in particular, escalating costs, lack of equality, and inflexibility. The SF has been promoted on the basis that it is both flexible and 'targets' benefits to those in greatest need. In reality the implementation of the SF has cut costs irrespective of the needs of people.

It has been argued that the SF is more equitable because people on IS like any others in work and on low income, will have to budget their resources to reduce dependence on the 'benefit culture'. But IS, even if the 'applicable amounts' were adequate for the purpose of day-to-day living expenses, does not contain an element for repayment of loans.

However, for many potential SF claimants DSS repayments should not be a problem as they will not get a loan in the first place. Far from being a more equitable system, claimants' chances of a grant or loan will depend, in part, upon where they live. The fund will be cash-limited and also run on discretion – claimants will no longer have a 'right' to anything. If their case is not judged by an SFO to be of high enough priority, they will get neither grant nor loan – and a high priority in a cash-limited situation can vary between not only where the claimant lives but also between the 5th and 25th of the month, depending on how well the local offices themselves are managing to budget. Once refused, a claimant has no right of appeal, only review by the same office.

SFOs are instructed to consider whether claimants will be able to repay a loan. The fund, it would seem, has a built-in mechanism to fail the very poorest and most in need. Officers must also see if some other body or person can help meet a claimant's needs. Charities have expressed grave concern that they will be expected to pick up the tab as research has already shown how, even in recent years, they have been unable to meet the growing demands made upon them.

Another remedy to explore where property is owned by the person with AIDS is to raise a bank loan with charge against the property and to request suspension of interest and capital repayments which would be paid on death.

Where life insurance is secured against mortgage and if the property has considerably appreciated in value and there being no dependants to necessitate continual protection of the mortgage, the life policy could be surrendered to realize disposable capital to discharge any indebtedness.

It is pure conjecture whether there is remedy for the newly diagnosed person with AIDS under the current SF provisions. No case-law exists at present to provide the advice worker with directives. It could be contended the spirit of the CCG could be the basis of argument to persuade an SFO to make an award for a 'whole cost diet' or any other additional expense which presents risk to the welfare, health, and life of a person with AIDS. A claim could be calculated and costed over a certain period, substantiated by medical evidence. A person who becomes severely dehydrated and malnourished will certainly require hospitalization which would basically defeat the object of the introduction of CCGs.

Conclusion: the available options for relief of poverty

With the introduction of Income Support and the Social Fund in April 1988, it is necessary to explore the available options to alleviate financial hardship and suffering. This section of the chapter specifically relates to those people with AIDS or HIV infection, with direction to the advice worker to seek an alternative. Alternatives may not be desirable at first, but as with any compromise, they are better than nothing. Thus, for example, meals-on-wheels might be met with a great deal of resistance but a client may soon realize that this affords the opportunity to have more money available, which would otherwise be spent on food. Where there is incontinence, laundry costs could be saved by using facilities provided by the local authority.

Liaison would seem to be the key word and with the permission of the person with AIDS, the advice worker should make contact with all the resources available in the area including social services, health authority, and the like.

1. *The Chronically Sick and Disabled Persons Act 1970*

   (a) Section 2 requires the local authority to assess the requirements of individuals determined by them to be substantially and permanently handicapped (including the mentally handicapped) as to their needs for the following services. If they are satisfied that an individual is in need of all (or any) of these they are to make arrangements that are appropriate to his or her case. They will be asked, in making assessments, also to take into account all relevant needs and not merely those referred to in the section and to judge whether these needs or others are of prime importance from a complete picture of the situation.

(b) The local authority must, when satisfied that it is necessary to meet the needs of handicapped persons, provide or give assistance to obtain all or any of the following services:

(i) practical assistance for that person in the home;

(ii) provision for that person of, or assistance to that person in obtaining, wireless, television, library, or similar recreational facilities;

(iii) recreational facilities for that person outside the home and assistance in taking advantage of educational facilities;

(iv) travelling facilities to enable the person to make use of these facilities;

(v) assistance in carrying out works of adaptations to the home or the provision of any additional facilities designed to secure their greater safety, comfort, or convenience;

(vi) facilitating the taking of holidays;

(vii) the provision of meals for that person whether in his or her home or elsewhere;

(viii) the provision for that person of, or assistance to that person in obtaining, a telephone or any special equipment necessary to enable him or her to use the telephone.

The Chronically Sick and Disabled Persons Act 1970 makes provision and the local authority has a statutory duty, but what if the local authority is in default in failure to perform? It is necessary to look no further than *Wyatt and Wyatt v London Borough of Hillingdon* (CA 9 May 1978) for the answer. It was held that because there is provision within the Act for complaint to the Secretary of State, the court was not willing to intervene in an administrative action.

A complaint could therefore be made to the Secretary of State that the local authority is in default of its statutory duty under the National Assistance Act 1948. On average it takes 2 years to have a complaint investigated by the Secretary of State for Social Services. Judicial review, even an expedited hearing, could not be entertained before receiving an answer to the complaint. The Local Authority Ombudsman could be requested to investigate for maladministration. An obvious choice is use of the Press to embarrass the local authority, but an advice worker must always be mindful of using his or her client as a pawn.

2. There are services available for the person with AIDS provided under the National Health Act 1977, which lists under Schedule 8 services which must be provided by a local social services authority – namely:
2.1 prevention of illness and the cure and after-care of sick persons;
2.2 the provision of home-help and laundry facilities.

3. Section 1 of the Child Care Act 1980 places a duty on a local authority to promote the welfare of children. Under this section, which

has been deliberately drafted in wide terms to maximize its use, local authorities have a duty to make available such 'advice, guidance and assistance' as may promote the welfare of children by diminishing the need to receive into care.

Money is available under this section of the Child Care Act 1980 but the problem for the advice worker, if dealing with young people who are either prostituting themselves and/or drug-users and perhaps homeless, is whether to alert social services to the needs of clients.

There is also difficulty where children are involved and one or both parents are HIV-infected to know whether to request help and support from the Social Services Department. A social worker without experience of the AIDS issue may consider the child to be at risk and will therefore feel obligated to seek a care order. Such action could have a devastating effect on the child and parents so it will always be necessary for the advice worker to be careful and be fully aware of the implications when taking advantage of the provisions of assistance under Section 1 of the Child Care Act 1980.

In conclusion, whenever possible, the advice worker should expose deficiencies of the system where there is a failure. Where application of either IS or the SF has not met a need and as a result the person with AIDS experiences hardship, a report should be forwarded to his or her Member of Parliament. Where there is evidence of maladministration, an application should be made for investigation by either the respective Parliamentary Ombudsman or Local Authority Ombudsman. Use of a sympathetic local councillor could be beneficial where failure by the local authority to perform its statutory duty is evidenced. The circumstances of individual cases could be collated and the deficiency highlighted by either local or national press.

Chapter four

Housing law and people with HIV infection

Ginny O'Brien, Jane Carrier,
and David Ward

Introduction

The following chapter looks at some of the main housing problems that people with HIV infection have encountered. Although the background information is given where appropriate, it does not attempt to provide a detailed manual of housing law. It is rather a discussion of the ways in which advice workers may apply the knowledge they possess to the specific problems of this particular client group: we therefore hope that the chapter will be read in full rather than simply used as a reference text.

We begin by highlighting some of the information about local housing provision that advisers will need to have *before* the client comes to seek help. This preparatory work is important: mistakes can be difficult to rectify and potentially very stressful.

The chapter then goes on to consider the major forms of tenures in the public and private sector and of owner-occupation. These sections are not wholly self-contained. Problems are considered in the text as they may be most commonly presented to advice workers. Thus, for example the main discussion of harassment occurs in the section discussing the public sector because often the problem will be encountered when the local authority insists that legal remedies for harassment be pursued rather than accepting the client for rehousing under the homeless-persons legislation. Harassment is discussed again in the section on the private sector, where the importance of providing support to the victim of harassment is stressed.

By far the largest section considers the problems of applying to a local authority as homeless and in priority need. Not only has our experience been that these problems have led to the greatest number of enquiries, but it is also, perhaps, the area where the law is more specifically related, particularly through case-law on vulnerability and intentional homelessness.

Throughout the chapter we emphasize the important role that advice agencies can play in influencing both housing policy and practice for people with HIV infection. Neither housing policy nor provision have kept pace with the development of the needs of people with HIV infection, and we believe that an approach that focuses exclusively on reactive individual casework will inevitably fall short of success.

Finally, a word about terminology. We have tried to use words with which readers will be most familiar; but we recognize the difficulties around such terms. For example the term AIDS-related Complex (ARC) is not unproblematic; it may be read *quite wrongly* as a less serious condition than AIDS. Further, the definition of AIDS has varied as our knowledge has increased, and certain conditions previously included with ARC are now regarded as indicating AIDS. We recognize too that for the sake of simplicity it may be useful to use such phrases as 'people with AIDS, ARC, or HIV positive'. However, advisers should be sensitive to the differences between each individual's experience of HIV infection and the problems he or she faces as a result.

We would of course like to express our thanks to all our colleagues whose experience we hope is reflected here, and to David Taylor and Russell Campbell whose comments were helpful and informative; but most importantly we thank the clients themselves whose courage and strength continues to demand admiration.

Information

When advisers are working with a client with HIV infection and who has housing problems, time is of the essence. There is a link between poor-quality housing, stress, and the progression of the disease. It is therefore important to be aware of all relevant housing procedures and options to ensure that the swiftest route to housing is open to your client.

Clients themselves must always play a central role in the resolution of their housing difficulties. Advisers should therefore ensure that clients are always fully aware of all the available options, so they are in a position to reach a well-informed decision about their housing. Similarly, visits to the local-authority housing department or to the building society are likely to be less daunting if the adviser takes the time to discuss with the client what is likely to happen to them.

The actions of advisers must always be informed by the stated needs and wishes of the people with HIV infection with whom they are working. There will for example be times when your clients may feel unable to carry out negotiations themselves for a variety of reasons, including ill-health. Advisers should be sensitive to this and be prepared to take a more active role when necessary.

Housing resources which need to be identified and explored include the following:

Emergency accommodation

Although most local authorities accept that they have a duty to house homeless people who have AIDS or ARC under the Housing Act 1985 Part III, it is increasingly rare for responsibility to be taken for homeless people who are HIV-positive and asymptomatic (unless of course, there are other factors involved, for example where the applicant is pregnant or has children). For people who are HIV-positive, asymptomatic, and literally homeless, advisers may have no alternative but to attempt to locate good-quality emergency accommodation.

Bed-and-Breakfast accommodation, which tends to be characterized by poor conditions and overcrowding, should be avoided if at all possible. If, however, there is no alternative, the Bed and Breakfast used should be warm and clean, with single rooms and with facilities which are shared between only a small number of people. Access to cooking facilities is also important, as this increases control over diet and nutrition.

Similar physical standards should be applied to emergency hostels. In this case, it will be useful to find out whether local hostels have yet addressed existing policies or formulated new ones to incorporate HIV infection. If they have not done so, it may be appropriate to suggest that they should consider this.

It is essential to be aware of all the good-quality temporary accommodation which exists in your area. However, are you also familiar with all local provision for people with special needs?: for example, are there any local emergency facilities which would be suitable for very young people or drug-users who are HIV-positive?

Local authorities

Local authorities still have a major role to play in providing good-quality housing for people with HIV infection. Advisers should be familiar with all local-authority policies which are likely to have an impact on people with AIDS, ARC, or who are HIV-positive. For example, what are the Homeless Persons Unit's policy guidelines on this issue, and what do they view as 'vulnerable' under the Housing Act 1985 Part III?

On a practical level, how does a homeless person make an application to the local authority? In some areas, applications are made at the Housing Aid Centre reception desk, in full hearing of queues of people. If this is the case, are confidential interviews available and is it possible to make an appointment in advance?

It is likely that the local authority's medical officer will have a strong influence over which applicants for rehousing are accepted on medical grounds (both through homelessness procedures and the housing waiting-list). It is often helpful to have as detailed an understanding of the officer's role as possible.

Does your local authority have any allocation priorities which may affect people with AIDS? For people with AIDS who are already local-authority tenants, how sympathetically is the Housing Department likely to view a request for an urgent transfer if their circumstances change, perhaps to accommodate a carer or to be closer to medical treatment?

Housing associations

Housing associations are well placed to respond quickly to changing local needs and they may be more flexible than local authorities. A number of housing associations have already formulated policies on AIDS/HIV, while others are developing a range of schemes suitable for the needs of this group. What are the policies of the housing associations which operate in your area?

Other resources

Housing advisers need access to information on a wide range of resources available to people with HIV infection in the area. While familiarity with possible housing options is central, it is important to be aware of complementary sources of advice and emotional or practical support. These could range from voluntary-sector organizations such as counselling agencies, self-help groups, and welfare-rights agencies to the services provided by statutory bodies. Support services provided by Social Services Departments, for example, include the home-help and meals-on-wheels services.

Public-sector housing

The public sector has a major role to play in offering secure, low-cost housing to people with AIDS, ARC, or who are HIV-positive. There are two access routes to public-sector housing: the housing waiting-list and the homelessness procedures.

The housing waiting-list

In many districts and for many households, the waiting-list is still a positive way to seek rehousing and people should be encouraged to register with their local authority.

People with AIDS and people who are HIV-positive are likely to experience a wide range of problems which highlight housing-related difficulties. This illustrates the deficiencies which exist in all sectors of housing in providing good-quality, secure homes that are responsive to the needs of the users.

For those people with HIV infection and in particular single households, the existing points-schemes may not easily reflect the full extent of their inadequate housing and its related difficulties. Wider aspects of poor housing which may affect a damaged immune system, but which may not necessarily attract any points (unless the adviser can strongly argue that they should do so) include the following:

Shared facilities

Problems for people sharing accommodation are multifold. All attempts at control over one's environment are affected by other residents. For somebody with HIV infection who is suffering from extreme bouts of diarrhoea, a shared toilet and bathroom may be a constant source of anxiety and embarrassment, quite apart from the obvious risk of contracting opportune infections from other residents. In some Bed and Breakfasts in particular, the standard of hygiene is very low and the individual has no control over it.

A nutritious balanced diet is important yet cooking facilities may not exist at all, resulting in people being forced to eat either in cafés or making do with unbalanced snack meals. Where cooking facilities do exist they are often shared and again it may be difficult to control hygiene standards.

Heating and hot water

Adequate heating is another important factor for balancing good health. For someone suffering from an illness or trying to maintain good health, lack of heat can lead to a range of problems from simply being permanently cold to dampness in beds and clothes which can aggravate (for example) chest infections. In many cases heating systems which do exist are inadequate and expensive, and in some cases are controlled by landlords.

Many shared houses only have small hot-water tanks or inadequate geyser systems in shared bathrooms. This lack of hot water is particularly distressing for somebody experiencing severe night sweats where sheets may constantly have to be washed and changed. There is also no relief available from muscular aches and pains by hot baths.

Lack of privacy and space

Lack of privacy in shared housing can be a major contributor to stress. Living this way can often be like living in a 'goldfish bowl' and neighbours may become suspicious about the person's health and begin forms of harassment.

For people with AIDS and people who are HIV-positive, wishing to have friends, lovers, or carers to stay can cause additional problems. Often there is opposition from sharers or landlords, while the resulting lack of space can lead to common infections being passed from one to the other. Relationships can become strained due to over-close proximity.

Areas of conflict which previously did not exist can be opened up. People who had previously lived side-by-side with the person with AIDS may suddenly be overcome with fear or prejudice or feelings of helplessness, and become totally unable to cope with the situation. Desperation sets in as the housing situation remains unresolved and the care and support which had been given freely can become an area of resentment. Often this situation is resolved as soon as the person with AIDS or the person who is HIV-positive acquires his or her own home. Relationships improve and the emotional and social support is back once again to assist the person with his or her other problems.

Telephone

Access to a private phone may be paramount to emotional stability and contact with the outside world to avoid feelings of isolation and depression taking hold. If phones do exist in multi-occupied houses they are mostly located in unheated hallways and offer no privacy of conversation at all.

Location

Home location is also a very important aspect for people with HIV infection. This factor is not reflected at all in the points systems. Many people will be living in their present locations not through choice but because it was the only option available to them at the time. For people who are in ill-health or vulnerable, the location of their homes takes on a whole new perspective. People with AIDS will need to be within easy access of their specialist medical and social care, and be able to travel easily and cheaply between clinics and home to avoid any unnecessary hospitalizations. Being near to shops and community facilities is of major importance as it is not always possible to have assistance with shopping. Close proximity to friends, lovers, and family is another factor in combating isolation.

Homelessness

In many parts of the country, access to public-sector housing will only be possible for people with HIV infection if they follow the homelessness procedures that are laid down in the Housing Act 1985. It is therefore essential for advisers to be familiar with the legislation so that they will be able to present a strong and effective argument to the local authority in support of their clients' applications for rehousing. A brief outline of the legislation follows.

The Housing Act 1985 Part III

Part III of the 1985 Act, as amended by the Housing and Planning Act 1986, gives a local authority the duty to secure permanent accommodation for anyone who is: (a) homeless, (b) in priority need, and (c) not intentionally homeless. Where they rehouse will depend upon the local connection; and what kind of accommodation is offered depends upon a number of factors including both the particular needs of the person and general housing circumstances. Both of these will be considered later in more detail.

Who is homeless?

Obviously people are homeless if there is nowhere that they are entitled to live – that is, if they do not have any legal right to occupy any accommodation. Included amongst the homeless, therefore, will be not only those who have literally no roof over their heads, but also those who have no legal right to remain where they are staying, for example squatters or people living in temporary refuges.

If your client has a restricted contract or a licence to occupy some accommodation, although the legal right to remain may be weak, it may exist and a local authority may insist that any right to occupy is formally brought to an end by a court order before considering the person as homeless. People who are threatened with homelessness within 28 days come within the terms of the Act.

Although the above may seem fairly straightforward, advisers will still find many problems faced by their clients with HIV infection. However, we should note, particularly in helping people with AIDS, the amendments introduced to the Housing Act 1985 which may extend the definition of homelessness. The amendments bring within the scope of the Act those who may have accommodation, and who may have a legal right to remain there, but where it would not 'be reasonable for him [or her] to continue to occupy' such accommodation. The test is not whether it would be reasonable to leave the accommodation, but rather whether it would be reasonable to stay.

The factors which may make it not reasonable to remain include the following.

The physical conditions of the accommodation If the accommodation is unfit for human habitation, overcrowded, or lacking in basic amenities, as defined by housing law, then a strong case could be made for your client being homeless. But you should be clear quite how low these standards are. A dozen or more people could live in a three-bedroomed flat and, if they were of the right age and gender, the property may still not be statutorily overcrowded. In one case of intentional homelessness, the case-law of which will certainly inform the new provisions, it was held that a rat-infested hut, 10 feet by 20 feet, without mains services, except from a nearby caravan site, was 'reasonable' to be occupied by two adults and two children. It only became unreasonable upon the birth of the third child.

However, housing standards set by law will not provide the only test. The local authorities may have regard to the general housing circumstances in their area. This 'one ray of hope for the authorities', according to Lord Denning, permits the local authority to take account of whether there are many people in the area living in worse conditions than the applicants –

although the local authority should not restrict itself to considering only this issue, and would have to provide evidence to merit its decision.

The personal circumstances of the individual It is the consideration of this area that may provide some benefit for our clients. For people with AIDS their health should be a major factor in determining whether it is reasonable to remain in occupation. Thus, for example, for someone with PCP (pneumonia) who has to climb three flights of stairs to poor-standard accommodation, it may be argued that it would not be reasonable for them to stay in that property, even though they had a legal right to occupy and that such accommodation may be satisfactory for others.

The Code of Guidance, which accompanies the Act and to which local authorities must have regard, suggests that it may be unreasonable for someone to continue to live in premises which they can no longer afford (for example mortgage or rent arrears because of illness leading to a drop in income), or in conditions causing severe emotional stress.

In this context, too, it is important to consider the issues around harassment: in the present climate of fear this is sadly a far from unusual situation. One area that may be difficult is where your client has a strong legal interest in premises suited to their needs, but feel they cannot remain because of harassment. Advisers should note that the response of many local authorities to this problem may be to insist that the applicant pursue every legal remedy that may exist before being accepted as homeless.

This approach rests on several test cases around intentional homelessness which have found in the local authorities' favour; but it should be very strongly resisted in the case of people with HIV infection, although in practice advisers may find difficulties except in bad cases of eviction or harassment, particularly when the client is very ill.

The housing law around the issue of harassment deals only with a narrow set of circumstances; behaviour which can be reasonably said to interfere with an occupant's peace and comfort, or is likely to cause an occupier not to exercise any legal rights. Harassment which takes place because the tenant is black, or a woman, or homosexual, or indeed if the tenant is HIV-positive or has AIDS, is not illegal under any existing housing legislation; although in the case of ethnic minorities some harassment may be an offence under sections 30/31 of the Race Relations Act.

To consider first, harassment from co-occupiers or neighbours. The major legal remedy open to a person with HIV infection who is being harassed by, for example, a flatmate, because of his or her HIV status, is civil action. There have been cases where a local authority has advised a person with AIDS to take out an injunction against a flatmate who was harassing him or her. Advisers may have no alternative but to argue forcefully that to subject a person with AIDS to such an intolerably stressful ordeal would clearly be unreasonable. However, in cases of this kind, where a client has been advised by the local authority to seek civil redress for harassment, it is important that the client not give up the accommodation, even if he or she has had to find temporary respite in another property: the client may well be deemed to be intentionally homeless if he or she makes an application for housing at a later date.

It can, however, be argued under Section 58 2a of the Housing Act 1985 Part III that it is clearly not 'reasonable to remain' in accommodation where an applicant is being harassed. If the harassment is severe enough and if it is provable, a local authority might well deem a person with AIDS or ARC to be homeless under the Act in this situation.

However, local authorities may also seek to rely on the Protection From Eviction Act 1977, as amended by the Housing Act 1988, in cases where the client is being harassed or evicted by the landlord. Advisers may well find themselves having to resist this argument too.

The present position is fraught with difficulties for a client with AIDS, and it is important that advisers understand the law in this area fully. To consider, first, the new civil wrong of harassment. While court action on the basis of this 'offence' may result in the payment of compensation, some legal authorities argue that this may make it more difficult to obtain an injunction to reinstate the occupier – in civil law an injunction is usually only obtained if financial damages alone would not compensate a person for his or her loss; and no damages are likely to be awarded if the occupier is reinstated by a court order or by the landlord. We must wait to see if problems emerge from such cases. Second, although the new provision strengthens the law, many people will be excluded from the protection of the 1977 Act if they began their occupation after the 15 January 1989 *or* if there is an agreed rent increase in an existing contract (except where such an increase is determined by a rent officer or a rent tribunal). It should be noted that these exclusions include, amongst others, those occupiers who share accommodation with the landlord and his or her family – exactly the situation in which many clients will find themselves. In such circumstances occupiers will lose the protection they might otherwise have enjoyed, and will now be evicted after whatever notice is required by the contract.

It can be argued that to rely on such legal protection is not sufficient if landlords would in the longer term gain possession anyway – as they would for example if they were resident landlords, or if the client had the limited protection of an assured shorthold tenancy. Further advisers should be prepared to argue the 'reasonable to occupy' test in such cases.

Finally, we should consider not only the applicant but also anyone who can reasonably be expected to live with them. In case law this will typically be a member of the family who normally resides with the applicant; but it can also include someone who normally resides with them *and* does so in circumstances in which it is reasonable for them to live together.

Homosexual couples may seek accommodation under this latter provision, and we should consider this matter carefully. Given the civil case law around homosexual relationships it may often be the case that such a relationship will not be treated sympathetically by some local authorities. It may be argued that the health needs of the person with AIDS, including the emotional health needs, form the grounds on which it is reasonable for the couple to live together, and this factor should certainly not be ignored. We anticipate problems, however, when the local authority actually reaches the point of granting a tenancy to the homeless person. Accommodation may be offered to the couple, but the tenancy is only granted to the person with AIDS, leaving his or her partner with few legal rights, including possibly no right of succession. If the couple wish to have a joint tenancy, it is important that advisers argue the case. The partner may themselves be HIV-positive, and this or other medical factors should be considered. However, equally importantly, it seems to us, is that the wishes of the person with AIDS should be taken into account, as with a heterosexual couple.

Many advisers have also experienced difficulty with clients who wish to live with someone who is their 'carer' rather than their partner or lover. This carer may be a close friend of long standing who was already living with the person with AIDS prior to his or her becoming homeless. Some local authorities seem reluctant to accept such a relationship, however, unless it is with a member of the family, only agreeing to consider the application as a couple. The significance, of course, lies eventually with the offer that may be made – as a couple it will probably be a one-bedroomed flat, as applicant and carer it should be two-bedroomed accommodation.

Priority need

As most workers in housing will be aware, it is, in practice, only those who fall within the priority-need categories who will be rehoused under the Housing Act. Section 59 of the Act defines the priority-need categories as pregnant women, households with dependent children, anyone who has lost his or her accommodation as a result of an emergency such as a fire or flood, and anyone who is vulnerable as a result of old age, mental illness or handicap, or physical disability 'or other special reason'. It is this latter case that will concern us here.

The starting-point is that medical vulnerability makes it such that the applicant is 'less able to fend for oneself so that injury or detriment will result where a more able man [sic] will be able to cope without harmful effects', and several cases have held that such vulnerability must be assessed in housing terms, rather than in any other context.

There is not much case-law on the question of vulnerability on medical grounds, and a fairly restricted interpretation is likely to be given by the local authority, usually allowing only those people with severe symptoms of HIV infection to be considered in priority need. Many of those local authorities that originally defined people who were HIV-positive as being in priority need have since backed away from their decision.

There has however been some movement in law, and advisers should be prepared to argue each case on its merits. Any evidence of vulnerability presented to local authorities must be taken into account: they cannot simply ignore it, but rather if necessary seek additional information for themselves. Nor would it necessarily be reasonable for an authority to rely solely on the opinion of its medical advisers. Medical opinion in itself may not be conclusive: for example, in cases where the vulnerability may lie in the more general category of 'other specific reason', the expertise of a housing or social-welfare worker may be important.

It may not be sufficient for a local authority to conclude that someone is not vulnerable simply on the evidence of a medical assessment form, which we will consider later, without the medical officer personally examining the applicant, or consulting with a practitioner who has examined him or her. There may too be some room to argue that the discrimination suffered by a gay man or drug-user who has contracted the virus could be a factor in determining priority need.

The question of medical self-assessment is important. Many local authorities will initially consider an application through a Housing Aid Centre, which may act as a filter for the Homeless Persons Section. It is at this stage that the applicant may be asked to complete a medical self-assessment form. For the applicant simply being HIV-positive may be enough to guarantee housing – but not necessarily for the local authority. Advisers must ensure that full information is given on such forms, with professional advice and an accompanying letter if necessary. The forms may also ask for the name of the person's doctor; but you should not assume that the doctor will always be contacted unless other information on the form were to give the medical officer grounds to believe that the person may be vulnerable under the Act.

It is in the case of borderline medical vulnerability that some of the problems of advising clients become most apparent. It is important that your client should be aware of both the purpose and the content of any negotiations you undertake on his or her behalf, and is allowed to remain in control. Thus, for example, it is unfortunately the case that you may not be able to guarantee the confidentiality of any information you disclose to the authority, and you should discuss this with your client. Advisers should bear in mind when considering this point the large numbers of people within the local authority who will inevitably know about the applicant's HIV status – not only the caseworkers at the Housing Aid Centre and the Homeless Persons Unit, but also the allocations or lettings section, the section that may arrange any short-term accommodation, the medical officer, and the support staff of all these sections.

Further, you should be aware of the emotional problems your clients may face in having to come to terms with their diagnosis. At the same time as they are trying to cope with being positive about their well-being, you may be arguing the seriousness of their case to the authority: that in itself may require some considerable sensitivity on your part.

Intentional homelessness

If any advice worker is not already aware of the fact, we should note that it is the area of 'intentionality' that has caused the most controversy in the law relating to homelessness. By far the largest proportion of reported cases deals with this area, and it is such cases that are most often reported in the media – perhaps contributing significantly to the continuing myths around homelessness and the undeserving poor. Yet some legal authorities, with good reason, have argued that the case law is far from being as unhelpful to the homeless as may appear at first sight. Many notable successes have been achieved, as well as the more noted failures.

It is not possible here to deal fully with the jungle of law around intentionality, but we aim rather to consider only some of the general principles as they might apply to people with HIV infection. It is important that you understand the general law in this area, and treat the following discussion as providing suggestions for applying the knowledge that you have.

First, to consider the definition of intentionality: the relevant section is fairly clear, namely that people are considered to be intentionally homeless if as a direct result of any deliberate act or omission they cease to occupy or are forced to leave accommodation that had been available to them and in which it was reasonable for them to remain! Several points should be noted. First, whether or not an act or omission is deliberate is judged from the point of view of a reasonable and fair-minded observer, not simply by the perception of the homeless themselves; but, second, an act or omission carried out in good faith and by someone unaware of a relevant fact will not be regarded as deliberate.

An example may best illustrate the first point. If rent arrears arose because of your partner's drinking, while you had consistently urged him or her to stop – or indeed, as in one reported case, physically assaulted the inebriate when told that you were about to be made homeless – the actions of your partner, which may lead to a finding of intentionality, may not necessarily apply to yourself, having acted in good faith.

The provision regarding the ignorance of a relevant fact may not include your client's ignorance of their legal rights, and will certainly not if they simply ignored any advice from the local authority.

The 'reasonableness' test is important. It is the same test that was imported, by the 1986 amendment, into the definition of homelessness; much of the case law around intentionality is now very relevant to the definition of homelessness itself. We need not repeat that discussion again, but you should note that in considering what is reasonable the local authority can and will take into account the local housing conditions; also note what other steps your client can take to prevent him or her becoming homeless. To continue some examples from the earlier discussion: the authority may expect a tenant to seek police protection from harassment or seek a civil injunction rather than leave the accommodation; they may argue that your client should have sought a legal remedy to force the landlord to undertake repairs to poor accommodation; or they may argue that the housing debt could have been renegotiated rather than simply ignored.

Finally, we should note that local authorities will look back to the initial, rather than only the immediate, cause of homelessness. This may involve considering your client's housing record over many years, and looking to the last secure accommodation your client had and examining the reasons why he or she did not continue to occupy it.

The reasons why people with AIDS or those who are body-positive may lose their home could include:

(i)   illness which leads to them not being able to pay mortgage payments, or increasingly rent (advisers should note the changes in Housing Benefit legislation, in Rent Act protection, and the poll tax or community charge);
(ii) giving up accommodation because it was physically unsuitable due to illness;
(iii) leaving secure accommodation because of harassment.

If properly handled many of these cases should not lead to a finding of intentionality. However, we do not think that advisers should anticipate that a local authority will apply any different standards to people with HIV infection than those they would apply to other groups. In most cases, if your client has accommodation that would have excluded him or her from the definition of being homeless under the law before the 1986 amendment, and if the choice is available to you, we suggest that you advise the client to apply to the local authority as soon as they are threatened with homelessness, and prior to his or her leaving the accommodation, and to argue the case at that stage.

Local connection

At law this is established by:

–   normal residence by choice (not Crown service or prison);
–   employment (not casual);
–   family connection (of at least 5-years standing);
–   other special circumstances (health care?).

People with AIDS have faced the problem of their being offered accommodation close to family, who do not support them, rather than to friends who do, but this may be open to challenge unless the applicant's wish were to seek to override statute.

The 'other special circumstances' is an important area for this client group. Some local authorities have accepted the importance of health-care facilities as establishing a local connection, and it is important that if it is your client's wish, this argument is pursued.

Offers of accommodation should reflect the availability of counselling and hospital services, friends and such factors as the location of public-transport systems. It should not be considered suitable to make an offer based on a 'local connection' to one's parents, for example, if that is not where the support lies. It will be more beneficial for a person with AIDS to be near to one good friend who supports him or her than to live close to an entire extended family who have cut them off. Under Part III of the Housing Act 1985 Section 61–d, if a person has a connection with a district because of 'special circumstances', then this must be considered.

Even if you and your client manage to get over all the hurdles outlined in the above paragraphs, the question of what kind of accommodation they are offered remains, and it is to this which we now turn.

Housing services should recognize that people with AIDS must be rehoused into suitable permanent accommodation as soon as possible and with the minimum of trauma. Rehousing processes can be fraught with stressful situations so it is important that at all stages the person with AIDS feels confident and in control by being properly informed. Interviewing procedures should be approached sensitively and attention given to the atmosphere created in advice agencies and housing departments.

Allocations and referrals should be guided by the stated needs and wishes of people with AIDS, involving them at all stages of the procedures, enabling them to have as much control as possible over matters.

Temporary forms of accommodation

If permanent housing is not immediately available, then only good-quality emergency or temporary accommodation should be considered.

Bed and breakfast

People with AIDS should not have to stay at all in Bed-and-Breakfast accommodation where facilities are lacking or inadequate. It is virtually impossible to find a single room in a Bed-and-Breakfast accommodation and most people end up sharing bedrooms with total strangers. Facilities such as bathrooms and toilets are shared between many people and cleanliness can leave much to be desired. It is unusual for cooking facilities to exist in most Bed and Breakfasts, and where they do, again they are shared by a great number of people.

Realistically, however, the problem will arise, especially in inner-city areas, and in situations in which a stay in Bed and Breakfast is unavoidable, it would be best for advisers to be aware of local B-&-B options and standards in order that a stay will be as comfortable as possible.

Short-life schemes

Some boroughs have developed short-life schemes managed by housing associations in which 'priority households' can live until permanent accommodation is allocated. Generally good-standard accommodation is offered by these schemes and although this option must be welcomed as an alternative to Bed and Breakfast, the only satisfactory long-term answer is for existing permanent stock to be made more readily available despite heavy demand.

Friends/relatives/partners

It should also be recognized that friends and partners may offer extended stays once a promise of rehousing by the local authority is forthcoming. Often, once the 'responsibility' of having to accommodate the person with AIDS has been lifted, relationships improve, and if this facility exists then it should be allowed without extending the waiting period for a permanent offer of rehousing. Advisers should be aware of the local authority's policy on this matter.

Attention must also be given to the cost of the housing offered. HIV infection is hitting a young group of the population and for many the illness may have come at a time when their earning capacity is at a maximum. As the disease progresses and at the very time when extra financial resources are needed, their earning power will decline or stop, leaving them to manage on limited resources.

The most important aspect of the entire rehousing procedure is that it should be as swift and clear as possible in order to minimize the period of uncertainty for the person with AIDS or who is HIV-positive. If there has to be a period in temporary accommodation, then the client should be made fully aware of any implications surrounding this, such as periods of possible additional expense and disruption in the future. In any circumstances where a less-than-ideal situation can be found, discussions must include the person with AIDS.

Succession of tenancy

Certain people have automatic right to succession of tenancy, for example a legal spouse or a common-law partner, providing that they can prove residence at the property over a reasonable time; direct members of the tenant's family *may* also have some automatic rights to succession, however, no such automatic right extends to unrelated friends and/or carers. It would follow, therefore, that same-sex partners could have considerably fewer rights. We would argue that a local authority should be urged to adopt policies which would address these issues and result in security for people in these circumstances. A similar situation also applies to the assignment of tenancies: the same unequal rights for same-sex partners and non-related friends and carers need to be addressed.

One further general comment is perhaps appropriate. The clear intention of the Housing Act 1988 is to reduce the importance of local-authority housing. No mention is made in the Act of 'homelessness', and at present councils still retain the responsibility to rehouse those homeless people who are in priority need. If the Act is successful in its aims, however, local authorities may face the position of having continued responsibility while its actual housing stock decreases. The issue of what kind of accommodation, where it is located, and on what terms of occupation, becomes all the more important.

The problems for people with HIV infection are not restricted to gaining public-sector accommodation. Problems exist for those who are already in, or who are about to move into, local authority stock.

Estates management

For those people who are HIV-antibody-positive or have AIDS, and who are living in public-sector accommodation, there may be a need to contact the estates management office to request modifications to existing accommodation or to request a transfer to somewhere more suitable. Good work-practices in these offices, with particular regard to sensitivity and confidentiality whilst dealing with people with AIDS, will be of major importance. The office will often be located directly within the community within which the person with AIDS is living, and for information to be leaked here would be disastrous, resulting in forms of harassment and persecution which could be extremely difficult to handle.

People working in Estates Management offices must at all times be sensitive of how situations might arise that could place the person with AIDS in confrontational circumstances. Gossip may surround a tenant who is having central heating installed whilst other people on the estate might have been waiting longer, questions about the person's illness, why meals-on-wheels are delivering, or why they are being collected by ambulance may be asked. It is absolutely paramount that swift action be taken against other tenants or workers at the offices who gossip, and that there are disciplinary structures to deal with breaches of confidentiality.

Transfers

The impact of AIDS on each individual is unique and it therefore follows that each housing resource should ideally be tailored as much as possible to that person's needs. Circumstances may also change during the person's life and as far as possible it will be necessary to address these issues by means of transfers and adaptations to existing properties. Whilst recognizing that some people who are terminally ill will chose to die in hospital or a hospice, services and facilities should be available to enable the choice to extend to being cared for and dying at home.

Accommodation originally offered might become too small for somebody needing 24-hour care; accommodation might not facilitate wheelchairs or special aids; a tenant might need a transfer nearer the hospital or away from a noisy estate. Each case should be handled as efficiently and carefully as possible, and although every effort should be made to assist tenants to remain in their homes if they so choose, equally, every effort should be made for a successful transfer if this is the request.

As in the waiting-list points procedures, transfers are generally judged fairly widely, with emphasis on such factors as mobility and harassment, but every effort needs to be made to tailor these systems to be more responsive to the individual needs and problems of the person with AIDS.

The new provisions for the 'change of landlord' under the Housing Act 1988, or for the management of an estate by a tenants' co-operative, may affect these procedures. To their credit, some local authorities have developed good work practices and procedures in the above areas. We wait to see if newer 'social landlords' adopt similar progressive policies.

All the above discussion has focused on local authorities, but much of the comment would also apply to housing associations. While potentially more flexible than council housing, the corollary is that associations' practices vary enormously. Some, particularly in areas where the initial impact of HIV infection was greatest, have responded positively; but it would be wrong to assume this is always the case. Many of the concerns expressed above apply equally to this sector, and advisers would do well to consider in advance their approach to such agencies on behalf of their clients.

The private rented sector

This century has seen a sharp decline in the importance of the private rented sector. Some of the sector is characterized by poor conditions, lack of security, and high rents. It therefore represents a standard of accommodation which may not be suitable for people with AIDS or ARC, or for people who are HIV-positive. However, the private rented sector has traditionally housed large numbers of single people, the group which, to date has been most severely affected by AIDS (although this situation is likely to change in the future).

People with HIV infection living in privately rented accommodation are likely to be affected by a wide range of difficulties associated with their housing. Although in many cases these may not be directly related to their medical condition, any housing difficulties are likely to affect their health.

Many of the problems faced by advisers will be those of clients trying to leave private-rented-sector accommodation. Issues of poor conditions, high rents, and harassment have therefore already been considered in the previous discussion. But not all clients will wish to leave their accommodation, or are likely to be offered public-sector housing were they to do so. People with HIV infection will therefore continue to face the same problems as everyone else in the private rented sector, but more acutely – and advisers must be prepared to deal sensitively with these issues.

Detailed knowledge of welfare and housing benefits will be invaluable. In cases of harassment not only will the adviser be called upon to assist in the more usual provision of legal advice, but he or she should also recognize that the person may need considerable support either from the housing adviser or from a more appropriate agency. The responsibility of finding both temporary and permanent accommodation will, from time to time, inevitably fall to the advice worker, and it will have been necessary to have planned well in advance. In particular, advice agencies have a crucial role to play in encouraging good work practices within hostels and special projects; and being aware of the services offered and the policies on health and safety and confidentiality clearly make for a more confident referral for your client.

It would not be appropriate or possible here for us to work through the detailed legislation affecting the private rented sector, but one area at least may be worth further discussion. Poor environmental conditions will inevitably have an adverse effect on the health of a person who has HIV infection. Local-authority Environmental-health Officer (EHOs) have wide-ranging powers regarding privately rented property which is in poor condition. The relevant legislation is contained in the Housing Acts (principally the Housing Act of 1985) and the Public Health Act 1936. The primary aims of the legislation are to prevent the fabric of the housing stock from deteriorating and to protect the health and well-being of occupiers.

For people with AIDS, ARC, or who are HIV-positive and living in privately rented accommodation, the intervention of an EHO can substantially improve the quality of their housing, although this may be a lengthy process. Where accommodation is in a poor state of repair, the EHO has the power to serve a notice on the owner of the property, requiring him or her to carry out the necessary repairs within a certain period. Depending on the nature of the repairs, the work may be grant-aided by the local authority. If the landlord fails to carry out the repairs within the specified period, the local authority has the power to intervene and carry out the works in default. The Housing Act 1988 strengthened the powers local authorities have to issue and enforce repairs notices, including the fact that non-compliance may be a criminal offence.

However, the greatest of care must be taken with these procedures given the changes introduced under the Housing Act 1988. The Act introduced wholly new ground for possession for assured tenancies, namely that the landlord intends to demolish, reconstruct, or carry out substantial works to the property and the work cannot reasonably be carried out without gaining possession. There is no requirement that the landlord must provide suitable alternative accommodation, only 'reasonable removal expenses'. If the landlord offers a reduced part of the premises for your client to occupy there would appear to be no requirement that he or she give back the original accommodation once the work is completed; and if the tenant refuses to co-operate possession may still be granted. Advisers should note that this is a mandatory ground, rather than discretionary – that is, the courts will have no choice but to grant possession if the circumstances apply.

In housing stock of very poor condition the result may be that the serving of a notice by an EHO results in the landlord instituting proceedings for possession.

Ironically, however, in the case of a person affected by the HIV, the intervention of the EHO may be required most frequently in support of an application for rehousing under the homelessness legislation, rather than in improving the housing in which they are currently living. This may particularly be so in local authorities that do not have specialist workers in housing or Social Service Departments who are dealing with issues around HIV infection. This can pose some problems, as EHOs may not necessarily be alert to the factors which may make accommodation unsuitable for a person affected by HIV. Thus, for example, an EHO who is requested to report on accommodation occupied by a person with HIV may note that the fire exits are inadequate while failing to identify a shared kitchen or constant traffic noise from a busy main road as environmental problems.

The person with AIDS may take the decision to inform the EHO of his or her HIV status before the inspection visit in order to resolve this difficulty, but this will clearly raise issues of confidentiality. A clear environmental-health report is a useful tool when assembling evidence in support of an application under the Housing Act 1985 Part III. However, it is important that the person with AIDS is aware of the implications of following this course of action.

Privately rented housing and legislative change

Deregulation of the private rented sector forms one of the central pillars of the government's housing policy. These changes are likely to have a direct impact on people affected by HIV, and those advising such clients should note some of the more important ones.

Under the new legislation, all new lettings will be either assured tenancies or assured shorthold tenancies. Assured tenants will pay 'market' rents, negotiated with the landlord. Mandatory grounds for possession are extended to include rent arrears of more than 3 months or 13 weeks if the rent is payable weekly or fortnightly; and persistent delay in rent payments is a further discretionary ground, as is 'arrears of rent'. The minimum period for a shorthold tenancy is reduced to 6 months, after which a landlord will be able to recover possession. Rents will again be at market levels.

It seems likely that the most common form of letting will be the assured shorthold tenancy, which will offer the tenant only 6 months' security. This low degree of security and resulting increase in stress is certain to affect people affected by HIV in an adverse way.

People with AIDS, ARC, and sometimes those who are HIV-positive are likely to be wholly or partially dependent on benefits during periods of sickness. They are therefore unlikely to be in a strong position when it comes to negotiating a rent with landlords. The importance of this point should not be underestimated. The intention of the Act is to allow landlords to be as free as possible to charge market rents, and new lettings will be at whatever rent is agreed between landlord and tenant. Further, the power of the new 'rent-assessment committees' to monitor the level of rents fixed is considerably undermined by the limited circumstances in which tenants may approach the committee without threatening their security, and by the fact that even if a market rent is set by the committee, a higher rent can be charged if both the landlord and tenant agree to a higher rent. It may not be difficult to imagine circumstances in which clients with HIV infection will be persuaded to 'agree' to higher rent levels.

The financial difficulties that may be faced by people with HIV infection may be illustrated by the fact that since the introduction of the social-security changes in April 1988, it has also been impossible for benefit claimants to make a claim for the deposit required by most landlords.

Similarly, people with AIDS living in assured tenancies may find that they lose their accommodation, either as a result of persistent Housing Benefit delays over which they have no control, or as a result of a reduction in earnings leading to difficulties in keeping up with rent payments. It seems unlikely that Housing Benefit will meet the full cost of market rents.

The government's proposals do not tackle unprotected private-rented-sector lettings (company lets, holiday lets, and licences, for example), so it seems likely that this section of the market will continue to flourish.

Legislative change affecting rights of succession will have a major impact on the carers and partners of people with AIDS living in the private rented sector. Even existing, fully protected tenants will be affected by the changes: only a surviving spouse will retain full rights of succession to a regulated tenancy. Any carer or partner who has been living with the tenant for less than 2 years when the tenant dies and who is not a joint tenant will forfeit any rights of succession under the new legislation. Even when they qualify, they will succeed only to an assured periodic tenancy. There will be no rights of succession attached to assured tenancies or assured shorthold tenancies, except for a surviving heterosexual spouse or partner.

Owner-occupation

A higher proportion of people than ever before now own their homes in this country and it is the government's stated intention to increase this percentage still further. It is therefore likely that a large number of the people affected by HIV fall into this group, so the specific difficulties facing them, as owner-occupiers, need to be addressed by advisers.

Obtaining a mortgage

Some 70 per cent of new mortgages are now of the endowment type, whereby borrowers pay interest only throughout the term of the loan. The total loan is repaid when a separate insurance policy matures at the end of the term. Most application forms for endowment policies now include specific questions on HIV. If applicants knowingly conceal their HIV status when they complete the form, the policy will become void if it later emerges that they did not tell the truth. For a few insurance companies, simply having taken an HIV test (even if the result was negative) is sufficient to prevent applicants from obtaining insurance cover. Once an applicant has been rejected by one insurance company, the others may follow suit.

Even applicants for capital-repayment mortgages may be asked to take out a mortgage protection policy which would repay the loan if the borrower died before the end of the term. A policy of this kind will invariably be required where the loan is for the full value of the property. However, for relatively small loans it seems that most building societies will not insist on a mortgage-protection policy. Current experience indicates that repayment mortgages can be obtained for between 90 and 95 per cent of the total value of the property.

Borrowers who already have insurance cover and who were not, to their knowledge, HIV-positive at the time of their application, should not experience any problems.

Difficulties with repayments

People with AIDS or ARC and possibly those who are HIV-positive may find themselves in difficulty with their mortgage repayments as a result of a reduction in their income. It is vital to inform the mortgage company of any difficulties with repayments at an early stage, before arrears are allowed to accrue. Once there are substantial arrears, most mortgage companies will have no hesitation in foreclosing the mortgage and then obtaining a court order, particularly if they are aware that the borrower has HIV. However, where people with severe symptoms are unable to keep up with their mortgage repayments, they should approach their local authority, as it would clearly not be reasonable for them to attempt to remain in a property which they could not afford.

Joint mortgages

For people with AIDS, ARC, or who are HIV-positive and who own their homes, joint mortgages present specific problems. Thus, for example, where a group of friends have purchased a property jointly, the discovery that one of them is HIV-positive can precipitate a rapid breakdown in relationships. If they choose to sell their share, however, they will be left with a lump sum which is unlikely to be sufficient to buy another property (even if they succeed in taking out a small mortgage), but may be large enough to make them ineligible for benefit. In addition, the legal status of joint owners is extremely complex and is governed by the type of contract which was drawn up at the time of the purchase. In the event of one joint owner wishing to sell his or her share, a new contract is likely to be required and this could incur substantial legal fees.

Although shared ownership may be an option for people affected by HIV and who are left with a lump sum, most schemes, particularly in the Southeast of England, are over subscribed.

Similar difficulties can arise when a person with AIDS, ARC, or who is HIV-positive owns a property jointly with his or her partner and the relationship breaks down. In this case, if the property is large enough, it may be possible to divide it into two separate units, although this is dependent on being able to raise capital to carry out the building works. Another option, which would admittedly require a great deal of commitment on the part of both partners, would be to attempt to resolve the difficulties within the relationship.

Advice workers will be well aware of the complexities of these problems and it is important to seek experienced legal advice when first attempting to assess the problem. In particular, advisers should be aware of the dangers of intentional homelessness in this area.

The way forward

All too frequently, AIDS is viewed in isolation as purely a health problem. The Department of the Environment, for example, whilst having overall strategic responsibility for housing provision, has been slow to acknowledge its role in initiating resources for people with AIDS. The Department of Health, meanwhile, recognizes the importance of good-quality housing for people affected by HIV, but has no housing responsibilities.

People with HIV infection who are ill cannot be cared for outside hospital unless they have somewhere suitable to live. People with AIDS who are suffering from specific infections such as PCP or have high care needs such as those related to HIV brain disease and are being assisted by hospitalization or schemes such as London Lighthouse should also have the choice to be nursed at home, if it is at all possible.

Similarly, for people who are currently asymptomatic and wish to maintain good health, housing will be an important part of their care package. The type and location of the accommodation offered to a person who is affected by HIV is of paramount importance. Housing is the linchpin from which all other caring services can run effectively.

This chapter has concentrated largely on gaining access for people with HIV infection to public-sector housing via the Housing Act 1985 Part III. In London, where to date the highest concentration of people affected by HIV is located, following this route to housing is, in effect, the only way in which access to secure housing can be guaranteed. Several of the London boroughs have responded sensitively and swiftly to the challenge of housing people with HIV infection, in spite of the financial restrictions placed upon them. In these areas, a close partnership between the statutory and voluntary sectors, working together with the frontline organizations representing people with AIDS themselves, has ensured that the development of policy and practice has been, at least in some measure, appropriate to the needs of this group.

Through their close contact with people with AIDS and awareness of the changing needs of the group, agencies which provide advice are well placed to promote good policy and practice and to make known the housing requirements. Advice agencies therefore have a central role to play in ensuring that local authorities work sensitively within the framework of existing legislation when dealing with people who are affected by HIV. Agencies' strategic role need not, however, be confined to local-authority policies. Other providers of housing, such as housing associations or hostels, can benefit greatly from help and guidance on how they can most effectively provide a service to people with AIDS.

Activities in which advice agencies could usefully become involved are discussed below.

Campaigning

Advice agencies have first-hand knowledge of the housing problems facing people with AIDS, and this knowledge should be used to help argue their case. Thus, for example, most agencies have on record large numbers of statistics which illustrate the extent to which people with AIDS are affected by housing problems. These can form the basis of a powerful argument for increasing housing resources, on both a local and a national level. Locally, statistics can be used in support of materials such as reports on the housing problems faced by people with AIDS. These could be presented to the local authority and other providers of housing to give some indication of the levels of need which exist in the area.

On a national level, locally based information has an important role to play in resourcing and feeding the wider campaign for housing for people with

AIDS, which is led by organizations such as the AIDS and Housing Project and the Terrence Higgins Trust.

Education

Advice agencies can play an important role in putting housing for people with AIDS on the local-authority agenda. It is therefore important for agencies to nurture existing links with both officers and members in order to ensure that a constructive dialogue with the local authority exists. Agencies should then be in a position in which they are more likely to be able to influence local policy, either by producing written materials or by providing training sessions, where that seems appropriate. Many local authorities, particularly those outside Central London, remain unaware of the housing needs of people with AIDS, nor is the strong link between poor-quality housing, stress, and the progression of the condition fully acknowledged. It is areas such as these which advice agencies may seek to address. Housing associations and hostels are also in need of information and guidance on similar issues.

While it is essential for advice agencies to educate both policy-makers and providers of housing, it is important not to overlook the needs of the client group, amongst whom are many people who will, at a later date, be affected by HIV. There is therefore a need to produce materials which outline the housing options available to people with AIDS, ARC, or who are HIV-positive.

Co-ordinated activity

Agencies which work together to promote good policy and practice will inevitably have greater success than those which work alone. However, the difficulty of providing a co-ordinated response to the needs of people with AIDS cannot be underestimated. A coherent local housing strategy for people with AIDS must involve representatives from the statutory and voluntary sectors, including the Housing Department, Social Services, housing associations, advice agencies, and, most importantly, people with AIDS themselves. Co-ordination at a local level is essential in order to avoid duplication of some services, while other important services remain unprovided.

It is also important for those areas which have not yet been affected by HIV to draw upon the different experiences of areas such as Central London and Edinburgh, which have been providing housing for people with AIDS for some time. Although all the experience and knowledge associated with AIDS and housing is clearly not confined to these narrow geographical regions, reinventing the wheel is a time-consuming process.

Case-study – Paul

The following case-study is an amalgamation of several cases dealt with by housing advice centres in London. We do not pretend that all went smoothly, but we hope it will serve as an example of the difficulties and lessons to be learnt.

* * * * * *

Paul first sought assistance with his housing problems, feeling very anxious about how some of these might be affecting his health. He had lived at his current address for over 3 years and was registered on the local housing waiting-list. The accommodation consisted of a bed-sitting room at the top of a house sharing bathroom, toilet, and kitchen facilities. The landlord was resident. His points on the waiting-list were low (mainly due to the fact that he had his own room) and in no way reflected the misery of his living situation.

Paul had suffered from mild anxiety and depression for many years and recently this had increased due to a positive test-result for HIV antibodies. For years he had coped with damp, with waste, from a stench pipe, deposited outside his window, pigeons making a noise and mess in the loft above his room, no hot water, and trying to cook in the overcrowded dirty kitchen and washing up in the shared bath. Now he had to come to terms with the knowledge that all these conditions could prove to be life-threatening.

An immediate problem for Paul and the advice worker was the possibility of notice to quit being served once the landlord was aware of any contact with the Environmental Health Department (EHD), which thus produced more anxiety. In addition, there was the issue of how to deal with confidentiality when contacting the EHD if a useful full report linked to medical evidence was to be obtained for the waiting-list application.

It was necessary to make Paul aware of the lack of security of tenure and how this might be affected by the EHD visit. The eviction and homelessness procedure was explained fully, emphasizing that if he were evicted there was no guarantee of rehousing as he might not be assessed as a 'priority' under the Housing Act. The advice centre suggested that if reports of his health were presented to the local authority, then it might be possible to argue that he could not be expected to stay somewhere where it was a danger to him and he should therefore be considered to be threatened with homelessness and these letters could act as a basis for a 'vulnerability' report. If he chose not to do this, then other avenues of housing could be pursued.

Paul was open about being HIV-positive and took the attitude that he had to solve his housing situation as it was the major health risk factor in his life. He decided that the most positive thing he could do was to take control of the situation, and he agreed to start the procedures with the help of the advice worker.

The environmental report was not helpful. Paul was disappointed. It was necessary to support him, explaining the restrictive nature of some reports, and it was suggested that it might be better to get additional facts from his social worker and consultant at the hospital, explaining how they considered his environment could be a danger to his health. These reports were then all presented to the local council, which agreed that he had some points due, but even if he obtained the maximum there was little chance of being rehoused quickly from the waiting-list; and as he was not threatened with homelessness, then there was nothing to be done.

At this stage, Paul developed skin lesions which would not heal and was admitted to hospital. The doctors wrote strong letters stating that he should not be expected to go back to a home where he could not wash properly and was in danger of infection from the shared bathroom facilities, but housing case-law does not easily address these problems.

Luckily Paul was able to stay with friends whilst the adviser arranged for the liaison officer responsible for matters concerning HIV at the council to visit and make a report which quite clearly outlined each aspect of the unsuitable and threatening environmental conditions; with this, and drawing on the credibility which had been built up over the years by the advice centre, Paul's case was immediately handed to the Emergency Housing Unit of the local council.

The Homeless Persons Unit at first offered Paul an interview appointment in 2 weeks' time. In the interim, it agreed to provide emergency accommodation. The case was then passed on to the temporary lettings section of the local authority, which offered Paul Bed-and-Breakfast accommodation. The section claimed that it was unable to offer alternative temporary housing, such as shortlife accommodation, unless authorized to do so by the Homeless Persons Unit. However, the Homeless Persons Unit was reluctant to do this before it had reached a decision on Paul's case. It said that it would be unlikely to be able to reach a decision until several days after the interview at the earliest.

Meanwhile, we received a telephone call from Paul's hospital social worker. He had been in contact with the local authority's Medical Officer of Health in an attempt to speed up Paul's application. The Medical Officer had no record of the case and was not in a position to make a decision until Paul's papers were sent on by the Homeless Persons Unit. They, in turn, were unable to complete the necessary paperwork until they had interviewed Paul. A frustrating 2 weeks followed, at the end of which the local authority offered Paul a bedsit. Paul accepted this gratefully as being sufficient to meet his needs at the time.

A year later Paul came back – his housing situation had changed considerably. Some 6 months previously he had become reconciled with his old lover of many years and they had been staying together. Both now had varying symptoms of ARC and were a source of great support to each other. The problems they faced, however, were lack of space, which was contributing to tension between them, and lack of adequate facilities for the two of them. One major problem was the lack of hot water needed for baths for relief from pain and for washing the linen drenched by night sweats. Another problem was their close proximity, leading to cross-infection.

Paul had gained some confidence about the way confidential information had been handled by the housing department but he was not sure about approaching the local estates-management office to see if he could apply for larger accommodation. He did not know whether homosexual couples would seriously be considered for a one-bedroomed apartment, and if he told the estates manager about their health, what could the repercussions be if information leaked on to the estate?

The adviser was able to act as a listening-post for these worries and answer them by assuring them of knowledge of local good practices and the fact that if information did leak then there were clear procedures set out to deal with this event. Reassured more by the knowledge that at least the issues had been raised than by actual faith in the system, Paul contacted the estates office and made an appointment for the manager to visit him at home. It has to be said that in this case the estates manager was very aware of many of the issues surrounding AIDS and was very co-operative. After the visit it was explained that any medical or social-work support would greatly assist the transfer section in making a decision, although he did not foresee any difficulties in actually getting a transfer agreed due to the increase in size of household coupled with medical factors.

This information then had to go before a transfer assessment panel, which proved to be a lengthy procedure and resulted in much anxiety for the clients, as they felt they were being judged in some way. The adviser kept up a constant contact until the decision had been made, and, this being positive, the long wait for a suitable offer began. It is still continuing.

Chapter five

AIDS and employment
Dai Harris

By 1985, the work-place had become a public arena where the facts and fictions about AIDS were publicly debated. At that time the daily Press emphasized the morbid, infectious nature of AIDS as a disease which afflicted groups like homosexuals and drug-users. The development of the HIV-antibody test and the knowledge that people were infected did not help matters. Rather than pacify those who believed AIDS was highly contagious, it created new fears about the 'carriers'. There was an absence of accurate public information when it was needed. Doctors responded by assuring the public that although there was a risk of infection through sexual contact or the sharing of needles, the virus had never been transmitted at work. They explained that HIV could not be transmitted by sharing cups and towels or toilet seats. But fears are never easily quelled.

Many trade unions responded quickly, prompted by the concerns of their members, who were readers of some scare-mongering newspapers. Large trade unions like NALGO, NUPE, and the TGWU had issued policies by the end of 1985. Equally, employers became aware that AIDS could pose social as well as medical problems. Employers took counsel from their medical and personnel advisers. The Health and Safety Executive and Department of Employment issued a booklet on AIDS, which was very well received and has been circulated to over 1.5 million employers. The CBI and the TUC worked closely on AIDS, issuing a leaflet and distributing information on the AIDS issue to their members.

Employment policies on AIDS

The formulation of employment policies on AIDS can positively raise the issue of AIDS and contribute to solving some of the employment problems posed by it. These policies are essential in the management of future as well as present problems. Policies can address the following areas of concern:

(a) the fear and risk of infection at work;
(b) fear of other workers who may be infected;

(c) discrimination or industrial action as a result of the above;

(d) a personal fear by employees about AIDS.

The Department of Employment guidelines provide concise and accurate information dealing with the above issues. The guidelines advise employers that workers are not normally at risk in carrying out their duties at work. The only exceptions apply in cases where employees come into contact with blood or other body fluids. The booklet suggests that employers ought to provide information to employees before problems arise. Most employers have followed the advice contained in the booklet and incorporated it into their own employment policies. The guidelines are discussed in more detail in other sections of this chapter.

The important issues tackled by AIDS policies include testing, confidentiality, and discrimination. Some employers have declared that they will not discriminate against people with AIDS. The Midland Bank, for example, has said that it will treat AIDS like any other serious disease. Nearly all employers in a comprehensive survey carried out by Income Data Services Ltd., in 1987, were not in favour of using the antibody test to screen employees.

A few employers – Bank of America, Wellcome, and Liberty's, and in the public sector, Manchester City Council and the London Borough of Lambeth – have developed policies which give support to people with HIV or AIDS. Manchester City Council's policy provides that there will be no discrimination in recruitment practices and that no employee will be under an obligation to take the antibody test. The council has identified the need to appoint people within each department to take responsibility to implement the policy, and has allocated resources accordingly.

Policy and the law

These policies are an improvement on the law and reflect an informed response by employers, trade unions, and the government to the problems posed by AIDS in the work-place. The policies described above are not law, but they are of potential legal effect. They could affect the general duties of employer and employee to behave reasonably when ill-founded fears about AIDS abound. Hopefully, by ensuring employees are informed about AIDS most of these policies will prevent cases of discrimination. The policies are an indication that employers no longer believe that HIV is highly contagious. This is significant, as we shall see.

Employment law

Employment law is based on the fiction of a legal contract between employer and employee. The employer agrees to pay the employee an agreed sum of money in consideration for the employee being available for work. If the employee becomes incapable of work, for example through sickness, then in theory the contract of employment ends. In practice, it continues because the contract of employment is supplemented with many additional legal terms and conditions – for example, a sick employee is entitled to sick pay. Although both parties work under a contract, in practice it is more and more like a relationship.

The law allows the employer to have the freedom to determine the conditions of labour and to treat employees according to the needs of the business. This is subject to protections and rights afforded to the individual employee by legislation. The principal legislation includes the 1978 Employment Protection (Consolidation) Act, the Equal Pay Act 1970, the Race Relations Act 1976, and the Sex Discrimination Act 1975.

Employer, employee, and the self-employed

An employer or employee can have other legal labels. An employer is often a company and employees can be directors, or agents of the employer. Individuals can also be self-employed, when they are both boss and worker. The self-employed work on a contract basis supplying professional or labour services to others under agreed terms. If they lose an opportunity of work they cannot claim it is unfair dismissal although they can sue another for contractual breach. If they are denied services on sex or racial grounds they can claim discrimination. However, the self-employed are in a vulnerable position when they are sick because there is no employer to pay them Statutory Sick Pay. They are advised to be covered by insurance which protects them or their business whilst they are sick.

Terms and conditions of employment

Every employee who has been employed for 13 weeks is entitled to know the terms and conditions of his or her employment. The law stipulates that an employer is obliged to provide terms as to remuneration, entitlement to holiday, sick pay, notice, pensions, disciplinary and grievance rules, and job title. The right is a limited one as the law only provides for minimum standards for sick pay, remuneration, holidays and notice. An employer is entitled to make application to a tribunal if the employer fails to provide any particulars.

All the above terms are expressed but there are also *implied* terms and duties which are unwritten. One of them is the mutual duty of trust and confidence. Trust and confidence is used by the courts to judge the behaviour of the employer and employee. If there has been a breakdown in trust and confidence an employee may be justified in resigning. The duty of trust and confidence has been held to include the obligation of the employer to provide support to the employee.

Terms can be incorporated into the 'contract of employment' if the contract so permits. An employment policy on AIDS could be so incorporated into a contract of employment if the parties have previously agreed to include such rules. The policy can then become legally binding.

Termination and enforcement of employment

There are two classes of contract: those which should end by notice and those fixed to expire at a certain date. In the absence of an express term the courts will imply that an employer will give reasonable notice to terminate the contract and the law provides minimum requirements as to such notice. The minimum is one week for every year of employment up to 12 years of employment.

No employee can be obliged to work for an employer but an employer can prevent a dismissed worker from working for another if there is a restraint clause in the contract. When an employee is dismissed, trust and confidence has broken down and so the courts will never force an employer to re-employ an employee.

Wrongful dismissal

Wrongful dismissal is not the same as unfair dismissal. Wrongful dismissal compensates for lost contractual rights, not the injustice of dismissal. Compensation is limited to holiday pay, any money due as compensation for lost notice, any other benefits such as the use of the company car or expenses, pension rights or entitlements accruing up to the earliest date of dismissal. There is no recovery for distress or hurt feelings. A case is brought in the County Court or High Court depending on the maximum amount of money recoverable. It will be small if limited to lost notice – a week's wages for each year. Larger compensation is due to a person employed under a contract for a fixed term. A case for wrongful dismissal needs to be brought within 6 years compared with 3 months for an unfair-dismissal claim. Advisers should note that any claim brought in the industrial tribunals will be stayed if an action is begun for wrongful dismissal. It is better to pursue the claim for unfair dismissal first.

Unfair dismissal

Unfair dismissal does not have an ordinary meaning, it is a legal phrase. The right to claim unfair dismissal is a right not to be dismissed for an unfair reason. This means that an employer can dismiss for a valid reason as long as the manner of the dismissal is fair. The industrial tribunal decides whether the dismissal was reasonable and fair.

People can only claim unfair dismissal if they have been employed for

2 years by the same or a related employer. They have to fulfil other conditions: in particular they must present their claim to an industrial tribunal within 3 months of being dismissed from employment. There are other qualifications which have to be satisfied before employees are entitled to claim. They must be employees, not self-employed, and normally work in the UK.

It is for the employer to prove a fair and valid reason to dismiss the employee. The only reasons which can be fair are related to capability, conduct, redundancy, the contravention of a regulation or law, or some other significant factor. At the tribunal, the employer has to show that, on balance, the given reason for dismissal was actually believed by the employer at the time of dismissal. There cannot be justification after the event. It is a common tactic to ask for written reasons for dismissal from an employer to ensure the employer sticks to the same reason for dismissal at the tribunal hearing.

Tribunal cases are heard by three people, the chairperson, who is a solicitor or barrister, and two lay members, who are representatives of management or trade unions. The panel makes up its own mind about what evidence to believe and unless its decision is perverse, there is no appeal on its view of the evidence. Its decisions are not law and are not binding on other tribunals. Tribunals are only obliged to follow the decisions of the Employment Appeal Tribunal or a higher court. There is no legal aid available for representation before tribunals but organizations which can assist in this area are listed in Appendix 1.

The law of confidence

The law of confidence obliges all individuals with a duty to keep secret all information imparted to them in a trusting relationship. This duty goes beyond the simple implied duty of employment. The remedies for breach of confidence are not limited to contractual damages. An individual can be injuncted to keep information confidential, or sued for the damage caused by any breach. *Any* information is capable of becoming subject to the duty. The information does not require a commercial or employment relationship to be protected. Indeed, a friendship is potentially confidential, and private details even if regarded as immoral by others, may be protected by the courts [*Stephens vs. Avery* (1988)].

Medical details will certainly be confidential as they are obtained through professional and legal duties of confidence and trust. Most commentators say, and quite rightly so, that the duty is not absolute and the courts will permit disclosure if it is shown to be in the public interest.

In *X vs. Y* (1988) it was argued that it was in the public interest for a national newspaper to publish and identify two general practitioners who had AIDS. Counsel for the newspaper agreed that medical records were confidential and in breach of confidentiality an NHS employee obtained the medical records of two patients with AIDS. However, the newspapers said that the public should know that there were doctors, diagnosed with AIDS, who were still practising and seeing patients. The defendants said the freedom of the Press overrode the private right of confidentiality.

The court did not agree. Medical evidence was called which showed that any risk posed by doctors with AIDS was theoretical and would be eliminated if they had the confidence to report their diagnosis to their employers. The judge was very troubled by the breach of confidentiality and did not accept that there was a public interest in the Press publishing medical records which identified people with AIDS. On the contrary, the judge said the records should be kept as confidential as the courts could ensure.

Health and safety

An employer must provide a safe environment of work for employees. Section 2 (1) of the Health and Safety at Work Act 1974 (HASAW) provides that 'It shall be the duty of every employer to ensure, so far as it is reasonably practicable, the health, safety and welfare of all [his] employees'.

The Health and Safety Executive has been instrumental in providing advice to employers about AIDS and has issued a special booklet giving guidance on the subject of AIDS and employment. It is not a comprehensive statement on AIDS and employment law but places in perspective the risks of HIV in the work-place. 'Normal social and work contact with an infected person is safe for both colleagues and the public', says the booklet, and it reiterates the fact that there has been no transmission of HIV in the work-place other than rare instances where, for example, a health care worker has injected him or herself with HIV. The Health and Safety Executive cites the occupations where there will be risks as including those of doctors, dentists, nurses, hospital support-staff, laboratory workers, and those responsible for the disposal of bodies. The booklet singles out *first aiders* and *health-care workers*, and advises that established practices of hygiene and safety will preclude risks of exposure when dealing with infected body fluids. They prescribe the use of plastic disposal gloves and bleach to deal with spillages.

Duties of employers

Occupational risks exist for health care workers and those likely to come into contact with the HIV infected blood or body fluids. The occupational risk is very small in these cases as HIV is not highly infectious outside the body. However, an employer in charge of a working environment where HIV-infected materials, particularly blood, are being dealt with on a daily basis has a duty to ensure that employees are as safe as 'reasonably practicable'.

Authorities would begin to discharge their responsibilities in this area by ensuring that *all* employees working in the sphere of risk were trained and instructed in handling waste. Hospitals generally use *Infection Control Guidelines* which identify the geographical areas of risk – for example, wards, surgery, STD clinic – and then prescribe for each department the necessary standards of cleanliness and safety practices. A hospital would be advised to keep all employees dealing with infectious materials informed and aware of risks involved in their work. It should be noted that health authorities can no longer claim immunity for acts of negligence.

If an employee were infected with HIV, *allegedly* at work, liability would be determined by examining whether the employer had breached a duty of care, by insufficient warning, training or safe practices. Two things come to mind as we speak in generalities. Infection has to be proved, so the employee would have to show that, more probably than not, infection took place at work. This could not be proved conclusively by one antibody-test result. Corroborating evidence would be required to show that infection had not occurred before the accident at work. An employee may also have to prove he or she did not agree to accept a risk of infection in choosing to work in an area or occupation where such risks, albeit very small risks, were known to exist.

Duty to provide information

An employer has a legal obligation to provide information so that people can protect themselves at work. Is the employer under an obligation to deal with misplaced and groundless fears about infection by HIV? There is no specific requirement under health-and-safety law, but an employer would be unwise to assume that the matter can be ignored.

Providing information at work is the most important step that an employer can take to prevent disputes occurring at work. Relevant health-education material can appease the fears of workers and the failure to provide information to employees can lead to distressing employment problems. In the USA, an employee brought a case of unfair dismissal against his employer after the employer failed in his obligation to reassure him that there was no risk of being infected with HIV in his job. The employee was a warden in an American prison and was required to search inmates entering the prison compound. He refused to do so, fearing that he might be infected with HIV by some of them, and he was sacked. The court upheld the employee's argument that the prison authorities had failed in their duty to provide information to employees about the risks of infection and consequently found the dismissal unlawful.

Discrimination

Much fear and prejudice about AIDS has manifested itself in discrimination against people who are believed to have HIV infection. Employees have been asked to take an 'AIDS' test, or are suspended from employment until they confirmed they were 'AIDS free'. The Terrence Higgins Trust, and other AIDS organizations, have heard horrific stories from people who have suffered at work and lost their jobs because of ill-founded fears about AIDS. In 1986, a woman contacted the Trust because she had lost her job, her boyfriend had been diagnosed with AIDS, and she had told her manager at work. She was then asked to take an HIV test. Even before the result of the test was known her employer decided to sack her. Her employer later alleged the dismissal was for a bad work-record. There are a number of legal issues around AIDS-related discrimination which we now need to explore.

Discrimination and the law

There is no single law which outlaws discrimination on the grounds of HIV-antibody status. Race and sex anti-discrimination legislation prohibits the unfavourable treatment of women compared to men, and men compared to women, and discrimination against one racial group compared to another. Both Acts may find application in cases of AIDS related discrimination. Black people have been subject to prejudice because of AIDS, and in the USA the Commission on Human Rights has taken action in many cases where coloured people have been discriminated against at work on these grounds.

Both the Sex Discrimination and Race Relations Act make it unlawful to discriminate in an indirect manner. This happens when a condition is applied equally to, for example, both sexes, such that only a smaller proportion of one sex *can* comply with the condition or qualification. This definition has application when an employer recruits new employees as discrimination is also outlawed in the arrangements made for the selection and recruitment of employees. These definitions of discrimination seek to eliminate sexist and racist practices and do not depend on proving that an employer intended to be prejudiced in its employment practice.

People with HIV can be disadvantaged by conditions which require job applicants to have a negative test result. Because there are more men with HIV and AIDS these practices could be considered sexist and unlawful. An employee subject to such discrimination can make a claim to an industrial tribunal but they must do so within 3 months of the act of discrimination. Advice should be sought from an advice agency listed in Appendix 1. The Equal Opportunities Commission (EOC) can also take action within 6 months of the discriminatory act and enforce general changes in the practices of employers. Indeed in 1987 the EOC did make a public investigation of the airline, Dan-Air, because of its recruitment practices. At the time of the investigation, Dan-Air admitted to a policy of recruiting only women for cabin-crew posts. This was direct discrimination against men and therefore contrary to the Act. The airline said that it had a defence under the Health and Safety Act, 1974, which permitted it to select women rather than men. It said that over 30 per cent of the men applying for jobs were gay. As AIDS mainly affects homosexuals there was a risk of infection if male staff had an accident aboard the plane. For these reasons a practice of employing women was preferable.

The EOC obtained evidence from two senior doctors which suggested that there was no health risk to passengers. The EOC issued a notice declaring its practices unlawful, requiring the company to change its recruitment practices, and to produce evidence every year, for 5 years, to show that it had done this.

The HIV-antibody test

The HIV-antibody test is a test which can be used to detect past exposure to Human Immunodeficiency Virus (HIV), the general virus proven to be a cause of AIDS. It is a blood test which detects antibodies in blood infected by the virus, which is limiting because HIV-antibodies take up to 3 months to appear. The test is never certain to detect recent infection. There are now tests to detect HIV in saliva, and DNA changes of the infected blood cell, which show recent infection, but these tests are not widely available.

The HIV-antibody test is a screening test which does not indicate the health of the donor. A positive test-result means that a person has been infected with HIV and it is assumed equally that they are infectious. The test cannot determine when the person has been infected, nor affirm or predict a diagnosis of AIDS. A negative test result means that a person's blood is probably not infected. Whether a person should take the test is a matter of personal choice. Many discover that the security of knowing whether they are infected or not leads to a more purposeful life, whereas others say that a test result can lead to an uncertain future. Either way, the test cannot protect against infection which really requires positively inspired changes in sex and drug habits. The Terrence Higgins Trust has published a leaflet specifically advising on the HIV test, called 'To test or not to test', and it is available free from the address listed in Appendix 1.

Obligations of the doctor

The HIV test can only be carried out by a doctor, and doctors must follow strict professional and legal rules when taking blood from a patient. It is necessary to warn the patient about the limitations and ramifications of the test, pointing out the implications of a positive result. Professionally a doctor will require a patient's complete agreement before blood is taken for HIV antibody testing. Furthermore, an occupational physician will always need the *express* permission of an employee. The law of medical negligence requires a doctor to obtain more than a simple consent as HIV testing is not routine. He or she must advise patients so they can make an informed choice about whether to take the test. In negligence, a person is liable for future loss, so a doctor who negligently tests an employee could be liable if he or she lost a job. The duties of a doctor who carries out an HIV test for occupational purposes are onerous. It seems that they would be ill-advised to require an employee to take a test which cannot prove fitness to work, but which could lose an employee his or her job.

The test and employment law

Employers are not free to require employees to take the antibody test. As we noted above, there is an implied and mutual duty of trust and confidence between employee and employer. Unless employees are unfit for work, requiring them or requesting them to take a medical test would undermine trust and confidence. It is agreed that such a request would be classed as conduct sufficient to entitle an employee to resign and claim constructive dismissal/unfair dismissal. The authority for such a principle of law was given in a Court of Appeal decision *Bliss vs. South East Thames Regional Health Authority (1985)*, where it was said;

> It would be difficult, in this particular area of employment law, to think of anything more calculated or likely to destroy the relationship of confidence and trust which ought to exist between employer and employee than, without reasonable cause to require a consultant surgeon to undergo a medical . . . and to suspend him from hospital on his refusing to do so.

Although there is no implied right to require an employee to take a test, there are cases where employees may be obliged to take a medical because their terms and conditions expressly require it. A medical of this nature is usually limited to employments which require employees to be at the peak of fitness, for example, pilots. It has to be said that the HIV test would not detect a change in mental or physical aptitude. A general medical check-up would discover any symptomatic changes in health which were caused by an immune deficiency. Because the HIV test is incapable of predicting the onset of AIDS and few conclusions can be drawn from a positive or negative result, it would not be considered as a routine test to be administered by an occupational physician.

If employees are asked to take an HIV antibody test they are perfectly within their rights to refuse, but they would be wise to seek expert legal advice *before* deciding to take any course of action.

Medicals for employee insurance schemes

Group insurance schemes for employees often necessitate periodical medicals when the scheme is renewed. We have seen that blood testing for HIV antibody has already been introduced by the insurance companies as part of these medicals. Some people have been tested for HIV and there has been disclosure to the employer. In cases like these the doctor is acting for the insurance company and is entitled to test and disclose information to the employer with the employee's consent. Consent to disclose the results of the test to the employer may be implied in membership of the scheme and attendance at medical. Employees are concerned that they are being tested at employment medicals and this could have serious implications for their employment. At the moment the Terrence Higgins Trust advises employees who do *not* wish to take a test, in the context of an employment/insurance medical, to take one of two courses of action. First, they can either attend the medical, and see whether they are testing blood. If the doctor wishes to take blood, refuse consent for HIV test, or do not allow blood to be taken. Alternatively, do not attend the medical and forfeit the right to the group insurance scheme. Neither course of action may be completely satisfactory but may be better than the risk of losing a job.

Case example 1: Taking the test

Paul was employed in the staff canteen of a large shop in London. One day, while preparing the lunch, he cut his hand with a kitchen knife. Because he was gay he knew that there was a remote possibility that he could expose others to HIV. Accordingly he warned people around him that he was in a 'high-risk' group.

The whole matter was reported to senior management at the office where Paul worked. After the incident Paul was asked into the manager's office and told that he was suspended from work until further notice. He suspected that his suspension was due to his admission that he was a member of a high-risk group for AIDS.

A few weeks later a letter was received asking him to 'clarify his antibody status'. He contacted the Terrence Higgins Trust for legal advice and we advised him that he was under no obligation to take the test. We wrote to his employer, on his behalf, explaining that even if Paul was infected, he posed no risk to others in ordinary daily contact. His employer responded with an unreasoned statement, repeating the fact that they could not consider re-employing Paul until he had a test. There seemed no way forward. Then we heard that the Health and Safety Executive had issued guidelines about AIDS and we asked them to comment on the case and sent their opinion to Paul's employers.

We received a reply from them some weeks later but they had not changed their minds. They wanted the whole matter brought to a close, and they attempted to contact Paul at home. The Trust also thought it important to take the initiative at this stage and contacted the senior personnel officer representing the company.

The company responded with a hint of negotiation, fearing no doubt that there could be some damaging publicity around this case. We were called to a meeting at their headquarters, with the senior personnel officer and a company lawyer. We all sat around in a comfortable room discussing the case, trying to put a price on the distress Paul had suffered. It was difficult but they were very civilized and polite. Paul was paid a large sum of money in compensation.

AIDS-related discrimination and unfair dismissal

Any type of conduct which undermines the trust and confidence of the employment relationship can entitle an employee to resign and claim unfair dismissal. As noted before, any investigation or enquiry into an employee's antibody status, any unwarranted request to take an HIV-antibody test, and any suspension from work, or threat of suspension until a test is taken, could be a breach of contract. This means that if an employee has 2 years' employment he or she could resign and claim unfair dismissal.

Alternatively, the employee may have the choice to resolve the situation by remaining in his or her job. In such a case, it is sensible for both employer and employee to seek the involvement of a third party. An outside conciliator, for example a representative of ACAS, can provide much-needed support to an employer. In a dispute where workers are putting pressure on an employer to dismiss an employee, a trade union will often relieve the employer of the need to take sides.

If enough information is provided to employees about AIDS, as the Department of Employment guidelines advise, there would be less harassment at work against people suspected of being infected with HIV. Most discrimination stems from the fear of employees that they might become infected at work by touching something used by another employee. In the case of *Buck vs. Letchworth Palace (1987)*, an industrial tribunal case concerning AIDS, the co-workers of the dismissed employee in a cinema refused to work with him because they feared he might be infected with HIV. One of the workers heard that the dismissed employee had cut his hand some days before and then began to clean and disinfect the door-handles at the cinema.

Employers are advised to avoid problems at work by ensuring that employees know that there is no risk of becoming infected by another employee through contact at work. The Department of Employment advice is succinct: 'There is a particular need to put to rest groundless fears by providing the facts about AIDS and to prevent discrimination against individuals. In most jobs there is little or no risk of becoming infected.'

If any employee is reluctant to work alongside an employee then he or she should be encouraged to discuss his or her concerns with a union, management, or a health-and-safety representative. Employees are required to obey the reasonable instructions of an employer and refusing to work, for whatever reason, is technically a breach of contract. Cases on race discrimination advise employers to take action against the individual responsible for discriminating, and moving the discriminator is sometimes, after persuasion, the only legal response. Most employees will be reassured by advice; only a minority will want to harass and discriminate. However, victimization around AIDS arose in the case of *Philpott vs. North Lambeth Law Centre (1986)* where two law-centre workers were dismissed for, amongst other things, dishonest conduct and bringing the law centre into disrepute. One of the dismissed workers had suggested that a new member of staff, who was gay, would 'introduce AIDS' into work. When the issue was later investigated, both workers denied saying this and blamed others for raising the issue. The tribunal found that both workers had been dishonest and were fairly dismissed.

An employer may also be encouraged by fellow workers to dismiss an employee whom they believe to be infected. It is not unknown for there to be threatened walk-outs and strikes unless an employer takes a line against a particular worker. Of course, an employer may be in a difficult position if there is no union to act as conciliator, and they may feel tempted to dismiss one worker to satisfy the majority. But they should be warned that dismissing for such a reason will not necessarily be considered fair. Section 63 of the 1978 Employment Act provides that an employer cannot rely upon a threatened strike or other industrial action as a fair reason for dismissal. The fears of workers about AIDS have figured in two other industrial tribunal cases. In *Buck vs. Letchworth Palace* an employee was dismissed after being convicted of having sex in public. Employees at the cinema where Mr Buck worked feared that because of his homosexual life-style he might infect them with HIV. The tribunal felt that the employees overreacted to fears about AIDS and failed to discuss these issues with Mr Buck and the other workers, but felt such consultation would have made no difference to the dismissal. It is hard to believe that the employees were so prejudiced that no amount of discussion or consultation could have influenced them. In any event, the tribunal found that the employee was fairly dismissed and the case went on appeal. It appears that the employer conceded, before the appeal hearing, that consultation might have avoided the dismissal.

In the case of *Cormack vs. TNT Sealion Ltd* (1986) another industrial tribunal took a different view. The case was about unfair selection for redundancy, which can amount to unfair dismissal. The employee was a chef on board a ship and was transferred and selected for redundancy after staff complained that he was 'an AIDS carrier'. The tribunal criticized the employers for accepting the complaints about AIDS without investigation: they said: 'This is a problem which is likely to arise with increasing frequency and a good employer who is fair to his employees must be seen to act promptly to lay at rest all unfounded suspicions.'

The need for discussion and consultation, and proper investigation in law

While the decisions in the above cases are not binding on tribunals it is clear that the principles of fairness and consultation are legally required as a result of other cases and legislation.

Unfair-dismissal cases have shown the need for consultation if employees are fearful or prejudiced towards an employee. In the case of *Bell vs. Devon and Cornwall Police Authority* the employee was dismissed from his job as the chef at a police canteen. The employers relied upon the statements of some of the staff who said they could not eat food prepared by a homosexual. The tribunal held that the employer behaved unfairly in simply relying upon these complaints without investigating the views of other staff.

When a tribunal decides the issue of whether a dismissal is unfair it will have regard to the procedure and manner of dismissal. In the past it was possible for an employer to argue that consultation would make no difference to the outcome of a dismissal. However, the House of Lords decided *against* this approach in *Polkey vs. Dayton* (1987), and resurrected consultation as a factor in deciding whether a dismissal was fair. In AIDS cases, consultation is most important because information will appease fears about working in close proximity with an infected employee. Realistically speaking employers should educate, inform, and advise all employees about AIDS now, if they are to avoid disputes in the future.

Case example 2: Applying for a job

Facts

We were contacted by Bill who had been refused a job with a British airline. He was very distressed when he arrived at our offices, because he had been told that he was antibody positive. A few weeks previously Bill had applied for a job to be an air steward. He was offered the job subject to a medical. He attended the medical at the employer's medical centre where they took some blood.

Some weeks later Bill received a letter. It said that he had not passed the medical as the tests carried out revealed an abnormality in his blood. Distressed by this news he telephoned the centre asking them to explain what they meant by 'abnormality'. The nurse at the other end of the telephone said she could not comment on what the doctor had said. Bill asked to speak with the doctor but was told that he would have to wait until after Christmas. He waited a week. He accordingly telephoned the centre and was told he was antibody-positive. Bill was devastated.

Legal issues

First, *negligence* on the part of the doctor, or vicariously by the employer. The doctor failed to advise Bill on the consequences of a positive test-result and the doctor could be liable for any foreseeable loss caused as a result. As this was a pre-employment medical the loss of the job could have been certainly recoverable.

Second, *unprofessional conduct by the doctor*. The doctor failed to warn Bill about the *consequences* of the HIV test and failed to counsel or to provide counselling before or after the test was performed. It is doubtful whether there was a good medical reason to carry out the test. There is a very important professional duty for occupational physicians to obtain consent from employees when acting for an employer. It is possible that this behaviour, certainly if repeated with other patients, could amount to serious unprofessional conduct. Such a charge, if brought before the General Medical Council, could lead to a doctor being disciplined.

Third, *direct or indirect sex discrimination* against the airline. The applicant would have to prove that the airline had followed a policy of discriminating against men.

People with HIV and people with AIDS

If perfectly healthy, a person with HIV will not encounter the same legal problems as a person diagnosed with AIDS. As long as they remain unsymptomatic, and most will for many years, there will be no question of their absence from work. Notwithstanding, people with HIV who are known to be antibody-positive have been treated as if they have AIDS and are terminally ill. Others who are also known to be antibody-positive find themselves isolated because people consider them infectious. People with HIV have been labelled 'carriers' as if they were capable of transporting the virus in baggage. There are no carriers of HIV, there are only those infected with HIV. They are people potentially infectious to others but not at work. HIV is not a virus which people can catch at work.

People with HIV are susceptible to stress like everyone else, but unlike others the stress is very harmful. It has been shown as a co-factor in the development of an immune deficiency in an HIV-infected individual. Unfortunately, people with HIV are exposed to harassment and victimization if their antibody status is known. People with HIV are vulnerable people who need protecting as much as people with AIDS.

People have AIDS if they have an infection or disease associated with an acquired immune deficiency. Two of the most important infections associated with AIDS include a pneumonia called PCP and a skin cancer known as Kaposi's sarcoma. They may also suffer infection from other viruses such as Epstein Barr or cytomegalovirus. These infections may cause considerable weight loss, drenching night sweats, exhaustion, and profuse diarrhoea. The infections are common and are easily fought by people with a healthy immune system. People who have AIDS fight many periods of infection. They are often very courageous and an inspiration for many others.

They generally encounter few serious problems at work but attendance at work, or retirement from work, are important legal issues which are considered below.

Fitness for work

Whether persons are unfit for work depends upon the length of their diagnosis, their medications if any, and how well their body and metabolism respond to drugs. The opportunistic infections and secondary infections of AIDS strike periodically; PCP may clear up in weeks, but it may not; Kaposi's sarcoma, the typical cancer of AIDS, may be very aggressive, or it may not be. It is never easy to say when a person with AIDS will be unfit for work. As a general rule most people with AIDS are fit for work and remain so for years rather than months. This is the experience of the Terrence Higgins Trust as an employer of people with AIDS.

Dementia

HIV is capable of attacking certain cells of the brain. Fortunately this only affects a very small percentage (less than 5 per cent) of people with HIV and it is only significant in about 20 per cent of people with AIDS. In these cases such dementia is only obvious in people who are extremely ill. It is impossible to identify this dementia through a single test, and it cannot be identified through HIV testing. The HIV screening of employees in jobs requiring high dexterity or mental agility will not detect dementia. It is very common for the other symptoms of AIDS adversely to affect a person *before* dementia.

The label and the reality

AIDS is a clinical definition, meaning that a person has both an immune deficiency in his or her blood and an opportunistic infection caused by the lack of immunity. It is not unusual for the infection to be treated very quickly and the person can then lead a normal life. A diagnosis of AIDS itself is a medical label used to identify a rare and fatal immune deficiency.

The law can distinguish between the label and the reality. Dismissing people *solely* because they have HIV infection or AIDS is unfair; medical classifications are not valid reasons for dismissal. In the same way, it would be invalid to dismiss people with dandruff, or double joints of the finger, unless as a result they were unable to do their work. Parliament has provided that there are certain valid reasons for dismissal but they have to be related to the ability to work or the employer's business. It is of course possible that these reasons may be applied to people with AIDS, but only in the way they apply to people who do not have AIDS.

When surveying the reasons for an employer wishing to dismiss someone with AIDS a number of possibilities arise: dismissal because of fear of infection by customers or fellow workers; simple prejudice, fear, or homophobia on the part of the employer; and absence from work. The former reasons have been explored in the previous section as fear and prejudice covers a wider field than that of people with AIDS. We now note the rules around dismissal for people with AIDS absent from work through illness.

Absence from work

It could be possible to dismiss people fairly because they have AIDS, if they are absent from work for an unacceptable period of time. It does not matter whether an employee is absent for a long period of time, or shorter intermittent periods; these are justifiable reasons for dismissal. The law is not so much concerned with the welfare of the employee as much as the effect of employee illness upon the employer's business. The law, as developed by the tribunals, asks one fundamental question – how long can the employer be expected to wait for the employee to return?: an economic question, in short, tempered by some respect for the employee's job. The issue is determined by looking at the length of the employee's absence in relation to the size of the employer's business. One factor to be weighed in the balance will be the work the employee is employed to do. An employer may have to obtain a replacement and employ alternative labour while the employee is away. Indeed, the law will look at the nature of the illness which is causing the absence. Is there a permanent incapacity? Is the employer entitled to treat the absence as long-term? Other facts may weigh in favour of the employee. Sometimes Sickness Allowance provisions create a presumption that the contract continues at least as long as Sickness Allowance is paid.

Each case will follow its own facts but in all these cases the employers have to show that at the time of the dismissal they had sought medical evidence of illness to justify the sacking. Assuming that a person has AIDS will not suffice.

A medical opinion

Employers have to show that they made reasonable attempts to obtain a medical opinion. Once obtained, an employer is not expected to assess the quality of evidence and it is no argument for the employee to say it is unreliable.

The only time industrial tribunals have rejected reliance upon medical evidence is when it fails to indicate whether the employee is fit or not. It is sometimes argued that an employer owes a duty to provide alternative work for employees unable through illness to do their usual work. The employer only has the duty to provide alternative work if it is available.

It will be necessary, as the law prescribes, to discuss any prolonged absence with the employee. The medical officer of the company may be unaware of a diagnosis of AIDS. The person immediately in possession of that knowledge will be the employee because sickness certificates will not usually show AIDS.

An employer dealing with a sick employee would also be wise to consult the employee's doctor as well as the employee. This is the best method of assessing the health of the employee. It is almost a rule of law that the employer should attempt to consult with those who have an opinion of how fit and able the worker is.

Likewise, an employee should also be advised to comply with the employer's request and to consent to the release of medical evidence to the employer. Refusal to allow an employer to contact the employee's doctor would not justify a dismissal. It could make a dismissal based on the *assumption* of incapacity perfectly lawful. An employee with AIDS would also be advised to provide evidence of periodic sickness to an employer even for short absences, as otherwise an employer can technically treat a person as guilty of misconduct because of unexplained absences.

The implication of these rules is that a tribunal would not look kindly upon an employer who failed to obtain a medical opinion and argued that the employee was permanently unfit for work, even if the employee were unfit.

Sickness Allowance

An employer may agree to pay Sickness Allowance. As a general rule it will be shown in the terms and conditions of employment. It can also be the custom and practice of certain trades and employments to pay an allowance. The right may be implied, rather than written, and the allowance is deemed to be payable for a reasonable period. Otherwise, Sickness Allowance is payable for as long as the employee has agreed. It may not be uncommon with large employers to agree full pay for 6 months and half pay for a further 6 months.

Statutory Sick Pay (SSP)

SSP is payable by the employer, not the DSS, and is the minimum payment which the law stipulates that an employer is obliged to pay an employee who is absent due to sickness. To be entitled, employees must notify employers of their sickness. Correct notification involves employees providing their own sick notes for 7 days and a doctor's certificate is required thereafter. The doctor's note requires certification that the employee is unfit for work and the reason thereof. It is both incorrect and undesirable to cite the cause of incapacity as AIDS. The most proximate cause of illness is often a chest or gut infection, or even the side-effects of a drug, but never just simply 'AIDS'. SSP is payable for 28 weeks, although it is not payable for the first 3 days off work. This waiting period can disqualify employees for more than 3 days if they have a number of separate periods off work. Usually only one waiting period will apply, if any two periods of 4 days or more sickness fall within an 8-week period. SSP is taxable, and is sometimes not recognized in the pay packet but will be indicated on the itemized pay-slip that every employee is entitled to receive. It is payable at three different rates depending on the level of the employee's usual wages. SSP rates are reviewed annually and employers can deduct SSP from national insurance contributions other-wise payable to the state.

Permanent health insurance

This is an insurance scheme arranged between employer (or the self-employed) and an insurance company which provides that a payment shall be made in the event that an employee is incapable of work. It is an insurance which is common amongst the self-employed, and the higher wage earner, who can afford to pay the premiums. Employees may have to exhaust their entitlements to Sickness Allowance and Sickness Benefit before they are entitled to claim. They have to show that they are incapable of work, but not necessarily permanently incapacitated or disabled. A certificate from a doctor will be sufficient proof of incapacity but an insurance company does have the power to require its own doctor to see an employee. Advisers should be aware that employers may consider an individual unfit to do his or her particular job, whereas an insurance company will consider the person fit enough to work. The definitions in the policy document need to be examined before anyone is advised and the broker who obtained the policy can also be a useful source of wisdom.

The payment eventually received is high compared to SSP, the eventual amount depending upon contributions made. A standard policy pays out two-thirds basic salary at time of sickness excluding overtime or bonuses.

Retirement

Of course, any employee may retire early from work. Unfortunately only those who have contributed into a private pension scheme, or whose employees have contributed into a scheme, can have any expectation of a payment. Contributions into a private pension scheme of the employer will be shown on a wage-slip or mentioned in the general terms and conditions of employment. The specific rules of the scheme will be summarized in a Policy book which is usually given to all employees.

General rules of a pension scheme

No benefit is payable for at least 5 years on most schemes. This means that a person cannot receive a [return of contributions, or an annual] pension unless he or she has been employed for at least 5 years. After this time the pension usually provides for early or ill-health retirement before a person reaches pensionable age. Early retirement in many pensions is taken as retirement at the age of 50, but ill-health could mean retirement at any age after 5 years' work.

People with AIDS who are unable to continue work due to ill-health should take ill-health retirement, even if over 50, as it will be a greater amount than the early retirement pension. Retiring on such grounds they will have to show either total or partial incapacity to work. The difference is financial as well as medical. Anyone who is anticipating ill-health retirement should seek expert advice as indicated in Appendix 1.

What is the final pension?

Pensions are calculated on the basis of the number of years worked and the final wages before retirement. There is a benefit in waiting for any forthcoming pay rise and retiring afterwards. Retirement is based on the number of years of pensionable service, which will be increased to compensate for ill-health. If incapacity is total there will be a further increase. This reflects the fact that people who retire because they are partially incapable can sometimes find alternative work.

Pensions are payable as annual income or a single lump-sum. Both can be taxable depending upon size, so expert advice is required to maximize the benefit of a smaller lump-sum payment. A lump sum can also affect entitlement to income support if it exceeds £3,000. Entitlement to other social-security benefits can be affected if the benefit rules treat pension as income. Pension payments are a fraction of an employee's usual salary and are found to be inadequate for many. An adviser does have the option of negotiating with an employer to make a discretionary payment. It is important to remember that claims on pension funds will put up premiums, whereas a one-off discretionary payment by the employer can leave both insurance and pension funds unaffected.

AIDS and employment law – checklist

Health and Safety

Governed by the Health and Safety Act 1974 which obliges employers to protect employees against any special risks in their jobs.

Duty on employers

In occupations, where there is a risk of exposure to sharps, needles, or blood infected with HIV, there is a duty to ensure that employees are warned, informed, and as safe as possible from exposure to infectious fluids or materials.

Screening for HIV amongst clients or employees is illegal, and is not a proper substitute in law for safety guidelines on HIV.

HIV testing

Putting pressure on workers to take the test for HIV could be illegal; forcing them, at the threat of losing their jobs, is unlawful.

If a company doctor carried out HIV screening on new applicants and tested them, without consent, the doctor and employer could be legally liable on various grounds.

Unfair dismissal law

An employer could face a claim for unfair dismissal if he or she dismissed an employee because he or she had AIDS or HIV. The employee could also sue in the courts for the failure of an employer to give proper notice.

Discrimination

Any discrimination against people with AIDS or HIV, haemophiliacs, or gay men, can be unlawful sex discrimination as most people with AIDS or HIV are male.

Law of confidentiality

A breach of confidentiality by an employer, disclosing that an employee or client has AIDS, could leave that employer open to being sued. Employers are also liable for the actions of other employees who breach confidentiality.

Travel abroad

Although it may be perfectly proper to request employees to travel abroad as part of their jobs, this does not necessarily mean they have to travel to countries where there is an increased risk of contracting HIV.

Legal change?

AIDS is a serious work-place and economic problem, particularly in the labour-intensive industries of Central Africa. As The Panos Institute (*Aids and the Third World Report*, 1987) states, 'AIDS in Africa does not only threaten individual lives. The survival of whole industries and national economies may be at stake.' UK industries are unlikely to see the scale and level of absenteeism prevalent in San Franciscan and Central African industries and businesses. Presently we are still dealing with social problems in employment.

First, there is very little health-education information provided in work time, despite the fact that most people at risk from HIV are working. Can we afford to lose the opportunity to provide information to working people? The work-place is not usually regarded as the place for education; but in the case of AIDS, employers may find that it is economical in the long term, to provide time for people to learn about AIDS during the working day. Many educationalists can be provided through existing training schemes. No new legislation is needed, just extra resources which should be released to the Health Education Authority and the Health and Safety Executive under a programme which has the support of the CBI and the TUC.

Second, there is an increasing amount of discrimination and prejudice towards people with HIV or AIDS, or those believed to be infected or infectious. This prejudice remains unchecked by the existing remedies of unfair dismissal. Indeed, no present law affords employment protection to people affected by AIDS. Between 1986 and 1987, the Social Services Standing Committee made an extensive investigation into the social implications of AIDS. It recommended that Industrial Tribunal hearings about AIDS should be heard in private and that the amount of employment service needed before a claim could be brought, should be one rather than two years. Certainly, there have been hundreds of people who have suffered victimization at work and decided not to pursue claims because of fear of publicity. However, a private hearing can be provided under the existing rules; the real difficulty is press reports *about* the hearing. Unfortunately, amending the qualifying period to bring a claim is unlikely to be well received. It was the present government which increased it to 2 years.

Legislation which clarifies existing employment rights is a preferred option. In 1987, the then Liberal Chief Whip, David Alton MP asked the Terrence Higgins Trust to make suggestions as to legislation which would assist in the area of AIDS. We drafted a Bill, to make amendment to the Employment Protection (Consolidation) Act 1978, and this is reproduced in Appendix 3. This is not a Bill which advocates a special case for people with AIDS. It is a Bill which makes it unfair to dismiss someone who is simply diagnosed with AIDS. An employer is still entitled to dismiss if the person is not fit, capable, able, or willing to work. Unfortunately, David

Alton decided not to proceed with the Bill after he was informed by a government department that there was no need for it.

In 1989, Gavin Strang MP tabled an unadopted amendment to the 1989 Employment Bill. The British Medical Association and the Terrence Higgins Trust gave support to a draft which provided anti-discrimination protection for people with HIV, outlawing discrimination in recruitment and employment as well as dismissal. The proposed legislation would have applied to make it unlawful, amongst other things, to refuse a job to a person with HIV because of his or her diagnosis.

Any future proposals will only be successful if they meet with the agreement of the CBI and the TUC. A suggested change in the law needs simply to qualify present laws in a non-contentious way to meet with the agreement of a wide section of Parliament. Of course the present government will not put forward legislation in this area; but the Departments of Health and Employment may not object to prospective laws which have a compassionate tone. It is possible that a private member's bill, which does not fall behind party-political lines, will get through.

Chapter six

AIDS and immigration
Michael Shrimpton

Introduction

The movement of people with AIDS and others infected by HIV across frontiers and the attempts of governments to restrict this has provoked much controversy. Although this chapter looks mainly at the position of people wishing to enter the United Kingdom or to stay here, a few words should be said here about the problems which British nationals may encounter in travelling overseas.

It is at least doubtful whether international law and the International Health Regulations in particular permit countries to discriminate against people with AIDS, for example, by compulsorily testing passengers for HIV antibodies on arrival. Most assuredly, the World Health Organization has not supported any such moves and there is little expert support for them. They were not recommended at the London summit of health ministers in January 1988.

Nevertheless some countries have imposed restrictions. Amongst them are Bulgaria, China, Cuba, Cyprus, Czechoslovakia, Egypt, India, Kuwait, Libya, the Philippines, Qatar, Saudi Arabia, Syria, the United States of America, and the USSR. Unfortunately, this list appears to get longer each year. Taking just two countries from the list, the Soviet Union's restrictions appear to be aimed at those intending to stay for more than 3 months (i.e. they do not affect the general run of tourists). The USA's provisions classify AIDS as a 'dangerous contagious disease', notifiable by a medical examiner (52 Federal Regulations 21,532). This restriction needs to be seen in the context of the long tradition of anti-homosexual discrimination in US immigration law, for example that contained in the Immigration and Nationality Act, which has been upheld as constitutional by the Supreme Court (*Boutilier vs. Ins* (1966) 363 F.2d.488).

These two examples should suffice to put advisers on notice as to the sort of difficulty likely to be encountered. New types of restriction are imposed continuously and the wisdom of checking the current position before travel is clear. Clearly one should not simply set off with the intention of coming straight back if there are any problems. Airlines may decline to carry passengers refused entry on AIDS-related grounds. It is also necessary to bear in mind the possibility (and great expense) of having to be brought home in an emergency while unfit to travel without medical attendants. This is a risk against which it may not be possible to insure. Furthermore, there is no guarantee of humane or cordial treatment at the proposed port of entry.

On the other hand if one takes too gloomy a view, the result is advice that clients should confine themselves to this country, precisely the result which responsible international opinion seeks to avoid. Not all of the restrictions affect holiday-makers and distinctions may well be drawn between those who are ill with AIDS or ARC and those who are simply HIV-antibody positive. A balance needs to be struck between allowing one's clients to face the humiliation and financial loss and doing the work of the foreign immigration official. Thought needs to be given and advice sought beforehand where an intending traveller has AIDS or ARC or is HIV-antibody positive.

Travel within the European Community

EC law will take precedence over the requirements of the law of member states when EC nationals are travelling within the Community for purposes recognized by Community law. This applies to a British national who wishes to travel elsewhere in the Community or to a national of another EC country wanting to come or remain here. In the UK, EC law takes precedence by virtue of the European Communities Act 1972, which incorporates EC law into British law.

Now Community law is aimed at promoting the freedom of movement of people for economic purposes, i.e. as workers and business people, as well as providers and consumers of services. The latter two categories are loosely defined and have given rise to much litigation. As a result it is right to regard the notion of providing or receiving services as a fairly broad one whose limits have perhaps not been reached. EC law might be prayed in aid, for example, by a British citizen, who was HIV-antibody-positive and who wanted to holiday in the South of France. In that instance a decision by a French immigration official to exclude the Briton could be challenged in the French courts, which would ultimately be bound as to the application of Community law by decisions of the European Court in Luxemburg.

These rights of movement between EC countries are qualified under the Treaty of Rome and may be restricted or rescinded upon grounds of public policy, public security, or public health. The obvious question in this context is the application of the public health qualification. The broad Treaty exceptions are set out in Directive 64/221 of the Council of the European Communities. Article 4 and the Annex deal with exceptions on the basis of illness and specify any disease subject to quarantine within the terms of the International Health Regulations: an 'infectious or contagious parasitic disease subject to provision for the protection of the host country', syphilis and tuberculosis.

AIDS is not subject to international quarantine and it is doubtful whether it could come within the definition of an 'infectious or contagious parasitic disease'. In addition, it is far from certain that the governments of member states have made provision for the protection of their nationals (as opposed to instituting educational programmes) in the manner contemplated by the Directive. The matter has not yet come before the European Court of Justice but it is submitted that EC nationals cannot be deprived of their rights of freedom of movement under EC law simply because they are HIV-antibody positive or suffer from AIDS and that such a restriction could only be brought about by fresh (inevitably controversial) Community legislation.

Advisers should bear in mind that the definition of an EC national is somewhat wider than might be thought, and includes French overseas departments (such as Martinique), Gibraltar (but not British passport-holders in East Africa or Hong Kong), and arguably many East Germans, owing to the particular definition of German nationality under West German law.

The scheme of UK immigration legislation

Historically British subjects have always been allowed to enter this country without let or hindrance, the definition of British subject at common law being a wide one embracing the citizens of all member nations of the Commonwealth, whether republics or not. Thus, the first wave of post-war settlers had the absolute and unfettered right to live here. Indeed, that remained the case until the passage of the controversial Commonwealth Immigrants Act 1962.

In contrast, aliens (otherwise defined as foreign, i.e. not Commonwealth, nationals) have never been able to assert a right to come here. It should be noted that non-British EC nationals remain aliens at common law, albeit aliens placed in an enhanced position by statute. Their position in modern times was governed by various Aliens Acts passed after 1905, until the Immigration Act 1971 replaced most of the previous legislation dealing both with aliens and Commonwealth citizens, who, by that time, had in any case been placed in virtually the same position as aliens. The Immigration Act 1971 came into force on 1 January 1973. Although Britain entered the EC on the same day, the Act did not attempt to assimilate the new system of control for EC nationals. It remains in force, amended in part by the Immigration Act 1988.

The British Nationality Act 1981 redefined our nationality in such a way as to accord with the immigration position, since numbers of British passport-holders had been denied the right to come here by the Commonwealth Immigrants Act 1968 and by the Immigration Act 1971. British Citizens are those who have the right to live here. British Dependent Territories Citizens have a connection with a particular overseas territory and have no right to come to Britain. British Overseas Citizens, who similarly have no right to enter the UK, form the bulk of the remainder of those with a British passport.

The adviser first needs to check the client's nationality. Possession of a British passport is no guarantee of a right to live in the UK. Conversely, the lack of a British passport does not necessarily mean that a person has no right of entry. Such an individual could well be entitled to full British citizenship, even perhaps without knowing it, for example by birth overseas to a British father before 1983 or to a British parent of either sex after that date (the British Nationality Act having come into force on 1 January 1983). Alternatively, such a person might have acquired the right of abode for life under Section 2 of the Immigration Act 1971 before that section was amended by the 1981 Act.

The old right-of-abode provision has not always been easy to apply in practice. The existence of the right often depends on looking into a family's history. UK citizens acquired the right either by living here as settled residents for five years, being born here or having a parent or grandparent born here. Other Commonwealth nationals could acquire the right through having a UK born parent or, in the case of a woman, marrying a UK or Commonwealth citizen with the right of abode. The existence of the right can be far from obvious (for example, the UK-born parent may have left this country years ago, or in the case of women the right may have been acquired by virtue of a marriage long since dissolved), and advisers need to be on the alert. Once the right is established, it is an end to the matter as far as immigration officers are concerned.

Irish nationals

Although Irish nationals do not possess the absolute right to enter enjoyed by British citizens and Commonwealth citizens who have the right of abode, by and large they are able to move freely between Ireland and the UK and vice versa. Britain and Ireland are part of what is known as the Common Travel Area. Whilst anti-terrorist provisions have made inroads into this free movement, having AIDS or being HIV-antibody positive should not present any difficulty in travelling between the two countries.

Immigration control on entry into the UK

The immigration rules, currently HC (House of Commons Paper) 169, specify certain countries whose citizens require a visa. The list is a rich source of confusion for the uninitiated, first because the nationals of all countries require visas for settlement, and second because the rules refer to foreign countries, by which is meant countries other than Commonwealth countries. There are also now five Commonwealth countries whose nationals require visas for all purposes: India, Sri Lanka, Bangladesh, Ghana, and

Nigeria. Most foreign countries in Africa and Asia are on the list, as are virtually all members of the socialist bloc. Of the American nations, only Cuba and the Argentine are on the list, so US passport-holders do not require visas for purposes other than settlement. Where a visa is required, application must be made to a British post overseas, usually to the visa or entry-clearance officer (note that these two terms are interchangeable). On the Indian subcontinent and in West Africa the queues for entry clearance are long and waits of a year and more are not uncommon in the case of a spouse. In other parts of the world the position is much better, to the extent that a visitor's visa could be issued over the counter. There is no reason why a visa cannot be issued even in a non-visa country and, as will be seen in the section on procedures, possession of a visa provides a substantial advantage in the event of difficulty at the airport. However, most consulates in non-visa countries will simply advise the traveller to go without, as a visa is not required.

The actual decision about whether to give leave to enter is made by an immigration officer at the port of entry. Possession of a valid visa does not assure entry but simply means that entry can be refused on narrower grounds than would otherwise be the case. These grounds include the use of fraud to obtain a visa, a change in circumstances since it was issued, restricted returnability, medical grounds, the existence of a deportation order, or a determination by the Home Secretary that exclusion would be to the public good. Lack of a visa where one is required can itself be a ground for refusal. Where no visa is required or possessed, the decision on entry is made by the immigration officer exercising the discretion allowed by the immigration rules.

With regard to the grounds on which entry may be refused even when the traveller has a visa, fraud and change of circumstances are self-explanatory and will probably not occur very often. The other grounds apply whether or not the traveller has a visa. Restricted returnability simply means that the passenger may end up being stranded in the UK, for example, if the traveller arrives with a passport which is just about to expire.

In the present context it is the power to refuse entry on medical grounds which gives cause for the greatest anxiety. An immigration officer has power to refer a passenger, except a returning UK resident or the spouse or child under 18 of someone resident here, to the medical inspector (HC169, Paras 13(c) and 79–81). Medical inspectors are appointed by the Department of Health and are qualified medical practitioners. They have powers to board any aircraft or ship in order to exercise their functions under the Immigration Act (see Immigration Act 1971, Schedule 2). If the immigration officer is minded to grant leave to enter but is advised by the medical inspector of a risk to public health, then leave may be given, qualified by a requirement to report to a specified medical officer of health for further tests or examination. The medical officer may also ask for tests to be carried out by a qualified person, who probably need not be a doctor. Under the immigration rules the immigration officer is likely to refer anyone wishing to stay in the UK for more than 6 months to the medical inspector. Anyone, regardless of length of stay, who is coming here for medical treatment or who 'appears not to be in good health or who appears to be mentally or physically abnormal' is also likely to be referred. Other than these cases, the power to refer to a medical inspector is to be 'exercised sparingly' (HC169, Para. 79).

How would these rules apply in cases of AIDS and HIV infection? The stated policy of Her Majesty's Government is that neither AIDS nor HIV infection of themselves justify refusal of entry on health grounds. The screening of passengers upon arrival for HIV infection has been firmly rejected – and rightly so. However, this does not mean that people with AIDS or HIV-antibody positive are exempted from the normal requirements of the immigration rules. The best illustration of this is where entry is sought in order to obtain private medical treatment. If the cost of the necessary treatment is likely to be beyond the passenger's means, entry would normally be refused. The immigration rules have not been amended to deal specifically with AIDS and there is no reason to expect that they will be.

The Home Secretary's powers to direct refusal of leave to enter on the ground that it would be conducive to the public good are exercised sparingly and it is most unlikely that they would be exercised because a person was affected by HIV. Indeed, it is doubtful whether it would ever be a proper exercise of the power and, if it were used in this way, consideration should be given to whether it is appropriate to make an application to the High Court for judicial review.

A traveller who is a person with AIDS may well be in possession of expensive medication. Customs officers should exercise great care when searching baggage to ensure that drugs such as Ziduvodine (AZT) are not destroyed or contaminated. Unwarranted interference could easily cause damage running into thousands of pounds, for which the Commissioners of Customs and Excise might be responsible – although obtaining compensation might not be easy.

Substantive rules

It is beyond the scope of this chapter to go into lengthy detail on the various categories of entry and the qualifying requirements; however, they will be described briefly. The main kinds of temporary-purposes applications are from visitors and students. (There are other more obscure categories, such as *au pairs*). The current rules on visitors (HC208) provide for a maximum stay of 6 months, which will be the usual length of stay granted. Visitors cannot claim social-security benefits and must be able to demonstrate that they can support and accommodate themselves without recourse to public funds, which are defined for immigration purposes as Income Support, Family Credit,

Housing Benefit, and housing under the homelessness provisions contained in Part III of the Housing Act 1985. It is no longer possible, as it once was, to extend a stay up to 12 months.

Students also need to be able to show that they can support and accommodate themselves. It is not possible to get leave to enter as a student in order to attend a local education authority maintained school but only a private school, although, at the higher-education level where fees are paid in any event, the status of the college or university does not matter, provided that it is a bona fide educational establishment. The usual stipulation is that at least 15 hours of organized study be undertaken each week.

The immigration rules do not automatically allow wives, husbands, or children of those settled here to join them. Indeed, there are difficult hurdles to be surmounted which, since the Immigration Act 1988, apply to almost all applicants.

In the case of children under 12 years old, there is no difficulty, as they are allowed to enter by virtue of a concession. Children over 18 will not be allowed in at all, except for unmarried daughters under 21 who were part of the family unit overseas (HC169, Para. 50). Children joining both parents here should have little difficulty. However, problems arise when only one parent is here: this is because the 'sole responsibility' and 'exclusion undesirable' rules are difficult to satisfy and expert advice will be needed.

Similarly, the spouses rule (Para. 40) can cause problems because it contains the primary-purpose concept, which requires parties to a marriage to prove that the primary purpose of the marriage was not to ensure that the spouse subject to immigration control could enter the UK. Clearly expert advice is required on the application of the rule. If one of the spouses has AIDS and is the breadwinner, then it may be difficult to satisfy the means requirement which is imposed on all those wishing to settle. On the other hand if the married couple are going ahead in those circumstances it is difficult to conceive of a refusal. It will be at once apparent why the rule has been so controversial and difficult in its application.

The same may be said for the parents and other-relatives rule (Para. 52), although if a parent or other relative with AIDS is living alone abroad, it should not be hard to demonstrate the exceptionally compassionate circumstances which the rule demands.

Application to the Department of Employment for a work permit (which must be made by the proposed employer whilst the subject of the application is abroad) for a person with AIDS may present difficulties. The same will be the case for a self-employed person making an application to the Home Office under the immigration rules in order to come here to carry on business.

Application can be made to come as a person of independent means, but the means requirement is substantial (£150,000 at the time of writing).

Refugees

The immigration rules specifically state that account is to be taken of the Geneva Convention on the Status of Refugees of 1951 and the 1967 New York Protocol to the Convention. What is the position where people present themselves here and ask for asylum on the grounds of persecution in the country of origin because of having AIDS or HIV infection? This is far from being an unlikely prospect, given the treatment of people with AIDS in some parts of the world.

A refugee is defined under the Geneva Convention as someone unwilling to return to the refugee's country owing to a well-founded fear of persecution on the grounds of race, religion, nationality, membership of a particular social group, or the holding of a political opinion. The meaning of 'well-founded' has been the subject of recent litigation (R-*vs*-Secretary of State enp. Swakymaran [1988] All ER 193). More relevant for the purpose of this volume is whether the definition would extend to homosexuals or someone being persecuted for having AIDS. There is no case-law in this country, although Dr Richard Plender in his outstanding work, *International Migration Law* (see Appendix 2), gives examples of Dutch and US cases suggesting the term that 'social group' might encompass a group defined by sexual orientation, and a Canadian case which went the other way. Plender also cites resolutions of the Executive Committee of the United Nations High Commissioner for Refugees and the European Parliament in 1985 and 1984 respectively, urging the inclusion of those excluded for having transgressed sexual mores. It is submitted that the Home Secretary should treat someone persecuted for being homosexual or having AIDS or being HIV-antibody positive as a refugee within the meaning of the Convention, and one foresees a legal battle if that view is not taken. It may be that in practice the Home Secretary will use discretion and grant 'exceptional leave to remain', a device used in the absence of willingness to concede full refugee status.

The determination of refugee status is a matter for the Home Secretary and not an immigration officer at the port of entry. Should a claim for asylum be made at an airport, an immigration officer is bound to refer the matter to the Home Secretary and the person concerned will not be returned until the case is considered. This is a specialist area and the advice of one of the agencies listed in Appendix 1 should be sought.

Immigration control after entry

It is possible to vary leave provided that an application is made before the leave expires. Once the application has been made in time, the applicant may remain until the Home Office has made its decision, which may be for some time. The numbers of such applications are to reduce sharply, however, since changes to the rules adopted in 1988 limit stay as a visitor to 6 months. Someone here as a visitor will therefore have to point to some other claim to remain under the rules, perhaps as a student or on the basis of marriage.

The last-mentioned basis of stay has pitfalls. The Home Office is very wary of people trying to get round the entry clearance system by coming as visitors when their intention all the time was to marry. Thus, if the application is on the basis of marriage to someone who was known to the visitor before arrival, the first question likely to be asked at the interview is, 'Did you plan to marry, when you came?' If the answer is in the affirmative (or in the negative and disbelieved), a probable consequence is the service of notice of illegal entry by deception of the immigration officer on arrival. What if a gay man or lesbian meets someone during his or her visit and wishes to remain in a permanent relationship? Valiant attempts have been made to try to bring such a relationship within the definition of marriage for the purposes of the immigration rules. They failed. Application can still be made outside the rules but the applicant is then thrown on the Home Secretary's discretion possibly with no right of appeal.

Another situation encountered in practice has been where someone here as a visitor or student either develops AIDS or has a partner who contracts the disease. Application can be made in these circumstances for an extension of stay. The Home Secretary can waive the strict requirements of the rules where there are compassionate circumstances and indeed adjudicators on appeal are empowered to suggest such a course of action. When such considerations arise in this context, they are likely to be of an overwhelmingly compassionate nature and considerations of immigration control ought to give way.

Deportation

This term is often used loosely to describe all forms of forcible removal from the UK. Deportation, properly so called, is only one of three ways in which the authorities can achieve this objective and has at times been the least used of all. Most removals are of those who have been refused leave to enter and can easily be confused with deportations, as they can take place a year or more after the traveller's arrival. This sounds odd until it is realized that passengers subject to control are only legally considered to be in the UK when granted leave. Thus, although they may be in the country, for legal purposes they are not treated as if they are.

The Home Office also makes substantial use of its administrative powers to remove illegal entrants. 'Illegal entrant' is defined, not very helpfully in Section 33 of the 1971 Act, as a person 'seeking to enter in breach of a deportation order or of the immigration laws'. It used to be thought that this applied to people arriving off a little boat at Thanet at 2 o'clock in the morning, but the courts have interpreted the applicable section to encompass entry by deception of an immigration officer. There is no appeal against a determination that one is an illegal entrant (other than a perfectly useless procedure which may only be invoked *after* removal) and the only challenge would be by way of judicial review or habeas corpus. Even habeas corpus would be met by a response from the Home Office that it does not apply in illegal-entry cases. Expert legal advice should be sought in any case in which illegal entry is said to be involved, from the moment that the suggestion is first mooted.

The obvious question in this context is: what are the consequences of concealing HIV infection or AIDS from an immigration officer? The argument that, had the officer known, leave to enter would not have been refused is not likely to find favour with the courts, given their attitude in refugee cases where, if the officer had known the true position, entry or temporary admission would have had to have been allowed in any case. The answer is that concealing the true position is always going to carry some risk. Again, however, the use of this power against a person with AIDS could prove legally controversial.

There is, in many cases, a right of appeal before deportation, where all the circumstances of the case, including the compassionate ones, may be explained. Where AIDS is involved, there is almost always an argument on compassionate circumstances at least.

There is no such right of appeal where the ground of deportation is that someone has overstayed his or her leave and the last leave expired less than 7 years previously. Appeal rights will also be lost where the Home Office has no address on which to serve notice of intention to deport. The notice is the preliminary step before the making of the order itself.

Deportation can take one of two forms. It can occur following a recommendation by a criminal court after conviction on an imprisonable offence. (Note that the defendant may only be fined by the court but can still be deported if the court could have imposed a sentence of imprisonment.) It can also happen following a decision by the Home Secretary to deport. Section 3 of the 1971 Act sets out three possible grounds for deportation by the Home Secretary:

(a) Overstaying leave or breach of a condition attached to the leave;
(b) Where deportation is deemed to be to the public good; and
(c) In the case of the wife or child under 18 of a person who is to be deported.

It must be open to doubt whether the Home Secretary would try to deport a person with AIDS or infected by HIV on the second ground; but this is at least a theoretical possibility. The exercise of the power could affect someone who was settled here, unless the person could show exemption from deportation, as having been resident on 1 January 1973 (the date when the Immigration Act 1971 came into force), provided that the residence requirement contained in the Act could be met. It is not thought likely that the Home Secretary would use this power given the domestic and international repercussions. Arguably, such deportations would amount to a breach by the

United Kingdom of its international obligations under human rights conventions. At the very least such an exercise of power would be subject to the closest legal scrutiny.

Challenging immigration decisions

It will have been appreciated that immigration law has its own appeal system. This consists of immigration adjudicators at first instance and the Immigration Appeal Tribunal (a three-person body) on appeal. However, the Tribunal sits at first instance when hearing appeals against deportation on the ground that it is conducive to the public good or by family members of a deportee who have themselves been served with notice of intention to deport.

Appeals may be lodged against refusal of entry clearance and refusal of leave to enter. The difficulty is that appellants in entry-clearance cases are generally, albeit perhaps wrongfully, barred from attending the appeal. Furthermore, on port-refusal appeals only those with valid work permits or visas may actually remain in the country for their appeal; others are liable to be removed. An appeal *after* the person has been sent back is not the most useful legal right. What is more, the would-be entrant can only apply for bail if there is an appeal right exercisable here, except where the decision to grant or refuse leave to enter has taken more than 7 days. It is these provisions which make an entry clearance such a valuable thing to have in the case of trouble. It is suspected that this factor is not always in the minds of those in overseas posts who advise nationals who do not *require* visas that there is no point in obtaining a visa before travel. There is, in fact, a good reason to do so.

Challenging a decision when there is no right of appeal is becoming more difficult. It is usually necessary to secure the intervention of a Member of Parliament or a peer, who can make representation to the Home Secretary. Removal will usually be postponed in these circumstances, although it is no longer possible to be categoric about this. The legal source of MPs' ability to hold up removal is obscure and is thought to depend on parliamentary privilege, if anything. Representations can be made to the Home Office to regularize the stay of people who are in the country illegally, either because they entered unlawfully or because they overstayed their leave. Discretion has a large role to play in the immigration system and the Home Office can always be more generous than the rules demand. Turning that scope for discretion into advantage for one's clients is an acquired art.

Chapter seven

Powers of attorney, wills, and probate

Nigel A. Clarke

Introduction

Preparing for death or for the possibility of being mentally or physically incapable of handling one's own affairs is something that few relish. Yet one of the few certainties of life is that all people die, and with improving medical care, increasing numbers survive with impaired mental or physical abilities. The legal aspects of these matters, so far as persons with AIDS and those persons HIV-positive are concerned, are no different from those applying to any other member of the public and generally no special provisions apply. Nevertheless, a person with AIDS, and those trying to assist such a person, may well feel that the possibility of death, or of being mentally or physically incapable, may occur sooner rather than later, and that preparation therefore ought to be made without delay. The diagnosis that a person is HIV-positive whilst not in itself demanding that an arrangement be made, may act as a reminder of the steps that ought to be taken by any individual.

It is hoped that the following contribution to this volume will give guidance on how individuals may arrange their affairs so as to ensure that others can attend to their wishes if they are no longer mentally or physically capable of doing so, and so as to ensure that in the event of death, their wishes are carried out. In addition, guidance is offered to relatives, partners, and representatives after a death.

Assisting in the organization of the affairs of an individual

Preparing for the possibility of mental or physical incapacity

(a) The principle of one person appointing another to carry out duties for such a person has long been enshrined in English Law. It is known as the Principle of Agency and arises whenever one person, called 'the agent', has authority to act on behalf of another, called 'the principal', and consents so to act. Thus, an infirm pensioner may arrange for a relative or friend to collect a pension from the Post Office by signing the requisite authority on the pension book. With a properly signed authority by its customer, a bank may permit another to sign cheques for those unable to do so. Even the act of arranging for another to do domestic chores, such as shopping, creates in law a relationship of Principal and Agent. However, piecemeal arrangements may well prove unsatisfactory and having one legally binding document will invariably prove to be more useful. This document is known as a Power of Attorney.

(b) A Power of Attorney may be defined as a document by which one person ('the donor') gives another person ('the attorney') the power to act on his or her behalf and in his or her name. It may be completely general, entitling the attorney to do – almost – everything the donor could do, or it may be limited to certain defined objects. The donor can appoint one, two, or more people to act as attorneys. If they are appointed joint attorneys they must always act together – this may prove a useful safeguard against improper acts by one attorney; if they are appointed joint and several attorneys, they may either act together or individually. The practical purpose of a Power of Attorney is not only to invest the attorney with power to act for the donor, but also to provide the attorney with a document defining the extent of the attorney's authority, which he or she can produce as evidence to the third parties with whom the attorney is to deal.

In every case a Power of Attorney must be in the form of a deed, that is properly executed under seal. The donor must also have sufficient mental capacity to grant the power and this generally coincides with the ability of the donor to enter into a binding contract; nevertheless it has now been held that an enduring Power of Attorney is valid when, at the time it is made, the donor fully understands the nature and effect of the power, but on account of recurrent mental disability could not be said to be capable of managing and administering his property, (Re K, Re F, [1988] 1 AllER 358). The signatures must be attested by a witness who should not be related to either the donor or the attorney and who must give his or her full name, address, and occupation. The two statutes that deal in any comprehensive way with Powers of Attorney are the Powers of Attorney Act 1971 and the Enduring Powers of Attorney Act 1985. Unless it is proposed to use one of the forms prescribed in these Acts, the donor should always consult a solicitor in connection with the preparation of a Power of Attorney.

(c) The Powers of Attorney Act 1971 simplified and codified the law relating to Powers of Attorney and by Section 10 provided a simple form which is suitable in the majority of circumstances. The prudent donor will consult a solicitor to ensure that the wording is sufficient for the purposes required. On occasions it will not be; an important example of where a simple power is not suitable is where property is owned jointly with another. A simple Power of Attorney will not give the attorney any right to deal with the donor's share and interest in such property (*Walia vs. Michael Naughton Ltd* [1985] 1 WLR 1115). In these circumstances a power must be granted under the Trustee Act 1925, and the solicitor will advise. Where it is desired to give the attorney limited powers only, such as to buy or sell a particular property or to deal with certain investments only, the advice of a solicitor should always be sought. It is much more difficult to draw up a limited Power of Attorney, as it must be drafted in very precise terms: if there is any ambiguity as to whether a particular power has been delegated, a court will rule that it has not been so delegated.

The advantages of such a simple power are that it is easily entered into, gives the attorney wide powers, and is easily revoked if the donor no longer wishes the attorney to deal with his or her affairs. The disadvantages are, first, that the power given to the attorney is extremely wide, giving the attorney almost unlimited rights over the donor's property, with the resultant possibility of irresponsible behaviour by the attorney – although the chance of this may be reduced by appointing two or more attorneys to act jointly; and second, in all cases involving an ordinary Power of Attorney, that the power is automatically revoked if the donor becomes mentally incapable. Not only is this the time when the donor might reasonably be expected to need the assistance of the attorney but it gives rise to two major inconveniences. First, it is often not clear when the donor becomes incapable, particularly in the case of the donor gradually failing with the onset of old age or illness. The validity of the power may therefore be frequently questioned. Second, there is no way in which a person can privately arrange in advance to give someone the authority to handle his or her affairs when, at a later date he or she becomes incapable. The only mechanism that the law provides is an application by someone to the Court of Protection to be appointed receiver. That application is made after the patient has become incapable and without his or her having any say in the selection of the person concerned.

(d) The purpose of the Enduring Powers of Attorney Act 1985 was to meet both these objections while introducing safeguards to avoid abuses. An enduring Power of Attorney must be granted in the prescribed form which makes it clear to the donor that the power will continue to be effective even if the donor becomes mentally incapable. It must also be executed by the attorney. This achieves two ends. It ensures that the attorney accepts that he or she should be appointed: an ordinary power can be granted to an attorney who knows nothing of the appointment and is not prepared to accept it. Further, the attorney must acknowledge the statutory duty that he or she may later have to register the power. That duty arises when the attorney has reason to believe that the donor is, or is becoming, mentally incapable. The attorney must then apply to the Court of Protection to register the power. The powers of an attorney appointed under an enduring power vary, depending on the status of the donor, and the stages in the registration procedure. The

Court of Protection has a general jurisdiction over enduring Powers of Attorney.

(e) Most individuals will therefore find the enduring Power of Attorney is more suitable for their needs. It is most important to note that an enduring Power of Attorney is only valid if completed in accordance with the strict statutory requirements and therefore on the prescribed forms. Care should be taken not to copy out sections of the prescribed forms as the headings and side-notes form an integral part of the form. The forms can be obtained from legal stationers, although many donors will wish to consult a solicitor to ensure that all the legal formalities have been complied with, not least that the correct form has been used – although the statute only came into force in March 1986, already the initial prescribed form has been replaced by another. The prudent donor may also consider that in the event of his or her mental incapacity, the validity of the power may be called into question, particularly where a partner or friend has been appointed and there might be conflict with blood relatives. In the event of there being any doubt at all as to the mental capacity of the donor, the cautious donor and attorney might also wish to obtain the opinion of the donor's doctor as to the capacity of the donor before making the power.

What acts an enduring Power of Attorney (or any power) authorizes the attorney to carry out is a question of the construction of the document. The donor may in completing the form both limit the powers given and also exclude powers over any particular matter. Where particular powers are to be delineated, legal advice should be sought in drafting the particular clauses required. The enduring Power of Attorney has the additional advantage that it may be drawn in such a way that it becomes valid only when the donor becomes mentally incapable.

(f) Once the Power of Attorney has been completed, signed, and sealed by the donor (and the attorney where appropriate), the attorney, if acting immediately, will usually take possession of the power and register it with any organizations with which the donor has dealings: these will commonly include the donor's bank and building society, and may well include government organizations such as the Department of Social Security. The attorney takes or sends the power to the organizations concerned, and they will make a note of it in their registers and usually stamp the power to show that it has been so registered, and return it to the attorney. At a bank the attorney will then be able to sign cheques on behalf of the donor, make withdrawals from accounts, and collect pensions. In practice many attorneys will prefer to open a separate bank account in their own name as attorney to pay into it the donor's income and to pay out on behalf of the donor as the donor may instruct. The basic rule is that duties are not imposed on the attorney, but that the attorney is given the power to deal with the affairs of the donor.

Assisting the person suffering from mental incapacity

(a) In the previous section it was mentioned that where an individual has created an enduring Power of Attorney the attorney may continue to act even when the individual becomes mentally incapable, either temporarily or permanently. However, the attorney has a duty to apply to the Court of Protection to register the power as soon as practicable when he or she has reason to believe that the donor is, or is becoming, mentally incapable. It should be noted that for the duty to arise, the attorney does not have to be sure, or have proof, that the donor is actually mentally incapable. Belief of a gradual decline into incapability should be enough [1985 Act, s4(1), (2)].

Before applying to register, the attorney has to give preliminary notice of intention to do so. Written notice must be given to the donor and to the donor's relatives. At least three relatives, if there are three who qualify, must be given notice. The relatives are placed in classes, in order of priority, and if the obligation to give notice to three relatives means that any one person in a class has to be notified, then all in that class must be given notice (the enduring Power of Attorney Act 1985, Sch 1, Para. 2[4]). The Act sets out the following classes of relatives to be given notice:

- the donor's husband or wife;
- the donor's children;
- the donor's parents;
- the donor's brothers and sisters, whether of the whole or half blood;
- the widow or widower of a child of the donor;
- the donor's grandchildren;
- the children of the donor's brothers and sisters of the whole blood;
- the children of the donor's brothers and sisters of the half blood;
- the donor's uncles and aunts of the whole blood; and
- the children of the donor's uncles and aunts of the whole blood.

No notice need be given to a relative whose name and address the attorney does not know and which cannot be reasonably obtained, or to relatives believed to be minors or mentally incapable.

The prescribed form (form EP1) of preliminary notice should be used. Registration in the court is made by letter or by completing the prescribed form (form EP2) addressed to the Court of Protection at Stewart House, 24 Kingsway, London WC2B 6JX. There are five grounds of objection set out in the Act: one or more of them if established will defeat a registration application. The grounds are:

(1) that the power purported to have been created by the instrument was not valid as an enduring Power of Attorney;
(2) that the power created by the instrument was no longer subsisting;
(3) that the application is premature because the donor is not yet becoming mentally incapable;

(4) that fraud or undue pressure was used to induce the donor to create the power;

(5) that, having regard to all the circumstances and in particular the attorney's relationship to or connection with the donor, the attorney is unsuitable to be the donor's attorney.

These two last grounds may be of particular concern where a partner or friend has been appointed and there are objections from blood relatives. The importance of ensuring that the power is properly created and that proof of mental capacity is obtained when creating the power can be seen.

In all the circumstances a prudent attorney may wish to consult a solicitor in the event of it being necessary to consider registration. The procedural steps laid down need to be carefully and accurately followed.

Once the power has been duly registered, subject to the jurisdiction of, and any directions from, the Court of Protection, the attorney may continue to manage the affairs of the donor.

(b) Where no enduring power has been entered into before mental incapacity, any person wishing to continue to assist in the management of the affairs of an individual can only do so after having been duly appointed by the Court of Protection to be receiver of the individual, always then known as the patient. There are exceptions to this rule, the principal one being that the Department of Social Security has power to appoint an appointee to receive and administer Income Support and other benefits for the patient; and therefore unless the patient has other assets which require an order of the court, no application need be made. In addition, where the assets are small and the patient's needs are otherwise provided for, application need not be made.

The application for the appointment of a receiver is normally made by the nearest relative of the patient. However, if such a person is unable or unwilling to apply, another relative or friend of the patient may do so, but that reason should be clearly stated. Relatives of degree equal to or nearer than the applicant should be notified of the application and the court should be informed that this has been done.

Printed forms for use in all proceedings in the court are obtainable free of charge from the Court Office, Stewart House, 24 Kingsway, London WC2B 6JX. Upon written request the court will supply a set of application forms comprising the form of application, the certificate of family and property, and the medical certificate. The applicant completes the application form and the certificate of family and property, which is a lengthy form upon which the whole of the income and property of the patient, are set out together with details of the patient's family and any Will that might have been made. A section in which to give a short history of the patient is included in the form and if the applicant has any suggestions to make with regard to the disposal of the patient's property, or what ought to be done with it, such comments can again be made on the form. The medical certificate is completed by the patient's General Medical Practitioner, if the patient is at home, or if in hospital by the appropriate doctor having charge of the patient. The doctor will charge a fee for the report.

Although applications can be made personally and by post to the Enquiries and Applications Branch of the court, in most cases the applicant will wish to instruct a solicitor – in particular when, for example, questions of title to property and the sale of the patient's land or house property arise, or in applications which will result in the preparation and execution of deeds. All the costs involved, including those of the solicitor and of the doctor, will be assessed by the court and are payable out of the assets of the patient.

Once the application has been lodged at court it will be processed by the court and a date fixed for the consideration of it. Attendance is not required or usual in most applications. The form of application, with the hearing date endorsed, is duly returned to the applicant who must arrange to serve the patient with the document together with a covering letter of explanation from the court. Where a solicitor is instructed, all these steps will be dealt with by the solicitor, who will complete all the forms for the applicant ready for signature.

A fee is required (at present £50.00) to support the initial application, and further fees become payable from time to time, which are paid out of the patient's assets. In addition, the receiver may be required to give security for his or her dealings with the cash passing through his or her hands as receiver and for his or her act as receiver generally, the amount being fixed on the hearing of the application. The security is normally given by means of a fidelity guarantee bond obtained from an insurance company approved by the court. The premium is paid out of the assets of the patient.

After the hearing the court will send the applicant, or the solicitor, a draft of the proposed order to be made. The applicant has the opportunity of commenting on it before the court makes the order final. The applicant, thereafter known as the receiver, may only carry out those steps that he or she is specifically authorized by the court so to do. If at any time the receiver requires further directions these are applied for by letter to the court.

The receiver registers the final order, endorsed with the seal of the court, with such organizations as may be directed by the court, and in order to carry out the directions of the court. Registration is effected by taking or sending the sealed office copy of the order to the organizations concerned, who will enter and record the order in their registers and mark the order accordingly. Often the order will contain direction to an organization such as a bank to lodge monies in the funds of the Supreme Court; the bank carries out such steps without further reference to the receiver. Normally the receiver will also be required to open a bank account as receiver of the patient.

Receivers are required to keep a careful record of all income and expenditure received or made on behalf of the patient and each year on the anniversary of the appointment a detailed statement is required to be lodged at the court showing this information and the resultant balance in the hands of the receiver. The advantages of ensuring that all income is paid into the bank account and all expenditure paid out of the bank account will be seen. The form of account to be completed will be sent to the receiver by the court some short time before the account is due. Many receivers instruct their solicitor to prepare the annual account and again the cost of so doing will be assessed by the court and paid out of the assets of the patient.

The court also has the power to make a new Will for the patient upon an application being made, and in addition to next of kin, the court will consider those for whom the patient, if in sound mind, might be expected to make some substantial provision. The court has powers to deal with such an application on an emergency basis. Where it is proposed to consider an application, the receiver should take legal advice.

Although the procedure in the Court of Protection may seem cumbersome, the Court stresses it is trying to help those who are unable to help themselves and is normally very helpful and considerate to deal with.

What should an individual do to ensure that his or her affairs are in such an order that his or her wishes will be carried out in the event of death?

(a) Any person who dies without having made a valid Will, or who has made one that has been revoked either deliberately or, for example, by marriage, is known as having died intestate. All the estate of the deceased (with certain exceptions dealt with later) will be distributed in accordance with the Administration of Estates Act 1925 (as amended). Provision is made in that Act for properly married spouses of the deceased and for blood relatives. The amount of the lump sum that a spouse is entitled to, known as the statutory legacy, and any other interest of the spouse in the balance of the estate, depends on whether the deceased is survived by children and/or parents. The levels vary from time to time, but at present the spouse, where there are children, would receive a statutory legacy of £75,000; where there are no children but, say, parents surviving, the statutory legacy is £125,000. The claims of the blood relatives are laid down in a strict table. Such statutory provision may not in any way reflect the wishes of an individual, even if married and wishing to benefit family only. Unmarried partners have no claim, notwithstanding the length of any relationship that may have existed. Only by the execution of a valid Will can the wishes of an individual be effectively carried out. The vital importance of making a Will is therefore appreciated.

(b) Where an individual desires another both to be in a position to handle his or her affairs and to benefit from his or her property entirely, in addition to the preparation of a valid Will and an enduring Power of Attorney, the individual may wish to consider vesting any property, bank accounts, and other assets jointly with the other person it is intended to benefit.

The advantage of this is that upon the death of one of the individuals, such property will in most circumstances belong automatically in its entirety to the survivor. Not only can the survivor continue to operate any accounts that there may have been and that have been put into joint names, but also, it may be unnecessary for the survivor ever to have to take out a grant of probate or letters of administration to the estate of the deceased partner. Nevertheless, joint property should always be carefully checked, and in particular, the title to joint land, houses, and flats should be checked by a solicitor. The fact that the land, house, or flat is in two names does not necessarily mean that the two owners hold the title 'beneficial joint tenants'. Only where property is so held does it pass to the survivor. Another, perhaps less obvious, advantage is that in a situation in which there might be aggrieved blood relatives, a transfer in lifetime may be more difficult to challenge than a Will, the grant of probate to which can sometimes be held up for a considerable period of time. A solicitor should always be consulted before land, a house, or a flat is transferred into joint names.

The disadvantage of vesting property into joint names is that without the consent of the person to whom the property is transferred, the transfer is irrevocable. Any individual must therefore realize that unlike a Will or Power of Attorney that, with mental capacity, may be changed at any time, the transfer into joint names, without the consent of the person to whom the transfer is made, is a once-and-for-all step.

(c) A Will may be defined as the declaration in a prescribed manner of the intention of the person making it with regard to matters which the person wishes to take effect upon or after death. A Will is normally made for the purpose of making dispositions of property to take effect on or after the testator's death, but it may also be made for the purpose of appointing executors or other persons whom the testator wishes to manage or assist in managing any part of his or her estate, for appointing guardians of the testator's children after death, for revoking or altering any previous Will, or for any similar purpose taking effect on or after death. Every Will, however, has this essential characteristic that, during the lifetime of the testator, it is a mere declaration of intention and may be freely revoked or altered in the prescribed manner. Until death it is ambulatory, or without a fixed effect, and capable of operating on property which the testator acquires after it is made.

A valid Will can only be made by a person of at least 18 years of age. It must be in writing and properly executed. Section 9 of the Wills Act 1837, as amended by Section 17 of the Administration of Justice Act 1982, provides that a Will is duly executed if it is in writing, it is signed by the testator or by some other person in his or her presence and by his or her direction. It must appear that the testator intends by his or her signature to give effect to the Will; and the signature is made or acknowledged by the testator in the presence of two or more witnesses present at the same time, and each witness either attests and signs the Will or acknowledges his or her signature, in the presence of the testator (but not necessarily in the presence of any other witness).

Although, therefore, the legal requirements of a Will are not particularly complex, unless the form of the document in relation to the date and signatures of the testator and witnesses is correct, almost invariably difficulties will arise when trying to prove the Will after the death of the testator and an affidavit of due execution will be required to be sworn by one or both of the witnesses. Unfortunately, errors in a Will are, by the very nature of the document, usually not discovered until after the death of the testator, when it is too late to attempt rectification. Further and in addition, although the contents of a Will only have to be in clear and unambiguous form to express the wishes of the testator, in practice a testator may easily use words that do not have the desired effect and which cause considerable expense and difficulty to executors and beneficiaries. An individual wishing to make a Will would be well advised to consult a solicitor.

Before taking legal advice and consulting a solicitor, the intending testator should consider in particular the following factors. First, the appointment of executors and trustees: there must be at least one, and where there are infants benefiting it is better that there are at least two. In preference they should be close relatives or friends, but if none are suitable, or prepared to act, or if the testator prefers, a bank can be appointed, or professional executors such as solicitors. Where the appointment of a bank or professional as trustee is considered, the testator should be aware of the fees that are likely to be charged: in particular, some testators are surprised at the level of fees charged by banks. The duty of the executor is to administer the estate of the testator upon death. The executor may attend to the duties personally or instruct a solicitor to carry out all or some of the tasks. The burden on the executor depends on the size and complexity of the estate.

Second, the testator should also consider what particular powers the executors should be given and whether the testator has any particular wishes to make with regard to the disposal of his or her body. Thus, for example, the testator may wish to give the executors power to advance money to minors who would not otherwise be entitled to it until attaining the age of 18 years; or the testator may wish to give directions as to cremation or burial, or as to a particular type of funeral ceremony or service, although such directions do not actually bind the executor. The testator may wish to leave his or her personal possessions to the executor to deal with at his or her discretion. If the testator has children, guardians of the children may be appointed by the Will, who have the power to act alongside any surviving parent or other guardian appointed by the court.

Third, the testator should then consider how he or she wishes the estate to be disposed of: does he or she wish to leave bequests to any individual or charity, and to whom is the residue left? Where there is a number of beneficiaries, because of the difficulty of establishing the balance of a testator's estate, it is normally better to express shares of the estate as percentages of the residue, rather than as fixed monetary amounts.

The individual should make his or her wishes very clear to the solicitor instructed, who will then be able to draw up the Will in the correct form, to ensure that the wishes of the testator are carried out and that those intended to benefit actually do so.

The testator should note, as mentioned above, that he or she cannot generally give away any interest that he or she might have in property owned jointly with another. It is possible for alterations to be made to the legal title to land, houses, and flats to enable the testator to divide his or her interest in property owned jointly with another: this is known as severing the equity in property, and the advice of a solicitor should always be taken before such a step is carried out.

(d) Every testator in making a Will must consider the provisions of the Inheritance (Provision for Family and Dependants) Act 1975. This provides the following categories of persons (applicants) who may apply to the court on the ground that the disposition of the deceased's estate effected by his or her Will or the law relating to intestacy, or the combination of his or her Will and that law, is not such as to make reasonable financial provision for the applicant:

- the wife or husband of the deceased;
- a former wife or former husband of the deceased who has not remarried;
- a child of the deceased;
- any person (not being a child of the deceased) who, in the case of any marriage to which the deceased was at any time a party, was treated by the deceased as a child of the family in relation to that marriage;
- any person (not mentioned above) who immediately before the death of the deceased was being maintained, either wholly or partly, by the deceased, and it is defined that such a person shall be treated as being maintained by the deceased, either wholly or partly, as the case may be, if the deceased otherwise than for full valuable consideration was making a substantial contribution in money or money's worth towards the reasonable needs of that person.

The 1975 Act considerably widens the classes of those who can apply for reasonable provision to be made out of the estate of a deceased. There has been relatively little authority about claims in the last category, but decided cases clearly show that it applies to what is known as the 'mistress' type of case and it is contended that there is no reason why it should not apply where there has been dependency by one partner on another in a homosexual relationship. Testators should therefore ensure that they have made adequate provision for dependants, otherwise the other intended beneficiaries and executors are almost bound to be met with a claim that may be expensive, lengthy, and deplete the estate.

(e) It should also be stated that there are a number of exceptions to the rules relating to intestacy and with regard to Wills. First, assets such as national-savings certificates can be or may have been nominated in favour of another. Such nominations take priority over the terms of a Will or over intestacy and, if they are no longer desired, have to be specifically revoked in writing to the director of National Savings.

Second, joint property (see above) will usually pass to the survivor.

Third, and perhaps most importantly, many individuals of working age are now, through their employment, members of pension or other schemes which provide for substantial death in service benefits, commonly two, three, or four times annual salary. It is often thought that such benefits belong to the member of the scheme and therefore may be disposed of as the member thinks fit. This is usually not the case: the benefits belong to the trustees of the scheme and do not constitute part of a testator's estate. Payment is at the discretion of the trustees. Normally, trustees invite written requests as to whom payment is to be made in the event of death: such a written request must be made to ensure that the benefit goes to the desired person. Often the request can be contained in a sealed envelope that does not need to be opened until death. Trustees, upon the death of a member of a scheme, would normally expect to pay out to spouses and blood relatives and it is therefore prudent not only to complete the appropriate form of nomination, but also to give reasons in writing where an unmarried partner is intended to benefit. Trustees invariably will pay to the person in whose favour the request is made, but they are not bound to do so.

Assisting relatives and partners in the event of death

Expected deaths and most deaths occurring in hospital

(a) When a person with AIDS enters hospital, particulars of next of kin will be taken. The next of kin will normally be the nearest blood relative or spouse, but may be a close friend. If the death occurs in hospital the ward sister will contact the person named as next of kin. The body will be removed to the hospital mortuary, where it can be kept until the person responsible for making the funeral arrangements – the executor if there is a Will or the next of kin if there is not – arranges for it to be taken away. It will be noted that the only persons entitled to make such arrangements are the executors of the deceased or in default the nearest blood relatives. Normally, funeral directors have a chapel of rest which can be used for a small fee, and arrangements are usually made for the body to be taken there. However, if a post-mortem is required the body cannot be removed from the mortuary until authorized by the pathologist. Where the deceased was a person with AIDS it may be appropriate for the body to be removed directly from the hospital mortuary to the crematorium for the funeral. Should such a situation arise it is important that legal advice is sought immediately: please consult Appendix 1 for relevant advice. The ward sister will arrange for the nearest relative to collect the dead person's possessions.

(b) If the death occurs at home, but was expected, the doctor who attended the dead person during his or her final illness should be contacted. If the cause of death can be certified immediately the doctor will say so. The executor or nearest blood relative can then arrange for the funeral director to remove the body.

(c) In both cases the doctor will give the executor or next of kin a Medical Certificate that shows the cause of death (this will be in a sealed envelope, addressed to the Registrar of births and deaths), and a formal notice that states that the doctor has signed the Medical Certificate and explains how to register the death. If the death was known to be caused by a natural illness but the doctors wish to know more about the cause of death, they may ask the relatives for permission to carry out a post-mortem examination. This is a medical examination of the body which can find out more about the cause of death.

The unexpected death and where the Coroner is involved

(a) If the death occurs at home and is sudden or unexpected, the family doctor and the police must be advised. The doctor may be able to give a Medical Certificate, but in the following circumstances cannot do so and must report the death to the Coroner, when:

- no doctor has treated the deceased during his or her last illness;
- the doctor attending the patient did not see him or her within 14 days before death, or after death;
- the death occurred during an operation or before recovery from the effects of an anaesthetic;
- the death was sudden or unexplained or attended by suspicious circumstances;
- the death might be due to an industrial injury or disease, or to accident, violence, neglect, or to any kind of poisoning.

(b) The coroner may be able to ascertain that the death was due to a natural cause and that there is a doctor who is able to certify the cause of death. If this is not the case the Coroner arranges to have the body removed for an examination to be made. This is known as a post-mortem. The examination often shows that the death was due to natural causes and in such a case there is no inquest. Instead, the Coroner sends a certificate (known as the Pink Form) to the Registrar of births and deaths. At that stage the Coroner can, if required, issue a certificate for cremation. Alternatively, after registering the death, the Registrar can issue a certificate for burial or cremation.

(c) If the death is not due to a natural cause, the Coroner is obliged by law to hold an inquest. The inquest is not a trial, but an inquiry held to establish the facts. The Coroner decides which witnesses should be asked or summoned to attend and the order in which they should give evidence. Anyone who can give evidence is entitled to come forward at an inquest, but all the evidence must be relevant to the purpose of the inquest. Only a person who has a proper interest may question a witness, but such questions must be relevant and incriminating questions may not be asked. Any person who has a proper interest may be represented by a solicitor, although legal aid is not available for such purposes. The definition of a properly interested person may not necessarily include the unmarried partner of the deceased. The decision is one for the Coroner to make.

(d) The body may be buried or cremated as soon as the Coroner is satisfied that no further tests are needed and the necessary certificates have been issued. In view of the fact that the death can only be registered after the inquest, the Coroner may upon request supply a letter stating the fact of death and explaining that the death cannot be registered until the inquest has been completed.

The registration of death and funeral arrangements

(a) Deaths must be registered within 5 days, unless referred to the Coroner. The death must be registered with the Registrar of births and deaths for the area in which the death occurred. The registration is usually made by the nearest blood relative. If the death is to be registered by another, the entitlement to register is 'causing the body to be buried or cremated'.

(b) The Medical Certificate showing the cause of death, together with the deceased's medical card (if available), should be taken to the Registrar. If the Coroner has been involved the Pink Form must also be taken. The following information must be given to the Registrar:

- the date and place of death;
- the deceased's last address;
- the deceased's first names and surname (and maiden name in the case of a married woman);
- the deceased's date and place of birth;
- the deceased's occupation and the name and occupation of the deceased's spouse (if any);
- whether the deceased was getting any pension or allowance from public funds;
- if the deceased was married, the date of birth of the surviving widow or widower;
- finally, whether it is to be burial or cremation.

(c) The Registrar will supply the Certificate for burial or cremation (the Green Form) unless the Coroner has given an order or certificate for the purpose together with a short certificate of death for the Department of Social Security only: this is completed and handed in to the Department if appropriate. The death itself is entered into the Register, but a certified copy (known as a certified copy death certificate), although available, is not supplied unless requested and the appropriate fee paid. In almost all circumstances a certified copy of the entry should be obtained.

(d) Most funerals are arranged by a funeral director. It is a good idea to choose a member of the National Association of Funeral Directors. Estimates will be given, if asked, but the funeral director's fee will not cover things like the church or crematorium fees, flowers, or notices in the local paper. In cases of hardship an application to the Department of Social Security may be made. The funeral director should be instructed as soon as ever possible and the Green Form supplied by the Registrar handed over. The decision as to burial or cremation is for the deceased's executor or nearest relatives. The funeral director will make all the appropriate arrangements, in accordance with instructions given, including the removal of the body to the chapel of rest and completing the forms necessary to enable cremation to go ahead.

Dealing with the property and possessions of the deceased – obtaining the grant

(a) When a person dies somebody has to deal with the money, property, and possessions left, known as the estate, by collecting in all of the money, paying any debts, and distributing the estate to those entitled to it. The term Probate often means the issuing of a legal document to one or more people authorizing them to do this.

(b) Some property does not belong to the estate of the deceased, or does not pass under the terms of the deceased's Will or intestacy. Thus, where the deceased owned property jointly with another it passes in most cases to the survivor. A certified copy death certificate is produced to the bank or building society to enable the deceased's name to be removed from the account and permit the survivor to continue to operate it. So far as land, houses, and flats are concerned, the advice of a solicitor should be sought: if the joint owners hold the property as joint tenants it will pass to the survivor; if the title is not registered a certified copy death certificate merely needs to be placed with the title deeds; if the title is registered, the land or charge certificate will have to be submitted to HM Land Registry for amendment. If the property is held as tenants in common by the deceased and another, then the deceased's share falls in to be administered with the remainder of the estate.

As far as nominations of savings certificates are concerned, a certified copy death certificate is sent to the Director of National Savings, who will then send any form that needs to be completed with regard to encashment in favour of the nominated person.

As far as death in service benefits relating to occupational pension schemes are concerned, the certified copy death certificate is sent to the trustees, who will usually make enquiries as to any Will made, as to what blood relatives there are, and in particular to any request made to them by the deceased. The trustees will then make their distribution in accordance with their discretion.

(c) The legal document issued to enable the estate to be dealt with is known as a grant of representation. First, it has to be considered whether it is necessary to make any application for a grant. In the previous paragraph, circumstances were set out in which no grant is necessary. Further, if the whole estate of the deceased comprises less than £5,000 in value, it may be possible for it to be released without a grant. In such circumstances enquiries should be made of the organizations such as insurance companies, banks, and building societies, to see if they will release the money without a grant. They are not bound to do so, as releasing money without a grant is entirely at their discretion. The authority is therefore the Administration of Estates (small payments) Act 1965 as amended by the Administration of Estates (small payments increase of limit) Order 1984: this should be stated when a request in writing is made.

Where there are other assets such as shareholdings, experience shows that it is probably easier to apply for a grant in any event, as the forms to be completed without a grant are often complex and require guarantees by banks, which have to be paid for. The person making the application to deal with the assets without the necessity of obtaining a grant must still be the executor named in the Will, the principal beneficiary if the executor has died, or the nearest blood relative if there is no Will. The person retains all the responsibilities with regard to the administration of the estate that are referred to below.

(d) In other circumstances a grant of representation is required. This is normally: if there is a Will, a grant of Probate to the executors named in the Will, or if there is no Will, a grant of Letters of Administration to the spouse or nearest blood relatives. Where there is a Will and either the executors have already died, or none are named, a grant of Letters of Administration is granted to the principal beneficiaries: this is known as a grant of Letters of Administration (with Will annexed). The grant is issued by the Probate Registry of the Family Division of the High Court. In London, personal enquiries can be made at Room 526, 5th Floor, Golden Cross House, Duncannon Street, London WC2N 4JF. There are local probate registries and offices in most cities and major towns.

(e) There are two categories of estate to consider when applying to obtain a grant, those comprising less than £70,000 in value and those exceeding £70,000 in value. In computing the value of the estate the total assets of the deceased, including personal items and any share in jointly owned property, are taken. The relevance of these figures is that only where the estate exceeds £70,000 does a complex Inland Revenue Account have to be delivered, although Inheritance Tax is not payable until the value of the estate exceeds £118,000. Inheritance Tax is then payable at a fixed rate of 40 per cent on the excess.

(f) At most, four persons may apply for a grant. Where there are infant beneficiaries, at least two must apply, otherwise one person may apply. If there is a Will, the applicants will be the executors named. If no executors are named or those named have died, the applicant will be the principal or residuary beneficiary. If there is no Will a strict table is laid down, commencing with the spouse, then in order and in default of any category, the children, the grandchildren, the parents, the brothers and sisters, and more distant blood relatives.

(g) Applicants may wish to instruct a solicitor, but where they wish to deal with matters personally, they have to obtain and complete the application forms, return them with the certified copy death certificate and the original Will, if any, to the appropriate Probate Registry, and attend an interview.

The appropriate forms can be obtained from the Principal Registry or from local registries and offices. The probate application asks for details of the deceased and the applicants. Where the value of the estate exceeds £70,000, a detailed account of the estate for the Inland Revenue must be completed. The completed forms, together with the certified copy death certificate and original Will (if any), are sent to the Probate Registry chosen by the applicant as being most convenient. Applicants must attend one interview at the registry to confirm the details and to answer any necessary questions. A fee may be payable in accordance with the published scale and if inheritance tax is payable the amount payable must usually be delivered to the Probate Registry before the grant can be issued. In due course the grant of Probate or Letters of Administration will be sent to the applicants, then known respectively as Executors and Administrators. The executors may also ask the registry for a number of sealed office copies of the grant for use in the administration. The responsibility of the Probate Registry ends when the grant is issued.

Dealing with the property and possessions of the deceased – administering the estate

(a) Once the grant has been obtained by the executors they must proceed to administer the estate. The first responsibility is to gather in all the assets. This is done by producing and registering the original grant or one of the sealed office copies with all the organizations concerned, such as banks, building societies, and insurance companies. They in turn will supply the executors with forms to be completed and signed to enable the accounts to be closed and policies encashed. Personal items and furnishings may well have to be disposed of and any home owned by the deceased sold, or transferred.

(b) Once the monies have been gathered in, or part of them, the executors should start to pay out the debts: these will include the funeral account and usual household bills of the deceased. Reasonable enquiries must be made to ensure that all the debts of the deceased have been discovered: the executors can only ensure that they have protected themselves in this duty by advertising for claims. Enquiries should be made of the deceased's last employer to ensure that no other monies are due to an estate and also to the Department of Social Security that all benefits have been paid up to date.

(c) Executors should also remember that they are responsible for any taxation liabilities of the deceased and the grant should therefore be registered with the local tax office of the deceased. Often, tax returns up to the date of death have to be made, necessitating enquiries as to income, sometimes over a number of years. Executors are also responsible for making a return to the Inland Revenue of income arising during the course of the administration – that is, after the date of death, but before distribution. Whenever inheritance tax has arisen, the executors have to ascertain whether the values realized for any items differ from those originally estimated in the Inland Revenue Account; if so a corrective account will need to be filed. All correspondence is with the Capital Taxes Office, Inland Revenue, Rockley Road, London W14 0DF. If property is not sold, the Capital Transfer Taxes office may well ask the district valuer to check the estimates given, and if there is any disagreement the executors may need to instruct their own valuers. Finally, a clearance certificate from the Capital Taxes office must be obtained to confirm that the executors have cleared all the liabilities of the estate for Inheritance Tax.

(d) When the executors are satisfied that they have completed these steps and that the estate is therefore solvent, they should proceed to pay out any legacies and finally make the distribution to the residuary beneficiaries.

Is it necessary to obtain the services of a solicitor?

(a) Where the estate is small and no grant is required those responsible for the affairs of the deceased may well feel confident to deal with the administration in person. Similarly, where the estate is relatively simple and under the £70,000 level, executors and administrators may well feel able to deal with matters themselves, particularly where the executor and beneficiary is one and the same person.

(b) Nevertheless, often the period following the death of the deceased is a distressing time for the executors and beneficiaries and they may feel over-whelmed by the sheer volume of work in the administration with the many letters to be written and forms to be completed. Further, where the assets are large and the estate complex, or the estate includes property such as land, a house, or flat, legal assistance should be sought. The executors can leave all the work to a solicitor.

(c) The solicitor completes all the forms relating to the grant, including any Inland Revenue account that may have to be completed. The prospective Executor or Administrator will only have to attend the solicitor's office to sign and swear the papers. Once the grant has been obtained, the solicitor will deal with the administration and ensure that all the debts have been paid and will at the completion of the administration provide a complete financial account known as the estate account. Where there is a substantial number of beneficiaries and executors differ from them, the executors may prefer to have a solicitor accept responsibility for the administration of the estate, the solicitor's charges being deducted from the estate before distribution. The executors may also therefore be able to protect themselves in the event of their having distributed the estate and then finding that there are other liabilities to meet, for example a back claim from the Department of Social Security for overpaid benefits. The solicitors will have to accept respon-sibility for any error made by them.

Chapter eight

AIDS and insurance
Wesley Gryk

Introduction

The growing prevalence of AIDS in the United Kingdom has created difficult problems for the insurance industry. There is a number of factors related to the initial incidence of the disease in this country which have in particular forced the insurance industry to take rapid notice of its existence. These factors have alerted insurers to their potentially great financial vulnerability if they do not make provision now for the possible long-term effects of the spread of AIDS.

One such important factor is that the disease has thus far largely affected the younger segment of the population. This includes many individuals who, under ordinary circumstances, might be considered good insurance risks likely to lead long and healthy lives in this medically sophisticated final quarter of the twentieth century. Indeed, during the last two decades prior to the emergence of AIDS, actuaries had predicted falling mortality rates amongst males. Such predictions were taken very much into account in setting the level of premiums offered by life insurance companies keen to undercut their competitors.

A second important factor is that many of those affected by the disease have come from social groupings whose members frequently seek – because of the discrimination and disapproval which they face in society – to hide their membership of such groupings. To compound the difficulties, the virus itself which is responsible for the disease leads an elusive existence, lying dormant indefinitely within those whom it infects, often giving no indication of its presence. Finally and most unhappily, the prospect of prevention or cure by medical science remains unrealized.

Given this background, it is not surprising that the insurance industry has thus far been unable to develop sound actuarial projections about the long-term incidence of AIDS in the UK. In the absence of such projections, insurers face very real and legitimate concerns about their ultimate liabilities for AIDS-related claims. They have the clear obligation to make adequate financial provision now to maintain their solvency so as to be able to meet all future claims of those whom they insure; yet they find this necessarily difficult in the face of such uncertainty with respect to the AIDS threat.

The insurance industry has been struggling to resolve this dilemma over the past couple of years, and has discovered no easy solutions. Different approaches have been tried and the area remains in a state of flux as insurers continue to move in new directions. Unfortunately, they have been hindered by the very great difficulty of developing sound actuarial knowledge about the disease and its incidence. It is also unfortunate that the lack of an insurance regulatory structure in the UK has made it impossible to ensure that the very many public policy issues arising in this area are addressed. This has meant that many of the approaches taken thus far by the industry have been unduly self-serving and discriminatory, and largely based on surmise rather than fact. In particular, the insurance industry has failed to acknowledge that those at risk of HIV infection cannot be simplistically identified by seeking to establish the membership of individuals to particular limited groups.

This chapter attempts to outline for those who may be affected by these issues and for those advising such people the state of affairs as of early 1989. There are bound to be further developments and this must be borne in mind when considering the information included below. One can only hope that the various problem areas raised will become more manageable or disappear altogether as solutions begin to be found to the medical and the social problems which have been triggered by HIV.

Health insurance – the simple policy of exclusion

The two areas of insurance cover which have been most directly affected by the emergence of AIDS as a threat to health and life in the UK are – not surprisingly – health insurance and life assurance. In the area of health insurance, however, the existence of the National Health Service (NHS) has meant that insurers have in effect been able to evade or postpone their exposure to potential liabilities arising from AIDS-related illness. The trend has been that newly written private health insurance policies in the United Kingdom specifically exclude coverage for AIDS-related illnesses, either altogether or for a significant period.

Thus, for example, the British United Provident Association (BUPA), a leading provider of private health insurance in the United Kingdom, announced in 1987 that any claimant who joined a United Kingdom BUPA Scheme on or after 1 July 1987 would not be entitled to 'treatment which in any way arises from, is attributable to, or is consequential upon Human Immunodeficiency Virus Infection and which commenced during the first five years membership of any United Kingdom BUPA Scheme'. This limitation applies regardless of how or when the insured was infected, and whether or not the claimant was aware of infection – or, indeed, had even been infected – at the time of application.

Such exclusion clauses – absolving the insurer of liability for AIDS-related claims either for a set period or throughout the period of coverage – are now the norm with respect to ordinary private health insurance in the UK. The individual applying for a new health insurance policy should therefore examine the terms of a proposed policy closely in this regard and compare the terms of exclusion provided by different companies before signing an agreement with any company. Even with respect to those insurers who will cover the AIDS risk after a set number of years, variations exist as to the nature of that cover. Initial diagnosis and treatment of AIDS-related illness may be covered, for example, but not long-term treatment.

Those who already have private health cover may have contracted with their insurer prior to the institution of such exclusion clauses and their coverage may, therefore, include AIDS-related illness. In such cases, however, it is important that the cover be maintained continuously without break by prompt renewal on the originally agreed terms. If the insured individual allows the old policy to cease for whatever reason and then seeks to renew coverage, it is likely that this renewal will be on a new set of terms, including an AIDS exclusion clause. Again, it is important to read the terms proposed carefully before signing anything.

Obviously the existence of such exclusion clauses for AIDS-related illness is less problematic in the UK than it would be in other countries, such as the United States, where health care is mainly provided by the private sector. Private insurance cover remains something of a luxury here, taken out by some 10 per cent of the population and thus supplementing rather than supplanting the NHS. The privately insured individual contracting an AIDS-related illness during the effective period of an AIDS exclusion clause would simply turn to the NHS for treatment. Under present circumstances, this would occasion no particular hardship for the insured, given that most expertise relating to the treatment of AIDS-related illness in the UK is currently to be found within the NHS – as are compassionate staff and well-equipped facilities, at least in those urban areas where such illness is most prevalent.

At the same time, however, the response by private medical insurers to AIDS must raise difficult questions for the present British government. Margaret Thatcher's government would, on the one hand, appear to favour a shift of health-care provision to the private sector effectuated at least partly through the agency of private health insurers. On the other hand, that same government presently lacks – and presumably would be loath to take on – the regulatory power necessary to ensure that private insurers would perform this function adequately. The argument is made that the private insurance industry can be counted upon to take over to some extent the function of assessing the future medical needs of the population and then responsibly spread the financial burdens connected with the meeting of those needs through private insurance policies. If this is so, then it seems crucial that the industry not be permitted to opt out of the process when particularly difficult problems arise, such as the emergence of AIDS and the attendant uncertainties relating to its long-term effect on the medical needs of the British population. Otherwise, the danger arises that the NHS will find itself uniquely burdened only with the most onerous and unpredictable of case-loads.

As a final point, two particular special categories of health insurance should be mentioned – so-called 'permanent health insurance' and travel health insurance. Permanent health insurance (PHI) policies do not cover medical expenses as such but rather are intended to provide regular income payments to insured parties who are incapacitated by sickness, disability, or accident. The majority of such policies in the UK are group policies provided by an employer to cover the eventuality of employees becoming incapacitated. While, in 1988, such PHI policies continued to be available without AIDS exclusion clauses, it would appear that the trend towards including such clauses is likely to encompass PHI policies as well before long. To the extent that this did not occur, it might also be expected that the sort of procedures described below with respect to life assurance applications, might be applied in the PHI field. Already in 1988, for example, some PHI insurers were requiring HIV-antibody tests with respect to applicants requiring cover over certain limits (£15,000 and £25,000 maximum annual benefits were the limits cited by two companies). Failure to agree to such testing or a positive result would mean the rejection of an application for PHI cover. Again, an applicant for such a policy should examine the application and its conditions carefully before proceeding.

Travel health insurance policies are taken out by UK residents travelling abroad who want protection against the potentially very high cost of medical care should they need treatment for personal injury or illness in another country. Again, the general approach being taken by insurers is to exclude AIDS-related illness altogether. In some cases this may be done by explicit language in the terms of the policy referring by name to AIDS, while in others the approach taken may be more indirect. A policy may, for example, exclude liability for any illness 'directly or indirectly caused by or arising from or in any way attributable to' a sexually transmitted disease. Such an exclusion, however, would arguably not affect policy holders who had been exposed to HIV by a means other than sexual transmission. Insurers may also challenge AIDS-related claims on the basis of clauses excluding expenses 'arising from chronic medical conditions existing at the commencement of the insured period and not disclosed to the insurer'. Understandably, insurers have been sensitive to allegations that in the initial period after the emergence of AIDS some affected individuals travelled to other countries specifically to seek newer and more sophisticated treatments and sought to claim on such policies when doing so.

An interesting footnote regarding the effect of AIDS on the travel health insurance industry is that insurers doing business in this area maintain that the level of claims against them has grown appreciably because of another

AIDS-related reason. They cite the growing number of claimants who are demanding repatriation when afflicted with illness in countries where they fear infection from HIV attributable to contaminated blood transfusions, recycled hypodermic needles, or other treatments.

Life assurance: a more controversial approach

Because of the existence of the NHS and its ability thus far to assume responsibility for the treatment of the vast majority of AIDS-related cases in the UK, there has been little public comment or controversy with respect to the policy of private health insurers in excluding AIDS-related illness from their coverage. To the extent that there has been some public scrutiny and adverse comment on the policy of the insurance industry with respect to AIDS, this has been directed largely towards Life Assurance (LA) companies. At least until now, the LA industry has for the most part not followed the health insurers' approach of specifically excluding from their policies coverage related to deaths from AIDS-related illness.

One approach they have taken has been to use the threat of their potentially great financial vulnerability occasioned by AIDS to justify very significant overall increases in premium levels for life assurance. The year 1988 saw a spate of such premium increases effectuated by many LA companies – particularly relating to policies for males – in some cases amounting to 150 per cent increases. In light of the very unclear actuarial projections available to assess their eventual vulnerability in this area, it seems uncertain how these premium increases have been calculated and whether they are justified. Some have accused the LA industry of using the AIDS threat as an excuse to move premium levels higher. One approach which would avoid such charges but which thus far has been mostly ignored in the UK is the so-called 'German alternative', so named for its use in the Federal Republic of Germany. Under this approach, LA companies charge premiums which are in fact relatively high but with specific provisions to the effect that policy holders will be awarded bonuses (through reduced future premiums) if the actual mortality experience of those insured is lower than projected in setting the initial premium levels. Conversely, policies have also been written specifying that relatively low initial premium levels may be adjusted upwards on the basis of bad mortality experience in the insurance group.

Far more controversial has been the LA industry's two-pronged 'exclusionary' strategy which it has developed in the hope that this will minimize its future vulnerability to claims deriving from AIDS-related deaths. Under this strategy, insurers have sought means (1) to identify individuals who have been exposed to HIV, with the purpose of excluding all such individuals from coverage altogether, and (2) to identify individuals whom the insurers believe to be at risk of such exposure, with the purpose of either excluding them from coverage or offering coverage only at yet further increased premiums.

The pursuit of this strategy has necessarily involved the LA industry in seeking detailed, highly confidential information not only about the medical history of some applicants but about their private lives, sexual mores, and so on. On the basis of such information as it has collected, the industry has also attempted to draw presumptions about the future behaviour of applicants, in particular whether those who have not been exposed to the AIDS virus are likely to face eventual exposure in the future. In their attempts to balance their own commercial interests with the right to privacy of their applicants, LA companies have been walking through a minefield of personal sensitivities. It is not surprising, therefore, that considerable concern has been voiced about the approach taken. Such concern is only likely to increase as the risk of AIDS widens within the population and the number of people who find their personal lives under scrutiny by insurers increases.

One obvious question which arises initially is why LA companies, for the most part, have not so far followed the lead of health insurers and considered the widespread use of AIDS exclusion clauses in their policies. Industry representatives generally cite two main reasons.

First, LA policies are frequently taken out in the context of providing a form of security in a financial transaction. The individual or organization whose interests are meant to be secured by such a LA policy is likely to be seriously dissatisfied with a policy containing such an exclusion clause.

Endowment mortgages provide a good example of this use of a LA policy. A person takes out a 'term' LA policy which is to mature in a set number of years if the person survives for that period, providing on maturity a lump-sum payment sufficient to pay off the principal amount of a mortgage loan made by a bank or building society. In the meantime, the insured individual pays only interest on the mortgage loan and premiums on the LA policy, with no repayment of the principal amount outstanding on the mortgage loan. If, however, the individual dies before the end of the designated term, the LA company agrees to pay off the principal amount of the mortgage loan, leaving an unencumbered property in the individual's estate.

If such a policy were to include an AIDS exclusion policy and the insured individual died of an AIDS-related illness, nothing would be paid out by the insurer. This would be an unsatisfactory result from the viewpoint of both the bank or building society and of the insured's estate. The bank or building society, rather than receiving the automatic lump-sum repayment it had expected, would need to go to considerable additional trouble and expense, seeking repayment of the mortgage from the deceased's estate or, if necessary, taking possession of the mortgaged property and arranging for its sale to obtain repayment. At the same time, from the viewpoint of the deceased's estate, large LA premiums would have been paid pointlessly over a period of perhaps many years for the specific purpose of ensuring that the property would be fully paid up upon the death of the insured, for the benefit of the deceased's beneficiaries.

Of course, not all LA policies arise in the context of such financial trans-
actions. The individual seeking such coverage may simply want to make
provision for relations or other dependents in the event of death. Such an
individual may further feel confident that he or she has neither been exposed
to HIV nor faces the risk of such exposure. Even with respect to such cases,
the insurance industry has been reluctant to institute policies with AIDS
exclusion clauses.

This is because of the second problem cited by the industry in connection with
such exclusion clauses – the difficulty which would arise in policing the application of these clauses. In particular, industry spokespersons refer to the problems
inherent in ascertaining whether or not a given death was AIDS-related. The
immediate cause of death cited on the death certificate of an individual affected
by HIV may give no indication that a death was AIDS-related. Given the
prejudice and misunderstanding surrounding the disease, both family and
medical professionals connected with a given case may conspire to minimize the
chance for the AIDS connection to become public knowledge. In such an
atmosphere, the LA investigator will need to devote considerable resources to
sorting out each individual doubtful case. This sort of problem is much less
likely to arise for insurers in the context of exclusion clauses in health insurance
and PHI policies, because in such cases the insured individual is likely to be
alive and available. He or she may find that, as a condition of collecting under
the insurance policy, it may be necessary to answer questions, submit to medical
examination, and perhaps even to HIV-antibody testing if disputes arise relating
to the applicability of an AIDS exclusion clause.

For these two reasons, then – the unacceptability of policies with exclusion
clauses as security in the business context and the reluctance of insurers
themselves to police claims made under such policies – there has been no
large movement towards the writing of such policies by LA companies. A
few companies have expressed a tentative interest in writing such policies,
but early indications are that this approach will not prove popular. Policies
which exclude coverage for AIDS-related death are not likely to be
appreciably cheaper, and those whose financial interests are being secured by
an insurance policy are not likely to accept such terms.

Thus, LA companies have over the last 2 to 3 years been developing the
strategy, referred to above, of creating an application process designed to
screen out as many individuals as possible whom the companies themselves
decide to be at risk of AIDS-related death. As a result, the vast majority of
cases today in which individuals are likely to seek advice about AIDS and
insurance arise when those individuals are contemplating or are in the process
of making an application for LA cover. They may find themselves subjected
to intimate questioning about their sexuality and life-style, and to requests for
medical examinations and testing, without fully understanding the possible
personal and/or financial ramifications which may result from their compliance with such questioning or requests.

Much of the remainder of this chapter will, therefore, focus on the procedures followed by the LA industry in this area and attempt to draw attention to the potential pitfalls which may be encountered and should be anticipated by the individual applicant for a life policy.

Applying for LA cover: a checklist of steps

As already noted, the reaction of the British insurance industry to the possibility of substantial AIDS-related claims is still in an unsettled state, with various approaches being taken by different companies. With respect to LA, certain patterns have emerged which are described in outline below. It must be borne in mind, however, that there is no standardized procedure as such followed by all LA companies. Furthermore, whatever patterns do currently exist are subject to change as the companies seek greater sophistication in accomplishing their aims and, perhaps, as medical testing relating to the presence and effects of HIV evolves.

The following subsections are, however, intended to give some guidance to the individual applying for LA cover where questions relating to AIDS are likely to arise, and to those advising such individuals. They attempt to set out the most important features of the application process and to outline the considerations which an individual should bear in mind when deciding whether or how to pursue an application for LA.

Is the LA necessary?

A fundamental question which needs to be addressed by anyone considering taking out a LA policy is whether or not such a policy is in fact really necessary in the first place. This question becomes all the more important in a context where AIDS-related issues are likely to arise, since in that case details of a person's private life are possibly going to be probed, and the individual may be compelled to undergo medical testing which he or she would not otherwise desire. Furthermore, as will be discussed later, one must bear in mind that unsuccessfully pursuing an application for LA cover to the point of refusal will in effect preclude the individual from obtaining such cover for the foreseeable future, since the names of applicants who have been rejected for 'medical reasons' or who are offered cover only at a higher premium for such reasons are recorded on a master list by the insurance industry.

The question of whether to take out a LA policy can arise in various contexts. An individual may be considering a house purchase, and the financial institution approached for a mortgage may require LA with respect to loans over a certain limit or may be promoting the idea of an endowment mortgage simply because of the commission profits associated with selling an endowment-related LA policy. An employee may be offered a LA scheme at work. An individual may be considering appropriate plans for the financial security of a dependant in the event of death.

In each case, it is important that the individual weigh up the necessity of the proposed LA cover. It may be that the expense and potential difficulties which may be encountered in applying for such cover may not be worthwhile unless the proposed beneficiary under the policy is someone who is financially dependent on the applicant and whose security cannot be provided for in any other way. In the case of endowment mortgages, in particular, it may well be that there is no particularly strong reason for proceeding with the application for LA cover. A straight repayment mortgage – involving no insurance cover but where the house purchaser gradually pays off the principal as well as making interest payments – may be as suitable an arrangement. This may be especially so in cases where there is no special necessity that the mortgage be paid off in its entirety in the event of the purchaser's death.

Often, financial institutions are keen to promote an endowment policy simply because the sale of such policies earns extra commission profit for them. In other cases, a particular bank or building society may require insurance cover as a matter of policy with respect to mortgage loans over a certain amount. Sometimes, this may not be in the form of an endowment policy but rather a mortgage protection policy, which is a form of LA attached to an ordinary straight repayment mortgage, and which will pay off as much of the mortgage as remains outstanding upon the death of the insured. In any event, if an individual decides that he or she does not wish to seek an insurance policy with respect to an intended mortgage, it is essential to shop around to identify financial institutions which will be willing to provide a mortgage without such insurance cover.

The applicant's duty of full disclosure

Once, however, an individual has decided on the necessity of proceeding with an application for LA, it is essential that he or she understand the duty of full disclosure which then must be met throughout the application process. Under English law, contracts relating to insurance fall into the exceptional category of 'contracts of utmost good faith'. This means that when an applicant for an insurance policy is seeking to obtain that policy from the insurance company, both the applicant and the insurance company are under the obligation to disclose to the other all 'material facts' which the other party should take into account before entering into final agreement.

From the point of view of the applicant, the essential obligation arising from this is to answer fully and honestly the questions raised by the insurance company at every stage during the application process. It is not relevant that the applicant feels that the answers to any such questions should or should not be taken into account by the company in reaching a decision on the policy. The legal test, instead, is whether the 'prudent insurer' would want to know the facts in question in order to determine whether or not it should undertake the risk of providing the insurance policy being requested. Generally, it is a safe assumption that the 'prudent insurer' is entitled to know the answers to the specific questions posed by it, but the applicant ought not to be under an obligation to volunteer information which is not specifically requested in those questions.

The ultimate penalty against an applicant who fails to reveal or is otherwise dishonest relating to material facts is a severe one. In such cases, the insurance company may at any time void the contract of insurance it has entered into. In such cases, it will refuse to pay out any benefits under the voided policy and will seek a refund of any benefits already paid out. In cases where it can show that material facts have been wilfully or fraudulently withheld, it will also be in a position to keep the insurance premiums which have been paid to date.

An applicant who responds dishonestly to questions arising during any of the stages of the application process described below, therefore, risks obtaining, and paying substantial premiums towards, a LA policy which will ultimately prove worthless.

The initial application for a LA policy

The initial application for a LA policy is likely to appear to be an innocuous enough document. It is in the interest of insurance companies to make such a form appear to be simple, straightforward, and easy to complete. By creating a format which is brief and unthreatening, companies of course are seeking to lure as many potential customers as possible by stressing the ease of obtaining LA cover.

The applicant must recognize, however, that this initial application, while simple, will be used as an extremely important initial screening device by the LA company. In this respect, the most important question or questions will relate to the applicant's previous medical history and marital status.

While there is no standard format, questions may be asked, for example, about all contacts with a doctor over the previous 5 years, or about the nature and results of all previous blood tests. There may be a specific AIDS-related question, enquiring whether the applicant has been counselled or medically advised or had a blood test in connection with AIDS or any sexually transmitted disease. This last particular line of questioning would seem to be particularly overreaching since it would seem to require a positive response from anyone who had merely taken the sensible precaution of seeking basic information about AIDS. (Insurance industry spokespersons have however suggested that 'counselling' in this context is not meant to include the obtaining of such basic information about AIDS.) The applicant will also be asked whether any previous application for life cover has been delayed, refused, postponed, or accepted only on special terms.

Regardless of the particular format of questions used by an LA company in its initial application form, it is a virtual certainty today that such questions will be worded in such a way as to require an applicant to reveal that he or she has had a previous HIV-antibody test, if this is the case. In those instances in which an applicant has had an antibody test with a positive result, this will prove to be the termination point of the application since LA companies are rejecting out of hand applications from antibody positive individuals. An individual in this position should, therefore, not even consider making an initial application for life cover.

More surprisingly, in those cases in which the applicant reveals a previous HIV-antibody test with a negative result, the mere fact of having been tested will be interpreted as indicative that an individual is at 'high risk'. While this could potentially be treated as grounds for rejection of the application at this point, it will more likely lead to a request from the LA company that the applicant complete a 'supplementary questionnaire' and undergo a medical examination, including a further HIV-antibody test. Special factors relevant to these procedures are described in greater detail below. The use by the insurance industry in this way of a prior HIV-antibody test as an indicator of 'high risk' is one of the factors commonly cited by those who advise that caution and forethought need to be exercised by individuals who are contemplating undergoing an HIV-antibody test.

Even in cases where an applicant has not had an HIV-antibody test but reveals in the application that medical attention has been sought for sexually transmitted diseases, a supplementary questionnaire and a medical examination are likely to be required.

With respect to the initial application process, it should also be noted that other non-medical questions, seemingly more innocuous, can be and have been used by insurers to make their own assessment that an individual may be a member of a 'high-risk group'. This is an approach which thus far has been directed at determining possible gay men among applicants. Most obviously responses to the question on marital status are used in this way. Single men who have reached what a given insurer determines to be a 'marriageable age' are likely to be required to respond to a supplementary questionnaire and to undergo a medical examination.

This kind of approach can be extended further. In the United States, at least, very clear evidence has emerged of insurers using occupation, postal code of residence, and designation of a co-habiting male as beneficiary to be indicators that an individual is a gay male. In one example which would be laughable were it not for its seriously discriminatory ramifications, a US health insurance company circulated an 'AIDS Profile' which required its agents to segregate applications from 'single males without dependants that are engaged in occupations that do not require physical exertion'. These 'guidelines' went on to list the relevant occupations: 'restaurant employees, antique dealers, interior decorators, consultants, florists, and people in the jewelry or fashion business' (Great Republic Insurance Company, Memorandum of December 1985 to All Agents and General Agents, cited in Benjamin Schatz, 'The AIDS insurance crisis: underwriting or overreaching', *Harvard Law Review* May 1987, 1782). While there is no hard evidence of such practices being widely applied in the UK, it is known, for example, that underwriters have decided in some cases to include a question regarding occupation on all insurance application forms, specifically in the context of developing a strategy to identify members of 'high-risk groups'.

The supplementary questionnaire

As already noted, in those cases where an insurer's suspicions have been aroused by responses to the initial application form, the applicant is likely to be sent a supplementary questionnaire to fill out. The insurance industry is also moving towards a position whereby such questionnaires are used routinely when certain financial thresholds of coverage are reached. Thus, at least in some parts of the LA market, such questionnaires are automatically sent out with respect to applications for life cover exceeding a figure in the range of £60,000–75,000. If the application relates to a single, separated, or divorced male, this figure may be reduced to a threshold of £10,000 worth of cover. This practice has emerged in the last couple of years, and it is in this context that the LA company asks the difficult, intimate questions which might scare off the potential customer if they were included in the initial application form.

More particularly, the applicant is likely to be asked explicitly in the supplementary questionnaire whether he or she is a homosexual or bisexual man, an intravenous drug-user, a haemophiliac, or the sexual partner of a member of one of these groups. Fuller details of medical history will be sought. In particular, if these questions have not already been asked in the initial application, the applicant will be asked whether he or she has ever been tested, or received medical advice, counselling, or treatment in connection with AIDS or an AIDS-related condition or any sexually transmitted disease, including Hepatitis B. While not yet common practice, explicit questions relating to promiscuity and steady sexual relationships may be asked.

An applicant may be rejected at this stage by an insurer which believes that there has been a lack of frankness in the responses given, or if the responses given are unsatisfactory in some other way. The insurer has complete discretion to draw his or her own conclusions regarding the implications of the information gathered and an explicit explanation for rejection is unlikely to be given.

In many cases it would appear that an applicant is not likely to be rejected for the mere fact of admitting to be a homosexual. In such cases, however, the individual will almost invariably be required to submit to the medical examination and HIV-antibody testing procedures referred to below. As also discussed below, he or she is also likely to be charged a considerably higher premium if eventually successful in the application.

Oddly, an admission that one is a bisexual male is much more likely to lead to automatic rejection, at least by some LA companies. Perhaps this is on the rather unconvincing basis that by definition there is a greater likelihood of a bisexual male having multiple partners. An admission of intravenous drug-use is similarly likely to lead to automatic rejection. Haemophiliacs are not likely to be rejected outright but will certainly be required to submit to the medical examination and HIV-antibody testing procedures referred to below.

Medical examinations and HIV-antibody testing

Generally, an applicant who has been required to answer a supplementary questionnaire is also likely to be required to submit to further medical scrutiny, provided that he or she has not already been rejected outright in an earlier stage of the application process. It is common practice for insurers to require one or more medical examinations if they know or suspect that an applicant is a member of one of their 'high-risk groups' or if the application relates to a high level of coverage or if there are any particular indications that the applicant has health problems.

At some stage in the application process, the applicant will be asked to provide the name of a general practitioner and any other doctors who have been consulted during a given period. The applicant will also be required to consent to any such doctors being contacted for medical details.

While different LA companies may follow different approaches in collecting medical information about their applicants, three elements are fairly standard:

Obtaining information from the applicant's general practitioner

The applicant's general practitioner (GP) may well be asked to fill out a questionnaire about the applicant and, in some cases, to conduct a medical examination. It is important to note that the questions asked of the GP are not necessarily restricted to medical questions. GPs are frequently asked to express an opinion as to the applicant's life-style, sexual orientation, promiscuity, faithfulness within a relationship, and so on. Many GPs would refuse to answer such questions and it is the policy of the British Medical Association that doctors should not be put in the position of responding to such questions. At the same time, however, much depends on the attitude of the particular GP. An individual cannot be sure that a doctor will not tell an LA company that he or she is gay or in another 'high risk group'. It makes sense, therefore, not to volunteer information about such areas of one's life unless directly relevant to medical diagnosis or treatment.

Of course, an individual can and should ask to see a copy of any such form filled out by a GP before it is sent to the LA company. Until recently, GPs had no obligation to comply with such a request, but this has changed with the passage of the Access to Medical Reports Act 1988. Under that legislation, an individual usually has the right to see his or her own doctor's medical report prepared for an insurance company before it is sent. Generally this is triggered by the insurer asking the applicant at the time that the insurer first proposes to apply to the doctor, if he or she wants such access to the report. If the applicant requests this, the insurer must notify the doctor of this request and the applicant must then contact the doctor within 21 days to make arrangements to review the report. Alternatively, the applicant may initially apply directly to the doctor for such access to the report without first notifying the insurance company, but such application must be in writing, and it is, again, necessary to make arrangements within 21 days to review the report. It is always a good idea to notify the doctor in writing immediately when access to any report is desired, even when the insurer itself has been notified and is under an obligation to tell the doctor.

Under the Act, the applicant can make a written request for the doctor's report to be altered if it is incorrect or misleading. If the doctor refuses, as he or she is entitled to do, the applicant can then demand that his or her own statement be attached to the report. Finally, the applicant can always refuse to consent to the report being sent on at all, in which case the doctor is prohibited from supplying it to the insurers. In such cases, however, insurance cover is likely to be refused unless the applicant withdraws his or her application before the refusal can be made. (The applicant needs to bear in mind, of course, that such a refusal would probably have fatal effects on future applications for LA cover, as described below. It would, therefore, be important to withdraw the application *before* it can be refused. No reason for doing so need be given.)

Examination by LA company doctor

The protections afforded by the Access to Medical Reports Act 1988 only apply to reports prepared by an applicant's own doctor. In many cases, the applicant may instead (or in addition) be required to submit to an examination by a doctor employed by the LA company and will not in such an event be given access to any report prepared. Such a doctor is likely to ask explicit questions about the applicant's life-style.

HIV-antibody testing

When a medical examination is required of an applicant, whether by a GP or an LA company doctor (or both), the applicant may, and probably will, be requested to take an HIV-antibody test. If the applicant refuses to do so, or does so and is found to be antibody-positive, the application will be refused automatically. Even if the test result is negative, the applicant is likely to be offered coverage only at an increased premium if a determination has been taken by the LA company that he or she is in a high-risk group, negative result notwithstanding. In the case of term insurance, the premium charged can be as much as three times the ordinary premium.

The importance of avoiding a rejected application

The above description of the LA application procedure should make clear that, in cases where the applicant may be considered by the insurer to be in a 'high-risk group', he or she faces numerous points during the procedure when an application may be rejected. An application will, for example, almost certainly be rejected in cases where:

- The applicant has had a positive HIV-antibody-test result prior to, or during the course of, the application procedure. (Rejection in this case will be automatic.)
- The applicant has had a history of frequent sexually transmitted disease in recent times.
- The insurer suspects that the applicant is not responding frankly to questions posed.
- Information obtained from the supplementary questionnaire, a GP or elsewhere leads the insurer to believe that the applicant is 'promiscuous'.
- The applicant refuses to fill out a supplementary questionnaire when requested to do so or refuses to be examined by a doctor or to submit to an HIV-antibody test.

The insurer is under no obligation to explain the reasons for rejecting an LA application and is unlikely to do so. The basic effect of such rejection will be to make an applicant uninsurable with respect to life cover. The applicant will be obliged to respond on all future LA applications that he or she has been previously refused. Furthermore, the British insurance industry maintains a centralized computer record listing all individuals who have been refused life cover for 'health reasons'. Except in situations where the applicant can show that the rejection was the result of a mistake or some misunderstanding, the effect will be to prevent that applicant from obtaining life cover.

It is, therefore, most important that an application which is going to be refused either not be made in the first instance or, once made, should be formally withdrawn as soon as it becomes apparent that a refusal is likely. This should be done, for example, if a request for an HIV-antibody test is made and the applicant does not wish to have such a test. Any such formal withdrawal should be in writing and should indicate that the applicant wishes to withdraw the application and that the insurer should proceed no further with it. No explanation of the reason for withdrawal need be given.

In cases where the application has not been rejected, the insurer or the broker or agent will write to the applicant setting out the terms on which LA is offered. As already noted, individuals whom insurers consider to be 'high risk' may be offered cover at considerably higher premiums than the norm and a decision will need to be taken whether to accept these terms. It should be noted that, if any application is then made to another company, the applicant will be obliged to say that they have previously been offered coverage 'on special terms', and this will lead to extra scrutiny of the application.

In any event, if a decision is taken to accept the terms of cover, the applicant should write back accepting the terms. Under basic insurance law, the contract is completed when the first premium has been paid to the insurers and accepted by them. A policy acceptance letter or policy document will then be issued and sent to the applicant.

AIDS and insurance: summary of practical advice points

This chapter has attempted to review some of the main effects which the emergence of AIDS has had on the policies being pursued by the insurance industry in the UK. For those individuals who believe that they may be directly affected by these new policies, what follows is a summary of some of the principal pieces of practical advice which should emerge from the information included in the chapter.

* Individuals who obtained health or LA cover prior to the introduction of the insurance-industry practices outlined above would do well to maintain such cover. They should renew it promptly and avoid doing anything – such as increasing cover (unless this is provided for under the terms of the policy) or otherwise seeking a change of terms – which would make them susceptible to accepting new terms imposed by the insurers, such as an AIDS exclusion clause, intrusive re-application procedures, and so on. The insured should examine the terms of renewal carefully and, if in doubt, consult a reputable insurance agent. Following upon this advice, an old endowment policy ought not to be surrendered when a mortgage is paid off, since it can be applied towards the security for any subsequent mortgage loan.
* The terms of proposed new health or life policies should be examined carefully beforehand. If the terms set out seem to exclude AIDS-related sickness, incapacity, or death, a decision needs to be taken whether this is acceptable given the particular needs of the applicant seeking the insurance. An LA policy with an AIDS exclusion clause will probably not, for example, prove to be acceptable security for a mortgage loan.
* An individual considering LA who may for some reason face difficulties in obtaining it should consider beforehand whether, given the particular circumstances, it is necessary at all. In particular, in the

context of obtaining a mortgage, a straight repayment-mortgage may be obtainable without any insurance cover whatsoever. It is best to shop around for favourable LA and/or mortgage terms and a mortgage broker or insurance broker should be able to help. He or she should be a member of FIMBRA, the professional regulatory body for such brokers.

* If applying for LA in connection with a mortgage, an individual should be conscious of possible delays and not exchange contracts until the LA application has been accepted.

* An individual with ARC or AIDS or who has been tested to be HIV-antibody positive will not get LA and should not apply for it.

* Even an applicant who has had an HIV-antibody test with a negative result may be treated by insurers as a potential member of a 'high-risk group'. This needs to be borne in mind when considering having an HIV-antibody test. Such a test should be avoided before applying for LA unless there are other good reasons to be tested.

* Individuals whom the insurers believe to be gay or members of another 'high-risk group' are likely to be required to take an HIV-antibody test as part of the application process for an LA policy. Such individuals should always seek counselling before agreeing to undergo this test. In the event that such individuals do agree to be tested and obtain a negative result, they may get LA, though this will depend on other judgements drawn by the insurer, such as whether the individuals involved are thought to be 'promiscuous'. It is quite likely that any policies offered will be at inflated premiums.

* While an applicant for insurance cover is under a duty to answer any questions truthfully and completely, facts should not be volunteered which might be interpreted to indicate that the applicant is in a 'high-risk group'.

* An individual should also not volunteer facts about life-style to his or her doctor unless they are directly relevant to diagnosis or treatment. In the event that an individual's doctor is asked to prepare a report to an insurance company, the individual has the legal right to see that report before it is sent and should take appropriate steps to exercise that right.

* It is important to avoid getting into the position of having an application for LA refused. This will prejudice all future applications for life cover. If an applicant does not wish to proceed with the application, he or she should withdraw it in writing and instruct the insurer not to proceed any further with it. This should be done, for example, if the insurer requests that the applicant submit to a medical examination or HIV-antibody testing and the applicant does not wish to do so.

Some final policy considerations

This chapter, like this volume as a whole, has attempted to provide a straightforward guide to the effects which the emergence of AIDS has had on a particular area related to the law. It is primarily intended to afford some advice to the individual confronting the special problems which, as a result of AIDS, have arisen for some segments of the population seeking insurance cover.

The tone of the chapter, therefore, has been descriptive rather than critical. It would, however, be remiss to end the consideration of this subject without at least a brief comment on the policies and attitudes of insurers in the UK which have led to the procedures described above.

A discriminatory policy against gay men

Most notably, the response of the British insurance industry to the problems raised has been a highly discriminatory one. As should be clear from the procedures described, a primary aim of insurers here has been to develop LA application procedures calculated to identify gay males. The initial application, the supplementary questionnaire, and doctors' reports are all openly being used to determine whether particular individuals are gay males and, if so, to deprive them of insurance cover altogether or to offer it to them at substantially inflated rates, regardless of whether there is any indication that the individuals involved are at real risk of becoming infected with HIV.

It is a fact that the majority of those contracting AIDS in the UK up to now have been gay males; but this cannot logically justify a decision that any given individual should have his access to insurance cover denied or impeded solely on the basis of his purported sexual orientation, irrespective of whether his particular medical history contains concrete indication of an increased risk. A greater mortality risk arises not from membership of a particular social group but rather from exposure to HIV through sexual or other circumstances which may apply to a band of the population defined not in terms of sexual orientation as such, but in terms of specific sexual and other habits.

Indeed, gay males today are more likely than any other group to recognize the risk of such exposure and take steps to avoid it, precisely because their community has been so seriously affected. Fortunately, a very large majority of the gay males in the UK have not been exposed to HIV, and recent studies have indicated that the spread of the virus within this section of the population has been very sharply curtailed in the past few years through the adoption of safer sexual practices.

The experience in the UK on this subject contrasts with that in a number of other countries where similar initiatives by insurance companies have been closely monitored and controlled by independent regulatory authorities. In the United States, the National Association of Insurance Commissioners, the umbrella organization bringing together all state insurance regulators, has produced guidelines calling for the complete elimination of such discrimination and this has been implemented in the laws of the majority of states. Such discrimination is also forbidden in Canada and Australia.

The lack of a strong regulatory mechanism for the insurance industry in this country means that there is no real focal point upon which pressure for change of this discriminatory approach can be brought to bear. This situation is only exacerbated by what would appear to be openly anti-gay attitudes in some elements of the government and the media. The efforts of some, however, must be acknowledged. The British Medical Association has been staunch in its position that its doctors should not play a role in this selection process by answering 'life-style' questions about their patients. Archy Kirkwood, MP, promoted as a private member's bill the piece of legislation which eventually became the Access to Medical Reports Act 1988, affording individuals the right to see and comment on reports prepared by their GPs for insurance (and employment) purposes before such reports are dispatched.

An approach apparently not yet attempted would be a suit under the Sex Discrimination Act 1975. Section 29 of that Act makes it *prima facie* unlawful to provide insurance cover which discriminates between men and women. (Presumably one could cite discrimination between men who happen to be gay and women who happen to be lesbians.) Section 45 does go on to say that the treatment of a person in relation to insurance shall not be unlawful 'where the treatment – (a) was affected by reference to actuarial or other data from a source on which it was reasonable to rely, and (b) was reasonable having regard to the data and any other relevant factors'. The question which would need to be argued would be whether there is in fact reasonable data upon which reasonable calculations could be made to justify the highly inflated rates which gay men are being charged. On the face of it, at least, such rates would seem to reflect an arbitrary response by the insurance industry to the ignorance by which it feels itself confronted with respect to AIDS.

There also exists the entity of the Insurance Ombudsman, who is meant to be an independent official mandated to investigate and resolve enquiries, complaints, disputes, and claims between insurance companies and their policy holders. His or her mandate would not appear, however, to encompass such actuarial-related issues. (The Ombudsman's office would, on the other hand, seem likely to become involved in disputes regarding the making of payments on existing policies where, for example, a claim is being made and there is a dispute regarding alleged material non-disclosures relating to AIDS at the time of application.)

Use of HIV-antibody tests

Another area in which the insurance industry would appear to have unduly unbridled discretion relates to the use of HIV-antibody testing. Insurers routinely ask whether an applicant has had an HIV test and for the result. A positive test result leads to automatic disqualification from coverage and even a negative result is likely to be counted against the applicant – since the mere fact of having sought the test is presumably indicative of a dubious life-style! A large number of states in the United States has specifically prohibited questions about prior AIDS blood tests, so that individuals with particularly strong reasons to be tested – such as a woman considering having a child – would not be deterred for fear of becoming less insurable.

In addition, insurers are themselves requiring applicants to submit to such tests as a precondition to proceeding with an application. Tests are likely to be required if the amount of coverage sought is above a certain limit or if the applicant is believed for whatever reason to be a member of a 'high-risk group'. The result may well be that individuals find themselves compelled to take a test which they do not desire, which will not afford them information on which they can base remedial action, and which, at worst, may profoundly traumatize and stigmatize them. There is at least one documented case of a US soldier attempting to commit suicide after a positive result from a compulsory test.

Whether insurers ought to have discretion to impose such a condition is a complex question which should not be left to the insurers alone. So long as such tests are required, there need to be clear criteria for deciding when the test may be administered, the standards for testing, the provision of adequate counselling both before and after the test, and strict confidentiality. In the absence of an insurance regulatory authority, no clear criteria would appear to be operative in the UK today. Again, the British Medical Association has played a useful role in attempting to enforce a requirement that adequate counselling must be provided in connection with such testing by the insurance industry.

This chapter began by sketching the very real problems faced by the insurance industry in confronting the many actuarial question-marks raised by the emergence of AIDS. These problems must be acknowledged as substantial and challenging ones.

Also described above have been the solutions put forward to date by the insurance industry to these problems. These, unfortunately, can only thus far be described as haphazard, arbitrary, and discriminatory. One has no clear sense, for example, that the inflated premiums being charged to gay men who have tested antibody-negative are based on any reasonable calculation, but rather these would seem to represent numbers plucked from the ether in an attempt to seem to be doing something in the face of very great problems.

Always in the past when it has been argued that the insurance industry in the United Kingdom should be subjected to greater independent regulation – as is the case in many other countries – the industry has replied that it can be counted on to regulate itself responsibly and for the common good. Thus far, at least, in these difficult times it has failed to meet this promised standard.

Chapter nine

Legal structures of voluntary organizations
Timothy Costello

Introduction

If you are thinking of organizing a helpline or some other group, it must
have some structure. If it is to have its own funds, and perhaps employ
someone, it is important to ensure that the entity has the correct form, so that
unnecessary difficulties are avoided and everyone is enabled to function as
efficiently as possible. In this chapter the objective is to review the various
alternatives and the reasons for choosing each, in order to make your
decision easier.

What are the issues involved?

- First of all we must consider the possible forms of organization.
- Then we must ask how much the body will spend, and what the
  sources of its funding will be.
- Other important considerations are what the body will do and the level
  of legal commitments and other liabilities the body will assume: this
  will determine the appropriate form of the body. We must examine the
  implications of the various choices.
- We should consider the implications of charitable status, its advantages
  and drawbacks.
- Finally we must look at the second certainty in life – tax.

Form

There are a number of different forms of organization which could be
adopted. Simplest is the unincorporated association; then there is the trust,
followed by the industrial and provident society, and the company.

Unincorporated associations

This is like a village cricket club. It is simply a group of individuals who
agree to carry out certain activities in common. As far as the law is
concerned, it has no existence separate from that of its members; it has no

legal personality. An unincorporated association can also be a charity, but if it has any assets they must be held by trustees on behalf of the association. Such an unincorporated association will suffer from the same disadvantages as a trust.

Trust

The trust is the traditional form for a charitable body. The essence of a trust is that a person, the donor, gives property (which may be land, money, goods, or rights like shares or other investments) to someone else, the trustee, who holds the property not for the trustee's own benefit but on terms that oblige the trustee to give the property or the income which it produces to a third person, the beneficiary. In the case of a charitable trust there are of course multiple donors and the beneficiaries are defined by description – for example, people with AIDS – rather than by name.

Companies

The company is a common form of organization which is usually associated with trading activities. Most people are generally aware of the way commercial companies function. The company's business is carried on for the benefit of those who have invested in the company, namely the shareholders. The shareholders appoint the directors to manage the company's business. Non-profit-making companies are established under the same legislation. The main difference between such companies and a trading company is that, instead of having shareholders (who are often referred to in any case as members) who have invested money in the company, a non-profit-making company has members who agree, in the event that the company becomes insolvent, to contribute a fixed (usually nominal) amount to its assets. Such companies are called companies limited by guarantee.

Funding

The common sources of funds for voluntary organizations are:

- informal gifts (the subscriptions of those involved, proceeds of fund-raising events, flag days, and collecting boxes left in public places);
- central and local government grants;
- grant-making charities;
- formal giving by way of covenant or otherwise from companies and by way of covenant from individuals.

Of these only the first two are generally available to bodies which are not charities. It is difficult for charities to give money to bodies which are not themselves charities. To obtain the tax advantages available for charitable gifts, clearly the recipient must be a registered charity.

This is complementary to what is said below about the possibility of progressing from a relatively informal set-up to a more formal structure. As the body grows in size it will be necessary to establish it as a charity in order to take the fullest possible advantage of all possible sources of funds.

Before leaving the topic of funding, mention must be made of trading activities by the body. While minor trading activities, such as jumble sales, will not attract the attention of the Inland Revenue, other trading will usually give rise to an income or corporation tax liability. In the case of charities only, this liability can in practice be avoided by taking the steps discussed below under the heading Taxation.

Structures

Unincorporated associations

Informality is the order of the day. Unlike that which applies in the case of companies, the law prescribes few if any procedures which must be followed in the running of an unincorporated association. You can make your own decisions on how it should be organized. Will there be a committee of management? Will there be officers? Should they be elected and if so how often? Will there be an annual general meeting? How will accounts be kept? What are the qualifications for membership? Will the accounts be independently verified – audited? To all these questions and others you will be able to make your own decisions and the law will not force your hand, although perhaps funding bodies will have some requirements which you will need to satisfy, otherwise the body will not be eligible to receive funds.

Also, as the association grows and takes on more tasks, it is very simple to change the structure to meet the increased requirements.

An unincorporated association does not have to be registered. It is formed when as few as two people meet together to decide to carry out a common purpose. Unless the group is very small, it is desirable to have some rules so that everyone who belongs to the organization knows what is expected of members. All but the smallest associations will have a committee and the rules should establish how the committee is formed, what decisions it can take without consulting all the members, how often a general meeting of all the members must be held, and, if the association has its own financial resources, how these are to be accounted for.

As noted above, an unincorporated association does not have a separate legal personality. Accordingly it does not have limited liability in the same way that a company does. Thus, for example, if the office manager of a limited company places an order for stationery on behalf of the company, the supplier cannot make the office manager pay for the stationery, if the company is subsequently unable to do so. In the case of an unincorporated association it is different: while all the members usually (depending on the rules of the association) cannot be made responsible, the individuals who placed the order can be. This is a double disadvantage: first of all it puts an unfair burden on the people who run the organization and in addition, traders may be unwilling to give the organization credit – dealing with all purchases on a cash-with-order basis can be tiresome. If the time comes when the organization needs premises, it is probably not possible to continue with an unincorporated association, because the responsibilities undertaken towards the landlord by those who sign the lease or tenancy agreement on behalf of the organization, which probably has (or may, at the material time, have) insufficient assets to meet the costs involved, are too heavy.

There is no reason why a body should not start as an unincorporated association and subsequently change its status as the requirements of its activities dictate. Indeed, this is a common path followed by many bodies.

Trusts

A trust does not have a legal personality separate from its trustees. The trustees have no limited liability. So long as they have not committed any breach of trust, they are entitled to have recourse to the funds of the trust for any liabilities which they have incurred in their capacity as trustees. However, if the trust funds are insufficient or there is any outstanding breach of trust, the trustees will be liable to make good the shortfall from their personal assets.

Trustees must normally act unanimously and all the trustees must agree to any particular course of action. This can be inconvenient (because, for example, all the trustees must attend meetings in order that decisions can be taken) except in the case of a small organization. The trust deed establishing a trust will provide how new trustees are to be chosen. Trustees will remain responsible as trustees until they die or until a formal document is signed by all the trustees by which retiring trustees relinquish their responsibilities. New trustees will be appointed in a similar manner. Effectively this means that legal assistance must be sought with the preparation of these documents on each occasion when trustees retire and/or are appointed. This is cumbersome in an organization in which individuals may remain involved for a relatively short period of time. The trust is not an appropriate vehicle where democracy is to perform any role in choosing those responsible for running the organization. In practice, the document establishing the trust cannot be changed: there is a theoretical way of doing this but it would probably be ruled out by expense. This means that it must be drafted with the maximum amount of foresight otherwise the trust may not be able to respond to changes in circumstances. Almost all trusts will need to register as charities. The Charity Commission can rightly be expected to require precision in the trust document and this may limit flexibility in the future.

Trustees must always be in a position to account for the property in their hands. This means that books of account must be kept and, for the protection of the trustees, effectively audited annually, even though there is at present no requirement for a formal audit. This may seem to be a disadvantage by comparison with an unincorporated association but in reality all bodies will want to be in a position to demonstrate that proper accounts have been kept.

It is a cardinal principle of trust law that a trustee must not profit from the trust (unless the trustee is permitted to do so in the instrument establishing the trust). Accordingly, if the trust is proposing to buy goods or services from a trustee (or from an entity in which the trustee is interested), this cannot be done while that trustee remains a trustee; otherwise the trustee will simply have to hand back the cash or other benefit received. The position is not so stringent in the case of directors of companies.

It was accepted as a matter of public policy many centuries ago that generally speaking, property could not be put into trust for ever and that the terms of the trust must result in all the property which was subject to the trust coming into the hands of one or more individuals for their own benefit within a limited period. If this might not result, the gift to the trustee was void. However, charitable trusts are an exception to this rule. For this reason much of the case-law concerning charities centres on whether there has been a gift which is within this exception. Yet in the modern context this is of less importance than some other aspects of charity law, for example the tax advantages of being a charity.

For the most part (with certain very important exceptions) until the second half of this century, charities (other than educational and hospital charities which were usually incorporated in any case) were passive reservoirs of funds rather than active providers of services. For this kind of body the trust is probably ideal. However, for the modern charity, which spends as much of its resources as possible and resorts to governmental funding for some of its activities and which needs to be a charity not for reasons of property law but in order to obtain tax concessions, the trust is not the ideal vehicle. If it is chosen for some particular reason, it may need to have an affiliated body to which the individuals providing the services can belong.

The responsibilities of being a trustee are very heavy. The standard of care which a trustee is expected to exercise is much greater than that of a director of a company. If there is any subsisting breach of trust a trustee is not permitted to resort to the trust funds for liabilities which have been incurred as a trustee rather than in a personal capacity. In practice, in the context of a large organization minor breaches of trust may be almost impossible to avoid.

Companies

A company is regarded in law as a person separate from its members.

Trustees own the property of a trust; directors do not own the property of a company, the company does. A company exists to carry out the purposes (or some of them) set out in its memorandum of association (known as its objects) and for no other purpose. It has the powers specified in its memorandum of association and other powers reasonably incidental to those powers and required in order to carry out its objects.

Like the members of a trading company, the members of a non-profit-making company have a limit on their liability (i.e. the amount they agree to contribute) if the company cannot pay its debts. Similarly, the directors are not responsible for the debts of a company except in certain circumstances if they let it incur additional liabilities when they know it will not be able to meet them. This advantage of limited liability cannot be stressed too much. People undertaking voluntary activities do not expect to put their personal assets at risk. The modern kind of active charity carries with it the same order of risk as a trading enterprise; the individuals concerned in it should not bear these risks.

Another great advantage of the company is that it can be a charity. Most of the large charities are companies. Charitable status, which is examined later in this chapter, can be a great help in obtaining funding for the activities of the organization. The company basically has a democratic structure. Typically charitable companies have a small number of members who are admitted by the directors and a self-perpetuating oligarchy therefore persists. However, if this is not desired, for instance because the company exists to provide a medium for voluntary service for the beneficiaries of the charity, the articles of association can provide for the volunteer workers and staff of the company to become members. The directors of the company are elected by the members and it is easy to reinforce this by including provisions for secret balloting in its articles.

The company is also flexible. Directors are easily appointed in between elections and they can resign simply by writing a letter of resignation. Directors normally act by majority decision at regularly convened board meetings. If all the directors are not present, as long as there are sufficient of the directors present (called a quorum), a decision is validly taken. However, it would always be possible to provide that on certain matters the directors must be unanimous. It is also relatively easy to change the constitution of a company. There is almost complete freedom with regard to changes concerning the management of the Company and more latitude for changing the purposes for which the company was established, its so-called objects, than there is in the case of a trust. Commercial companies can in practice change their objects at will. Charitable companies, because they are subject to the tutelage of the Charity Commission and because they may be given property in such a way that they may be regarded as holding it on trust, are subject to more restriction; but nevertheless, changing the objects of a charitable company is much easier than is the case for a trust.

The management of the operations of a company is invariably placed by its articles of association in the hands of the directors: that is to say, in the hands of the board of directors as a collegiate body.

The board, and anyone purporting to exercise powers delegated by the board, must act only in the furtherance of the objects and using the powers contained in the company's memorandum of association. If the directors do otherwise, the company is not bound by any commitment which may have been made, and if the assets of the company are dissipated as a result, they can be called upon to make good the loss to the company.

The general power of the directors excludes any authority of the members of the company in general meeting. The general meeting may be asked to approve a particular course of action but it cannot initiate any conduct. If it attempts to do so the directors can ignore it and will not be absolved from responsibility if the initiative required by the members is taken and is a breach of their duties as directors. Individual directors have no powers at all in relation to a company unless particular powers have been delegated to them. The board is the fountain of all authority in a company save for matters which are reserved to the company in general meeting, such as, usually, changing the name and constitution of the company and the election of directors. Each individual acting on behalf of the company can do so only by virtue of powers actually or impliedly delegated by the board.

The board can only make decisions at meetings which are convened and held in accordance with the articles of association. The articles usually provide that any director may give notice of a meeting of the board, and the secretary shall do so, if required by any director. The length of notice required is normally not specified: it must be a reasonable time, and what is reasonable will depend on the nature of the business for which the meeting is convened. Notice of less than a week for matters of routine would be in danger of being unreasonable, if an objection were made. Assuming that the meeting is validly convened, it can only make decisions if a quorum is present.

The law about the responsibilities of directors is not simple for directors of commercial companies; it is even less straightforward for directors of charitable ones. The directors owe duties to the company, to those for whose benefit the company was established (the intended beneficiaries in the case of a charitable company), to its creditors, and to its employees. It is clear that the interests of the creditors prevail over those of the shareholders or charitable beneficiaries, but Parliament and the courts have given no guidance as to how conflicts involving the employees and the other parties are to be resolved.

The general duty of directors is to attend meetings of the board when not reasonably prevented from doing so. At meetings of the board and when carrying out matters delegated to a director, the director must act with reasonable care. The degree of skill required from an individual director is less than that demanded of a trustee and will depend on the experience and qualifications of that director. A higher standard will be required of an accountant or lawyer than of a teacher. More will be expected from a business-school lecturer than a chemistry professor.

The principal obligation owed to the creditors is not to allow the company to continue to incur liabilities unless the directors are satisfied that the company will be able to meet its liabilities as they fall due. Under the Insolvency Act 1986 directors of companies can be made personally responsible for some or all of the liabilities of a company if they allow it to continue in operation when there is no reasonable possibility that an insolvent liquidation can be avoided. This is known as a liability for wrongful trading. Although charitable companies do not usually trade, in the strict sense of the word, the directors could be made liable for the debts of the company, and in this context 'operating' should probably be substituted for 'trading'. Such liability is not automatic and is in the discretion of the court. It will be dependent on the conduct of the individual director concerned. Resignation is not enough to exclude liability once the company is in trouble: each director must do what the director can to ensure that the interests of creditors are protected. Directors of insolvent companies are also statutorily responsible for unpaid national-insurance contributions at the date of commencement of the liquidation. In the case of a trading company it is easier to establish when wrongful trading is likely to be occurring than it is in the case of a charitable company. A trading company knows that if it continues to do business, money will flow in and it can make a reasonable prediction of the amounts which are likely to be received. On the other hand a charity must to a large extent rely on donations to maintain its cash flow and whether or not it will be able to meet future liabilities is in the hands of third parties.

Finally, directors must avoid being in a position where their own interests conflict with those of the company, and if they inevitably occur, they must declare them. It is necessary for a director to declare any interest that the director may have directly or indirectly in any contract to which the company is a party or in any expenditure made by the company. This must be done at a regularly convened meeting of the board even if all the directors are individually aware of the matter in question. If this is not done, the director (like a trustee who would otherwise profit from the trust) becomes what is known as a constructive trustee. In other words, the director is regarded as holding the money or other benefit paid or given by the company on behalf of the company and must account to the company for the benefit which the director (or the entity in which the director is interested) has received.

This catalogue of directors' duties may be intimidating at first sight but in fact the liability of directors is substantially less than that of trustees and less than those incurring personal liabilities on behalf of an unincorporated association.

An alternative to the company limited by guarantee is the industrial and provident society. This is quick to establish provided that one of the forms approved by the Registrar of Friendly Societies is used for its constitution. If one of the standard forms is not used it must be approved by the Registrar, which is probably as time-consuming as having the constitution of a trust or company limited by guarantee approved by the Charity Commission (and the Inland Revenue). It seems likely that for the purposes with which readers of this volume are likely to be concerned, a special form of constitution will probably be necessary, if only to define the beneficiaries of the body. Accordingly, it is not proposed to discuss further the industrial and provident society.

Conclusion

For substantial organizations which may wish to (1) employ staff, (2) rent premises, or (3) make significant purchases of goods and services (rather than simply to collect and distribute money) and to obtain the income required to perform these functions, a corporate structure is the best option. Alternatively, it may be best to start as an unincorporated association and, as and when the need arises, progress to the incorporation of a company. As will be seen below in the section on taxation, the major advantage of being a charity is the additional income which can be gained from the tax refunded on covenanted donations. Equally, however, the procedures required to collect this money are complicated. This, combined with the initial work involved in establishing a charity, may not be worthwhile for a small body which is not likely to receive significant covenant income even if it is a charity.

A final point before we move on to consider the other aspects of establishing the body: to those who are not lawyers, a company may seem a very legalistic animal: indeed, it is a creation of the law. Given the healthy suspicion about lawyers in this country, some may wonder whether it is not better to have a body with a freer form rather than one which is not so hidebound. This might lead you to progress from an unincorporated association to a company later rather than sooner. This could be a mistake: apart from any inconvenience and unlooked-for personal liabilities, the great advantage of a company is its formal structure and the fact that there are rules for conducting its operations which are generally common to tens of thousands of other companies and well known. The rules of an unincorporated association are inevitably more likely to be unique to that association to a greater extent than would be the case if it were a company. Working for people with ARC and AIDS is stressful: often, the correct action in any given circumstances is open to debate and those involved may violently oppose the course proposed by those with whom they disagree. There is everything to be said for having a structure where such disputes which cannot be resolved by compromise can be disposed of cleanly and with the minimum of argument as to the correct procedure. This is more likely to apply if the structure of the body is formal.

Charitable status

It might be thought that any voluntary organization working in the AIDS field would be eligible to be a charity, but this is not necessarily the case. It will be as well to review what is considered to be charitable in law, but first, we should perhaps look at the significance of charitable status.

Significance

As might be expected it has advantages and disadvantages. Charities benefit from tax concessions which form a direct incentive to those who wish to give funds and which reduce the cost of operating the charity. On the other side of the ledger, charities must be registered by and are subject to the jurisdiction of the Charity Commission and their freedom to pursue certain courses is circumscribed by law.

Once again there is a trade-off. The small organization, which does not have the human resources to administer reclaiming tax on covenanted donations and which will probably not have many donors willing to make covenants and which does not occupy premises and so cannot make use of rates relief, is probably better off not being a charity. A more substantial body may view charitable status as vital. Strictly speaking there is not a choice because there is a duty on those in charge of a charity to register with the Charity Commission, but no one is likely to take the point against a small organization which does not misrepresent itself as a charity.

Eligibility

In order to be charitable a body must be established for one of the four 'heads of charity':

- the relief of poverty, human suffering, and distress;
- the advancement of education;
- the advancement of religion;
- other purposes beneficial to the community.

There is also the overriding requirement that it should be established for the public benefit and not for a private class of people. If the beneficiaries are limited, for example to the poor residents of a particular locality, this will be charitable, but not, it seems, if they are limited to the poor employees and former employees of a particular company.

Consideration of the 'heads' might lead one to think that any body formed to prevent the spread of HIV or help people with ARC and AIDS would inevitably be charitable, but the Charity Commission will not necessarily agree immediately, although ultimately it is likely to be possible to convince the staff of the Commission, perhaps by specifying more precisely the objects of the proposed charity and, for example, introducing education or the relief of illness so as to come within one or both of the first two heads.

Conduct of charities

As has been mentioned charities are circumscribed in their actions.

Accounts

As far as administration is concerned, even if they are not companies (which are obliged to produce periodical accounts and have them audited), charities must draw up accounts which comply with the Charities (Statements of Accounts) Regulations 1960 and submit them to the Charity Commission no less frequently than is stipulated by the Commission in each case. Usually this will involve the services of an accountant even if the accounts are not formally audited.

Disposals of property

If a charity occupies property for its own purposes and wishes to dispose of it, it must obtain an order of the Charity Commission.

Grants

A charity must apply its assets strictly to the purpose for which it was established and for no other purpose. There will not be a problem if one charity makes a gift to another charity having the same purpose. However, if the recipient is not a charity (although being established for the same purpose), the gift is likely to be unlawful. In relation to AIDS organizations, this operates in two ways: the small body not registered as a charity may not have access to funds on this account; the larger organization wishing to help fund a particular project may be in difficulty if the project is not being carried out by a registered charity. A possible solution is for the grant to be structured as a contract, obliging the recipient to operate the service concerned for a specified period. Then, provided that the service is within the purposes of the charity providing the money, there should be no breach of the law. It would be wise to try to insert in the powers of the charity a power to make grants to non-charitable bodies for the purposes only of providing services which it would be within the object of the charity to provide.

Political activities

It is often thought that a charity cannot carry on any political activities. This is not strictly true. It is true that a body established to change the law of the land is not charitable. The basic principle is that political activity must not be the prime purpose of the body, either in its constitution or in practice. A charity, however, may undertake activities which can reasonably be said to be directed towards achieving the charity's purposes and which are within the powers contained in its constitution. The Charity Commission has published some useful guidelines on what is and what is not permissible.

Fund-raising

It is beyond the scope of this volume to deal in detail with the requirements of all kinds of fund-raising. However, it is worth mentioning that street collections and house-to-house collections both require licences, to be applied for at least one month before the collection from the local district council outside London and from the Metropolitan Police in Greater London (except for the City of London, where the licensing authority is the Common Council). In the case of street collections, there is considerable demand for good days in the year, and the local authority is unlikely to allow two collections on the same day in the same area. Considerable forward planning is therefore required. There are no restrictions on leaving collecting boxes in private premises such as pubs and clubs. Lotteries and competitions are also subject to control, limiting the price of the ticket and the prizes which may be offered. The licensing authority in this case is the local district council outside London, the appropriate London borough council in Greater London (except for the City, where the licensing authority is the Common Council). Well before embarking on this kind of fund-raising and before, for example, having tickets printed, the applicable rules should be studied.

Taxation

Under this heading we must consider inheritance, income tax and corporation tax payable by givers of money to the body, and income tax, corporation tax, and VAT in relation to the body itself.

Taxation of donors

In the case of individuals, gifts to qualifying UK charities are now completely exempt from inheritance tax without limit and are deducted from the total amount of the estate: such gifts may take the estate out of a charge to inheritance tax altogether. Thus, a gift by will or during a person's lifetime (even if shortly before death) can benefit a charity significantly more than if tax is paid on the donor's estate paying tax, and the recipient then decides (independently) to make a charitable donation. There is always scope for a recipient to redirect a legacy (or other gift by will) to a charity within 2 years after the death and to obtain the same tax-free advantage.

Gifts to charity are not deductible in establishing the taxable income of an individual for the purpose of basic-rate tax, although gifts under covenants are deductible in calculating the income of an individual who is subject to the higher rate of income tax. However, if the gift is made pursuant to a deed of covenant under which the gift will be made annually during the shorter of 4 years and the life of the donor, the charity is able to reclaim from the Inland Revenue a sum equal to tax at the basic rate of tax on the grossed-up amount of the gift. Thus, while the basic rate of tax is 25 per cent, if the annual amount payable by the donor is £75, this is grossed up to £100 on which the basic rate of tax is £25; and this is recoverable from the Inland Revenue. Consequently, the charity receives £100 in all. Because of the treatment of higher-rate taxpayers stated above, the net cost to a higher-rate taxpayer of the £100 received by the charity is £60 (assuming the higher rate of income tax remains at 40 per cent). However, the procedure for reclaiming the tax due is quite burdensome: in principle the charity must obtain from the person who has given the covenant at the time of or after each annual payment a form (R185(AP)) confirming that the covenanted gift has been paid out of taxed income. However, in some cases where there is a large volume of payments, the Revenue in its discretion is, in respect of the second and subsequent annual payments of £175 or less, prepared to dispense with forms R185(AP) and accept a schedule (in form R248B) instead. Administering a charity's covenant income is time-consuming and requires good record-keeping.

As far as companies are concerned, they can obtain tax relief from gifts to charities in two ways: a company may give an amount equal to 3 per cent of its annual dividend to charity and deduct the amount given in calculating its taxable income. Additionally, like an individual, a company may make annual gifts to charity under a covenant which will cause payments to be made for at least 4 years. In this case the company deducts tax at the basic rate from the gross amount of the gift and pays this to the Inland Revenue (on account of its liability to pay corporation tax). The company then pays the net amount of the gift after deduction of tax to the charity, which can then immediately reclaim the tax deducted from the Inland Revenue.

If a company makes a payment wholly and exclusively for the purpose of its trade, this will be deductible from its gross income in establishing its taxable income. Certain payments to charities, if they secure some advantage for the company in the course of its trade, may be deductible as ordinary business-expenses. The most obvious example of this is sponsorship of a particular event, which secures publicity for the company sponsor.

Value Added Tax

Like any other purchaser of goods and services, a charity must pay prices which include VAT. Generally it is in no different position from any other person in this respect.

It may be worth pointing out that the VAT system effectively means that the whole amount of the tax is borne by the final consumer of goods and services, although amounts of tax are collected by businesses who are involved in producing the goods or services concerned on each occasion when a supply of goods or services is made. Thus, those who are registered for VAT can claim a credit for all VAT paid by them when purchasing goods or services (known as inputs) accounting to the Customs and Excise for the VAT charged when they have supplied taxable goods and services (known as outputs). A complication arises where some supplies (or goods or services) provided by the business are taxable (albeit at the zero rate) and others are exempt. In this case the fraction of outputs which is taxable will be applied to the gross inputs and only the result can be taken as a credit against output tax. If the input tax exceeds the output tax a refund is made by the Customs and Excise. This could be a good reason for carrying out tax-exempt activities in a separate company which would not be registered for VAT; while none of the separate company's input tax could be used, this might be relatively trivial (especially if the work in preparing the material for publication was done by volunteers). Provided that all the supplies of the main charity were taxable, the whole of its inputs would be available. The announcement that with effect from 1 April 1989 (in compliance with a ruling of the European Court), VAT will be imposed on construction costs and on rent means that charities will be faced with paying significantly increased amounts of VAT, although there is a 5-year phasing-in period for charities.

Taxation of a charity

It is a commonly held fallacy that charities are exempt from taxation. However, while they do benefit from some tax concessions, the only part of their income which is exempt from taxation is investment income and trading income in so far as it is derived from the activities for which the charity was established. To clarify this a workshop established to provide an opportunity for paraplegics to make baskets will be exempt from tax on the profits derived from selling the baskets but a charity importing baskets from India and selling them will not. It is likely that a charity established to provide health education will be exempt from tax on the profits arising from the sale of health-education literature and posters.

However, much of the trading activity of charities is done for more or less fund-raising reasons even if the goods sold have a relationship to the activities of the charity. This kind of trading is not exempt from taxation if it is carried out by the charity itself. However, there is a mechanism whereby these profits can also effectively escape taxation.

As has been mentioned, if a company enters into a deed of covenant to pay a particular amount to a charity annually for at least 4 years, effectively no tax is paid on the income used to fund the payment. As long as the sum to be paid is certainly ascertainable, it does not have to be expressed as a money amount. Accordingly it is possible for a company to covenant to give the whole of its net profits (after operating expenses but before tax) to a charity. If this is done, the company first determines its net profits for the year. This establishes the amount due under the covenant. Because of the tax law applicable to companies, the company must deduct tax at the basic rate from the gross amount and pay this to the Inland Revenue; the remaining amount is payable to the beneficiary of the covenant. The whole amount due under the covenant (including the basic-rate tax which must be deducted and paid to the Revenue) is deductible from the profits of the company in determining its taxable income, thus reducing this to zero, so that it pays no corporation tax. In addition, the recipient, as a charity, is in a position to claim a refund of the amount of the tax at the basic rate withheld by the company. Accordingly no tax is payable on the profits generated by the trading. Thus, charities which wish to raise funds by trading activities usually establish a wholly owned subsidiary company (which is a normal commercial company limited by shares) to carry out these trading activities. The subsidiary then covenants to pay the whole of its net annual profits to the charity. One point to note is that the deduction from taxable income can only be made for amounts actually paid under the covenant during the year in question: accordingly, it is necessary before the end of the company's year to estimate the profits for that year and pay the appropriate amount under the covenant.

When mounting fund-raising events, for which tickets are to be sold, it is common to include in the price of the ticket a 'voluntary donation'. This is necessary if the promoter of the event (and the recipient of the actual price of the ticket) is a commercial organization, otherwise all the profits of the event will be subject to tax. The actual price of the ticket is subject to VAT but the donation element is not. Care must be taken to ensure that the actual price of the ticket is commercially justifiable: the event ought not to make a loss based on the actual ticket price. The donation is receivable by the charity and is not taxable. If the event is promoted by a company which has covenanted to pay the whole of its net income to a charity there is little benefit in splitting the admission price in this way.

Rates

Charities can obtain relief from rates (but not water and sewerage charges) so that they only pay one-half of the amount which would otherwise be due. There will be relief from the Uniform Business Rate when this is introduced (at the same time as the poll tax or Community Charge), so that charities will pay at the most one-fifth of normal rates. As now, there will be provisions allowing local authorities to relieve charities of an even greater proportion of the Uniform Business Rate but this is at the discretion of the local authority. This means that charities will be better off paying their own rates rather than paying a rent inclusive of rates to a landlord which is not itself a charity.

Practical matters

Finally we turn to considering the practical steps which must be taken in order to set up a suitable organization. For some bodies it will never be necessary to go beyond the stage of an unincorporated association; for others this will be an initial step, to be followed in due course by a change to a more formal structure; but even where the need for this to occur as soon as possible is seen, the time taken to complete the required formalities will probably dictate starting as an unincorporated association.

Unincorporated associations

The basic idea of an unincorporated association is that it is formed by a contract between the members. The terms of the contract are set out in the rules of the association. Accordingly as soon as the decision is made to establish the association, the first thing to do is draw up some rules.

These should deal at least with the following issues:

- purpose – the activities which the association is established to carry out;
- membership:
  * eligibility;
  * admission to membership;
  * obligations of members;
  * removal as a member;
- how the association is to be run:
  * officers (e.g. chair, secretary, and treasurer) qualifications, appointment, removal, and powers;
  * committee (composition and powers);
  * general meetings of the members;
  * elections;
  * the conduct of meetings of members and any committee (what notice is required, how many people will form a quorum, that minutes are to be kept, and how they are to be published);
  * accounts (bookkeeping, preparation of annual accounts, whether they are to be audited, and how they are to be published to the members);
- special formalities required for changing the rules;
- how the association can be dissolved.

These matters should all be covered in clear everyday language. The object is to have a document to which all concerned can refer and which will give an appropriate answer to the questions which will arise in practice. Should the committee have embarked upon a particular course? Was it consistent with the purposes for which the association was established? Is it right that two members of the committee can reach a decision at a meeting of which some other committee members were ignorant? Should not the accounts from 2 years ago now be available? How does one deal with a member who is harming the organization?

If the rules do not provide answers to these questions and the others which will come up in advance, it will render a difficult occurrence even more troublesome. Voluntary organizations can be extremely beneficial. However, it is inevitable, human nature being what it is, that those who are giving their time do not feel as obligated as those who are being paid to do work. It is even more important to lay down what is expected in advance, so that performance can be compared with existing norms, rather than an individual's conduct being compared with a hazy notion of what is appropriate.

Time spent in formulating rules is unlikely to be wasted. As a start it will usually be possible to obtain copies of the rules of other similar bodies and to use these as a starting-point. Before finally adopting any rules, it is worthwhile, if funding is known to be required from perhaps a local authority, to enquire of the funding body whether they have any requirement with regard to the rules of bodies to which they provide money. The beauty of an unincorporated association is that once the rules have been prepared and adopted, you are up and running with no more ado.

It is possible to open a bank or building-society account for the association, although usually the association will need to retain a credit balance.

Companies limited by guarantee

It is possible to establish a company which is not and is not intended to be a charity. However, for this purpose we will assume that the company is intended to be charitable. If this is the case it is essential to apply for it to be registered as a charity before it has commenced its activities, although it must be in existence before it can be registered.

The constitutional documents of a company are its memorandum and articles of association. Broadly speaking the memorandum sets out the name of the company, where it is to be registered (and incorporated), the purpose for which it is to be established, the powers it will have to achieve its objects, and how any profits arising and any surplus left when it is dissolved are to be applied. The articles establish how the company is to be managed and its affairs conducted.

Drafts of these documents should be submitted to the Charity Commission for approval before the company is incorporated. Again it will be helpful to use the memorandum and articles of an existing registered charity as a basis. The Commission is chiefly concerned with the memorandum but the draft articles of association should also be submitted. If very few changes have been made to the model it may be worthwhile to inform the Charity Commission of the name and registration number of the existing charity, indicating what (if any) changes have been made: the staff of the Commission will examine it just as closely but they may be dissuaded from objecting to a provision which has been approved in a former case. It is sensible to submit the drafts with a letter explaining the reasons for the incorporation of the charity. The Commission is extremely overworked and the delay in replies to letters means that each exchange of correspondence can be expected to take 6 weeks as a minimum. When the Commission is satisfied with the draft it will be passed to the Inland Revenue, which may be expected to have some further observations. When the draft memorandum and articles have been approved, the company can be formed.

In order to incorporate the company, at least two of the initial members must sign the memorandum and articles of association. These documents, together with a form setting out the initial registered office and the details of first directors and the secretary and a statutory declaration (akin to an affidavit) to the effect that all the formalities required by the Companies Act have been complied with and a cheque for £50, must be sent to the Registrar of Companies. About 3 weeks later the certificate of incorporation will be issued by the Registrar and this marks the beginning of the existence of the company.

The first meeting of the board of directors should then be held. The company will not yet be a registered charity so its activities must be limited, but it is useful to proceed to open bank-accounts, appoint auditors, and perhaps admit additional members, and it is necessary for the directors to resolve to register the company as a charity. This requires the completion and signature on behalf of the company of a form obtainable from the Charity Commission. This is then sent to the Commission with a letter specifying the reference under which the Memorandum and Articles were approved. In due course the Commission will respond with confirmation that the company has been registered as a charity and will allocate a registration number.

Conclusion

Setting up and running an organization requires skill and time. However, this effort will not be wasted if it enables those at the sharp end of the project to function properly and without unnecessary administrative worries and, above all, disputes. It may be possible to obtain the services of a volunteer solicitor or accountant to assist in establishing and running the organization. Whether or not this is possible the National Council for Voluntary Organizations provides advice and information for charities and voluntary bodies and publishes a number of useful guides on setting up, funding, and running them. If you are embarking upon the establishment of a charity, you probably will need professional help. If this is not available on a voluntary basis, you will pay less to your professional adviser if you have thought out beforehand exactly what you want to do and are ready to give the person helping you the full details of your intentions and those of the others involved.

Appendices

Appendix 1 – Advice agencies

A list of agencies which can provide advice or help on AIDS, or organizations which can advise on legal housing or benefit problems.

Advice about AIDS

Terrence Higgins Trust
Tel. 01 831-0330 Admin. Line
Tel. 01 242-1010 Helpline
3–10pm Daily

– provides help, advice, and information on AIDS and a range of services which includes counselling, befriending, and support for people with AIDS; buddies information leaflets on AIDS; talks on AIDS; advice and help for drug-users affected by AIDS; health-education and safer-sex materials.

Body Positive
Tel. 01 835-1045 Admin. Line
Tel. 01 373-9124 Helpline

– provides help to people diagnosed as HIV-antibody positive; has support groups for people who are antibody positive; and an excellent newsletter.

Frontliners
Tel. 01 831–0330

– an organization set up by people with AIDS, providing support for people with AIDS and which has produced a booklet called 'Living with AIDS', an information and survival guide for people who have AIDS.

Haemophilia Society
Tel. 01 928-2020
contact
Johnathan Cooper

– besides helping haemophiliacs, the society also has an officer dealing with specific AIDS problems which arise.

SCODA – Standing Conference on Drug Abuse

Tel. 01 430-2341 — is the co-ordinating body for non-statutory services and individuals working in the drug field.

London Lesbian and Gay Switchboard

Tel. 01 837-7324 — advice, information, and help on all

24 hour service issues for lesbians and gays.

Legal and welfare rights and housing advice

For general and *non-AIDS-related* legal and welfare benefits problems, people are advised to contact their local Citizens Advice Bureau, Advice Centre, or Law Centre. The address and telephone number of these Advice Centres can be obtained from the telephone directory or the national organizations or federations listed below.

National Association of Citizens Advice Bureaux (NACAB)
115–123 Pentonville Road
LONDON N1 9LZ
Tel. 01 833-2181

Greater London Citizens Advice Bureau (GLCAB)
136–144 City Road
LONDON EC1V 2QN
Tel. 01 251-2000

Law Centres Federation
18/19 Warren Street
LONDON W1
Tel. 01 387-8570

Federation of Independent Advice Centres
Tel. 01 274-1839

Legal and welfare-benefits problems around AIDS

Terrence Higgins Trust Legal Centre
Tel. 01 831-0330 *Contact Administrator*
Mon–Fri 10–6
Tel. 01 405-2381 *Legal Line*
Wed 7–10

The Trust's Legal Centre provides advice on employment, immigration, medico-legal, housing, welfare-benefits problems, and Wills requests. Outside London the Trust will try to find an appropriate solicitor or advice agency to deal with enquiries.

Frontliners
Tel. 01 831-0330
Mon–Fri

Can help with general enquiries from people with AIDS about benefits.

Housing

AIDS and Housing Project
16–18 Strutton Ground
LONDON SW1 2HP

Established in 1987 to help housing organizations provide good-quality accommodation for people with HIV infection, it can be a valuable resource for further information and developments in the field.

National Federation of Housing Associations
175 Grays Inn Road
LONDON WC1X 8UP

The Special Needs Section can provide information on the work of housing associations, and also local contacts.

SITRA
16–18 Strutton Ground
LONDON SW1 2HP

Although currently working only in London, SITRA may be able to put readers in touch with special-needs housing co-ordinating bodies throughout the country.

Strutton Housing Association
16–18 Strutton Ground
LONDON SW1 2HP

Set up to develop good-quality independent housing for people with AIDS, it has sought to develop model housing schemes in self-contained units.

Housing initiatives for people with AIDS are being developed throughout the country – from housing associations in Wales to the imaginative use or shared use of church accommodation in London. Local helplines may have details of such schemes.

Legal structures

General advice about the legal or constitutional structure of a voluntary group should be sought from:

NCVO – National Council of Voluntary Organizations
26 Bedford Square
LONDON WC1B 3HU
Tel. 01 636-4066

Produces a specimen constitution for an unincorporated organization having a membership; a specimen deed for a charitable trust; and a specimen memorandum and articles of association for a charitable company limited by guarantee.

And on charitable structure from the:

Charity Commission
St Albans House
57–60 Haymarket
LONDON SW1Y 4QZ
Tel. 01 210-3000

Northern Office
Graeme House
Derby Square
LIVERPOOL L2 7SB
Tel. 051-227-3191

The powers and functions of the Charity Commission are set out in the Charities Act 1960. This gives the Commissioners the function of 'promoting the effective use of charitable resources by encouraging the development of better methods of administration, by giving charity trustees information or advice on any matter affecting the charity, and by investigating and checking abuses'.

Gay or lesbian legal problems
GLAD – 01 821-7672 Mon–Fri 7–10pm

A helpline specifically advising gays and lesbians. Also has a list of sympathetic solicitors.

Appendix 2 – References and further reading

An up-to-date list of legal and related authorities is available from the Terrence Higgins Trust Legal Centre.

Medico-legal authorities

Major statutory and case material

Aspects of treatment and consent

Sidaway vs. Bethlem Royal Hospital Governors et al. (1985) 2 WLR 480
Chatterton vs. Gershon (1981) QB 432
Bolam vs. Friern Barnet Hospital Management Committee (1957) 2 AER 118
GMC Guidance British Medical Journal (*BMJ*) 30.5.87, p.1436; *BMJ* 295
  p.1500; and *BMJ* p.1613.

Confidentiality of medical records

Stephens vs. Avery (1988) 2 AER 477
X vs. Y (1988) 2 AER 648

Specific AIDS legislation

AIDS (Control) (Contents of Reports) Order 1988. SI 1988/117. Amendments
  to NHS (Charges to Overseas Visitors) (No 2) Regulations SI 1982/863 have
  been made by SI 1983/302, 1987/371, 1988/8, and 1988/472.

Social-welfare law

Further reading

Findley, Lorna (1989) 'Annotated Housing Benefit Legislation' (Child Poverty
  Action Group).
Mesher, John (1989) 'Income Support, the Social Fund and Family Credit: The
  Legislation' (Child Poverty Action Group).
Ogus and Barendt *The Law of Social Security* (3rd edn) (Butterworths,
  Sevenoaks).
Williams, John *Social Services Law* (Format Publishing).

Housing and people with HIV

Housing Corporation circular HC 40/87, 'Housing for people with AIDS',
available from the Housing Corporation, 149 Tottenham Court Road, London
W1P 0BN

Association of London Authorities, 'AIDS: a model policy for Local Government', available from The Association of London Authorities, 36 Old Queen
Street, London SW1H 9JF, price £3.50

Resource Information Service, 'AIDS the issues for housing', available from RIS, 5 Egmont House, 116 Shaftesbury Avenue, London W1V 7DJ, price £4.50

Employment law

Department of Employment and Health and Safety Executive, 'AIDS and employment'.
Southam, C. and Howard, G. (1988) *'AIDS and Employment Law'* (Financial Trading Publications Ltd.).

On employment law

Tolley's Employment Handbook (1988), published by Tolley Publishing Co. Ltd.

Immigration Law

Fransman, L. and Webb, D. (1986) 'Immigration emergency procedures' (Legal Action Group, London).
Fransman, L. (1989) British Nationality Law, Format.
Hartley, T. (1978) *EEC Immigration Law* (North Holland, London).
Immigration Law and Procedure (Matthew Bender, New York) (1988 supplement).
Macdonald, I. (QC) (1987) *Immigration Law and Practice in the United Kingdom* (2nd edn) (Butterworths, London).
Mole, N. (1987) 'Immigration – Family Entry and Settlement' (Family Law, Bristol).
Nakonechny, E. (1987) 'The International Civil Liberties Implications of AIDS', unpublished study, University of Essex.
Plender, Dr R. (QC) (1988) *International Migration Law* (2nd edn, 2 vols) (Martinus Nijhoff, London and Dordrecht).
Supperstone, M. (1988) *Immigration: The Law and Practice* (2nd edn) (Oyez Longman, London).

Powers of attorney, wills, and probate

1. Aldridge, Trevor (1986) *Powers of Attorney* (Oyez/Longman)
2. Citizens Advice Bureau 'Information on Powers of Attorney'
3. Department of Health and Social Security 'What to do after death' (HMSO, London)
4. Home Office 'The Work of the Coroner' (a Guide) (HMSO, London)
5. Lord Chancellors Department 'How to obtain Probate'
6. Maurice, Spencer G. *Family Provision Practice* (Oyez/Longman)
7. Whitehorn, Norman (1986) *Court of Protection* (Oyez/Longman)

Appendix 3 – A Bill to outlaw discrimination in employment

Employment Protection on AIDS (Amendment) Bill 1987

A BILL TO MAKE PROVISION FOR THE EMPLOYMENT PROTECTION OF PEOPLE WITH AIDS AND THOSE WHO ARE INFECTED BY HIV, BY AMENDMENT TO THE EMPLOYMENT PROTECTION (CONSOLIDATION) ACT 1978, AND BY MAKING THE DISMISSAL OF A PERSON WITH AIDS OR WITH HIV INFECTION AN UNFAIR DISMISSAL AND INADMISSIBLE REASON FOR THE PURPOSES OF THAT ACT.

1. – (1)   After Section 58A of the 1978 Act, as amended by Section 7 of the 1980 Employment Act there shall be inserted –

Dismissal of a person with Aids or HIV

58B. (1)   An employee shall be treated for the purposes of this Part as unfairly dismissed if the reason or principal reason for his dismissal is that he has AIDS or is infected with HIV, or is for any other reason connected with being infected by HIV except one of the following reasons –

(a) that at the effective date of termination of his employment he is incapable of adequately complying with his terms and conditions of employment;

(b) that because of his medical condition his employer cannot continue to employ him without a contravention or restriction imposed under any enactment.

(2)   For the purposes of subsection (1) a person with AIDS shall include an employee whose employer or other employees regards as having AIDS and a person with HIV shall include an employee whose employer or other employees regard as having been infected by Human Immunodeficiency Virus (HIV), notwithstanding the fact that such employee may have had no medical diagnosis of AIDS or HIV antibody test performed by a fully registered medical practitioner.

(3)   Any reason by virtue of which a dismissal is regarded to be unfair in consequence of subsection (1) or (2) is in this Part referred to as an inadmissible reason.

187

Index

Index

HIV (Human Immunodeficiency Virus)
1, 102; transmission of 11–12
HIV-antibody testing 94–5, 97; consent
to 7–10; and life assurance 151–5,
160
homelessness 64–5, 74; intentional 70–1
homosexuality 2; discrimination 158–9
Hospital Complaints Procedure Act
(1985) 25
hospitals: complaints about 25–6; control
of infection 92; death in 17, 133–4;
detention in 16–17; removal to 15–16
Housing Act (1985) 61, 64–5, 67, 72,
76–7
Housing Act (1988) 74, 75, 76
Housing Act (1989) 40, 42
housing associations 62, 183
Housing Benefit (HB) 40–3
housing law 59–85; accommodation
65–6; case study 83–5; change 80–2;
costs, and IS 36–8; estates
management 74–5; homelessness 64–5;
individual circumstances 66–71;
information 60–2; local connection
71–2; owner-occupation 78–80;
private renting 75–8; succession of
tenancy 73–4; temporary
accommodation 72–3; waiting-lists
62–4

immigration 111–21; appeal 21; control
after entry into UK 118–19; control on
entry into UK 114–17; deportation
119–21; European Community travel
112–13; refugees 118; UK legislation
113–14
Immigration Act (1971) 113–14, 115,
120
Income Data Services Ltd 87
Income Support (IS) 29–40; board-and-
lodging 39–40; calculation of 34–5;
entitlement conditions 32–3; family
unit 34; housing costs 36–8; income
assessment 38–9; premiums 30, 35;
and Supplementary Benefit 29–31
Independent-Living Fund 48–9
Industrial Tribunals 90, 98–100, 104,
109
Inheritance (Provision for Family and
Dependants) Act (1975) 132–3
inquests 135
Insolvency Act (1986) 169

insurance 141–61; discrimination 158–9;
employment schemes 95–6; health
142–5; life assurance 145–56;
Ombudsman 159; permanent health
105–6, 144; travel 144–5
Invalid-Care Allowance (ICA) 44–5
Invalidity Benefit 43–4

Kaposi's sarcoma 102
Kirkwood, Archy 159

landlords, private 75–8
law and AIDS 1–6; employment
86–110; housing 59–85; immigration
111–21; insurance 141–61; medico-
legal aspects 7–27; powers of
attorney, wills, probate 122–40; social
welfare 28–58; voluntary organizations
162–80
Law Centres Federation 182
legislation, AIDS 14–19; AIDS Control
Act (1987) 17–18; Health and
Medicines Act (1988) 18; NHS
(Charge to Overseas Visitors)
Regulations 18–19; Public Health
(Infectious Diseases) Regulations
14–17
life assurance 145–56; applying for 148;
disclosure 149–50; initial application
150–2; medical examination and HIV-
testing 153–5, 160; necessity? 148–9;
rejection of application 155–6;
supplementary questionnaire 152–3
loans 55–6
local authorities: complaints about 57–8;
duties of 56–7; housing 61–2
London 2, 82; Citizens Advice Bureaux
182
London Lesbian and Gay Switchboard
182

Manchester City Council 87
medico-legal aspects of AIDS 7–27;
AIDS legislation 14–19; complaints
19–27; confidentiality of medical
records 11–14; consent to treatment
7–10
Mental Health Act (1983) 19
Midland Bank 87
Mobility Allowance 46–7
mortgages 78–80; endowment 146; and
Income Support 36–7; joint 80;